Cops, Crime and Capitalism

The Law-and-Order Agenda in Canada

Todd Gordon

Fernwood Publishing • Halifax

for Jackie and Breton

Editing: Debby Seed
Cover Photo: Beverley Rach
Printed and bound in Canada by Hignell Printing Limited

Published in Canada by Fernwood Publishing
Site 2A, Box 5, 32 Oceanvista Lane
Black Point, Nova Scotia, B0J 1B0
and 324 Clare Avenue, Winnipeg, Manitoba, R3L 1S3
www.fernwoodbooks.ca

Fernwood Publishing Company Limited gratefully acknowledges
the financial support of the Department of Canadian Heritage,
the Nova Scotia Department of Tourism and Culture and
the Canada Council for the Arts for our publishing program.

Library and Archives Canada Cataloguing in Publication

Gordon, Todd (Todd Stewart), 1973-
Cops, crime and capitalism : the law and order agenda in Canada
/ Todd Gordon.

ISBN 1-55266-185-7

1. Police--Canada. 2. Poor--Canada. 3. Discrimination in law enforcement--Canada.
4. Social control--Canada. 5. Capitalism--Canada. I. Title.

HV8157.G67 2006   363.2'0971   C2006-900313-0

Contents

Introduction

Over the last couple of decades the theme of law and order has penetrated deeply into popular discourse and come to shape state policy in very important ways. Its influence is profound. So too are the consequences for the targets of state policy and practices inspired by it. Law and order has become a popular mantra of politicians and media, especially those on the political right, but it is by no means exclusive to them. Repeated mention of this phrase can score popularity points for the politician or win a bigger audience for the media outlet. In so doing, it deflects attention away from other social issues. We are constantly reminded, on the one hand, that crime is everywhere. We are told that police and politicians, on the other, are waging the good fight against crime — never defeating it once and for all, perhaps, but with recourse to a tough law-and-order strategy, keeping on top of it. It is as if a thin line runs straight through Canadian society, precariously separating a civilized order from criminal chaos ready to overtake it if left unchecked for but a moment.

Law and order is certainly a central leitmotif of popular culture in North America, as witnessed by the proliferation of law-and-order themed movies and television shows since the 1970s. They have ranged from the uncompromising, no-holds-barred cop Dirty Harry (sometimes you just gotta break the rules to get the bad guys — a point we will discuss throughout the book), to Charles Bronson's stark mad vigilante anti-hero of the *Death Wish* series. Then there is the cold objectivity of the science displayed on the CSI series, as well as the hundreds of other law-and-order-inspired movies and TV shows. Since the 1970s, audiences have been presented with simple black-and-white moralistic narratives depicting the fight for justice and safety against the violent criminals lurking in the shadows of our society.[1]

But the real dynamics of the law-and-order agenda, following actual state policy and the related patterns of contemporary policing, are more complex than what is typically reflected in popular culture and politics. As law-and-order policies have been adopted by the state and police in Canada, what has increased is not a war waged on crime, which in fact has been decreasing for the past decade. Instead, what has increased is a less publicized war against displays of public disorder, such as begging, squeegeeing and hanging out in public spaces. This campaign is quite different than images of law-and-order policing we have become so used to. The campaign seems

1

much more mundane; it is in fact no less serious for the state than a war on violent crime. What is at stake may not be our protection from dangerous criminals run amok. It remains the case that a more serious agenda is at work: the consolidation of capitalist social relations in the era of neoliberalism.

To understand the law-and-order agenda, we must place it within the broader context of the political and economic changes associated with neoliberalism. Law-and-order policing is not an isolated policy endeavour or policing practice. It is, indeed, a central feature of a state power that, far from retreating with the demise of the Keynesian welfare state, is actively facilitating the establishment of a new capitalist order based on restructuring social relations. This new neoliberal order is very much about the role of an aggressive state and its relationship to the class struggle lying at the heart of contemporary Canadian society. Only by focusing on the issues of state power and social class will we be able to properly understand what is really driving the law-and-order agenda. Given the pervasive view of law-and-order policing espoused by its advocates, and current trends in social theory, it clearly warrants a fresh look.

A contemporary critical literature on policing does exist. The little attention, however, it gives to the role of the state and social class creates a significant blind spot, limiting its ability to see the full complexities of policing in capitalist society. Marxist theorists situated such complexities more prominently in the critical literature on policing in the 1970s. However, they tended to rely on a "crude functionalism," treating the police merely as a repressive agency whose principal role is to crush outbreaks of working-class struggle (Neocleous, 2000: xii; Young, 1979). The exhaustion of the theoretical limits of Marxist-oriented functionalism was expressed in the ascendancy of panoptic theories of policing. Influenced by post-structuralism and developed primarily in the disciplines of criminology and sociology, these theories represent a theoretical shift that specifically de-emphasizes the roles of the state and social class in shaping policing practices.

This book will show that the state and social class are in fact crucial to our understanding of policing in capitalist society. It situates policing historically as part of a state-centred strategy whose goal is to produce a social order based on the subordination of wage labour to the imperatives of capital accumulation. The panoptic break from the one-sided emphasis on repression contributes positively to our understanding of policing. Its theoretical refusal to meaningfully question the role of the state or class relations, however, means it misses much of what policing is actually about and its impact on working peoples' lives. In contrast, a non-functionalist Marxist approach refuses an overly simplistic emphasis on repression, but remains attentive to the role of the state and class relations. Such an approach shows the central dynamics of policing much more effectively. It draws our attention to the particular way in which policing, as a central and productive feature of state power, is an expression of a response to the day-to-day struggles of a working class as it responds to the vagaries of a new social order.

The approach employed here is informed by Open Marxism, which views the state as the political form, or mode of existence, of the class antagonism between labour and capital. From this perspective, the state is shaped by, and in turn shapes, this class antagonism. Mark Neocleous makes an important contribution to this theory. He defines state power as a form of political administration of the working class. As he develops his theory of political administration, he analyzes the historical role of policing in the creation of a class of wage labourers. This analysis significantly advances our understanding of policing in capitalist society. It also frames our interrogation of policing practices in Canada today.

The contemporary law-and-order agenda in Canada is in real need of a new critical study. The agenda, it will be argued, is part of the state's response to the problems posed to neoliberal restructuring caused by the unwillingness of working people to simply conform to the reordering of their lives. Its goal is to create a cheap, flexible pool of wage labour, something that has grown steadily with neoliberalism. Law-and-order policing, therefore, is best understood as part of a continuum of neoliberal strategies, including other things like cuts to social programs, which facilitates the generalization of a poorly paid and insecure work experience by diminishing any possible alternatives people may seek to it. In this respect, as with policing historically, fighting crime is not the principal aim of contemporary law-and-order policing. Instead, the aim is to produce a new social order based on the severely diminished expectations of working people. Fighting crime matters only insofar as it helps in this process.

The examination of the law-and-order agenda offered here will also be useful in another important way. It further develops our understanding of policing in capitalist society and, by extension, Marxist theories of state power. The analysis highlights the way in which these things are racialized and gendered. This aspect of policing is absent in both the panoptic literature on policing and Marxist writings on the state. This is a glaring omission, given the growing wealth of evidence showing the racist and gendered character of police work and the day-to-day encounters of people of colour and women, especially immigrants, with public police officers. The work of writers like Kelley (1997), Bannerji (2000) and McNally (2002), among others, who are attentive to the ways in which the capitalist mode of production and its classes are historically materialized through racist and gendered social relations, will be incorporated into the analysis to help understand the disproportionate focus on communities of colour and certain women in the law-and-order agenda.

Furthermore, this book will also make an important contribution to the critical literature on neoliberalism. By focusing on policing, and its relation to the overall agenda of neoliberal restructuring, it advances further Sears' assertion that the retrenchment of the "broad" welfare state does not mean there is now less state — as is the popular perception — but simply a different role for the state (2003: 1999). Often this role is more coercive.

Policing, of course, is not the only avenue by which classes are constituted or class experience is shaped in capitalist society. Other institutions, some of which are part of the state, can also perform this role in their own ways. Certainly religious institutions, educational systems, the family and even organized sport, have been important in forming social classes. Far be it for me to suggest that only the police or the state fulfill this role. But policing, as will be shown, is a strategically important and forceful part of this process. Given how misunderstood it is by advocates of law-and-order policies as well as by critics, it deserves our attention. The aim here is to cut through all the misconceptions surrounding the role of policing and to show that our understanding of it as an integral feature of state power is vital to understanding the development of neoliberalism.

The point here is to examine an important aspect of state power, which has been misunderstood and which has escaped serious examination in the studies of neoliberalism, particularly in Canada. Without developing our understanding of state power in general, and of policing in particular, as a constitutive force in capitalist society, our understanding of neoliberalism is incomplete. To put this point slightly differently, and perhaps a little more sharply: even though the operation of state power may not be, on its own, sufficient to the formation of classes and the persistence of capitalist social relations, it is nevertheless necessary. This is what in part makes our state capitalist: without a class of wage labourers to be exploited, capitalism cannot function. The aggressive intervention of the state in people's daily lives has persisted throughout the period of neoliberalism. The study of this aspect of the state, in turn, also forces us to pay more attention to the equally persistent struggles at the heart of capitalist society — the day-to-day expressions of aspirations for a life outside of dehumanizing exploitative relations. The desire for something more humane persists, and policing is an expression of this.

As we proceed, it will become clear that the state actively pursues a neoliberal order, and that the police are on the frontlines of this struggle. The book will begin, however, by first looking at the panoptic writing, which is the main framework from which a critical perspective of contemporary policing is advanced. Following the work of Foucault, this writing is marked by three problematic assumptions about policing: it is done primarily at a distance, rather than directly; it is done from multiple sites of power, not the state; and it targets everyone equally regardless of class, race or gender. This "electronic panopticon" form of policing, further, is said to produce self-regulating docile bodies. Using government and police statistics, together with studies of zero-tolerance and community policing, we will show that this body of literature actually misses on all three counts much of the reality that makes up contemporary policing. The panoptic theory is fundamentally inadequate despite its popularity to our task of explaining the law-and-order agenda.

The second chapter will establish the theoretical framework for the rest of the book. The theory is based on the analysis of Open Marxism, supplemented by the anti-racist and feminist analysis. The theory of state power based on class struggle is the key to understanding how policing has developed in a capitalist society. Modern policing emerged with the rise of industrial capitalism in Britain in order to produce a working class. The state's fight for public order, involving the criminalization of a large segment of the working class, was in fact the fight to consolidate private property by establishing a market in wage labour. Such a perspective offers more valuable insights into the reality of law-and-order policing today than the panoptic writings.

The third chapter will begin by looking at the global economic downturn, beginning in the early 1970s, and its economic and political impact on Canada. Readers here will find the argument that neoliberal strategies pursued by the state in advanced capitalist countries are a response to the opposition of the working class to economic restructuring. Employers initiated the restructuring to restore profitability. The state has helped employers regain their profitability, driving down the cost of labour. In Canada in the late 1970s labour costs were higher than the Organization for Economic Co-operation and Development (OECD) average (Wolfe 1984). The result: the Canadian working class was recomposed by creating an increasingly cheap pool of labour. This process has been facilitated, in part, by diminishing any alternative to the wage for subsistence.

Diminishing alternatives to the wage is achieved in different ways. Cuts to social-assistance programs, for example, have been one prominent strategy. Law-and-order policing has been another. As Sears suggests, "State disciplinary activities reinforce market discipline by visibly suppressing forms of 'deviant' conduct which threaten the norms of commodity exchange" (1999: 105). Law-and-order policies in this respect complement government restructuring. They are crucial to the success of neoliberalism.

The fourth chapter will look more concretely at how the law-and-order agenda has developed in Canada since the 1990s. The chapter begins with an historical examination of the vagrancy law in Canada. The vagrancy law was historically a key feature of the state's strategy to form a class of wage labourers. It targeted activities that might provide an income outside of formal market relations, until the law was declawed in the 1950s and again in 1972, in the context of the postwar boom and the higher employment rates, a significant increase in relatively well-paying wage work and a somewhat progressive shift in attitudes towards poverty and criminality. The focus will then shift to Ontario's Safe Streets Act and various municipal bylaws that target begging. Both the act and bylaws represent a de facto return of the vagrancy law. We will look at the laws themselves, the discussion of government officials surrounding their implementation, and the police practices associated with them. Such an analysis is revealing. A central aim of these laws, like the former vagrancy statutes, has been to target behaviour that potentially undermines peoples' dependence on market relations to survive. These laws, and the related police practices, have been as integral to neoliberalism as state restructuring.

The final chapter will look specifically at the law-and-order agenda as it relates to immigrants. Most of the recent immigrants to Canada come from the Global South. They experience a disproportionate amount of attention under law-and-order policies, but the attention they receive is also unique to them in some important ways. The state's aggressive effort to turn them into an extremely vulnerable source of labour is also influenced by the historical view of them. They represent a dangerous Other that threatens to contaminate Canada's precarious white Anglo-Saxon order. Bringing with them customs, habits and languages foreign to most Canadians of British or Western European background, immigrants of colour are viewed by authorities as physical and moral pollutants to Canadian society. Thus their criminalization is profound: simply being an immigrant in Canada is to be potentially criminal. This further increases their vulnerability to the worst forms of wage labour Canada has to offer.

After explaining this theme in some detail, we will look at two very interesting examples showing how criminalization plays out for many immigrants of colour. The war on drugs is one example. It has been well studied in Canada but is still largely misunderstood. The war on drugs has developed historically as an aggressive tool to target immigrant communities and the signs of disorder they represent. It also criminalizes alternatives to working for an income. The other example is the increased use of detention against immigrants. It serves as a stark reminder to them of the lengths the state is willing to go to assert its control over such immigrants and to increase their vulnerability.

Note

1. The proliferation of law-and-order themes in movies and television since the 1970s cannot receive the attention it deserves in this book; indeed, this is worthy of a study of its own. One show that perhaps can be described as part of a law-and-order genre, but which does not succumb to the simplistic and moralistic black-and-white narratives typical of so many shows, is *Da Vinci's Inquest*.

1. A Critical Look at Panoptic Theories of Policing

Often tied to a discourse on law and order, policing has become a marked political feature of advanced capitalist states over the past two decades. This is the case not simply in response to political protest, but also in the day-to-day experiences of many people in these countries for whom policing is an all-too-common feature in their lives. Although academic writers have tried to examine contemporary policing from a critical perspective, most of the literature is severely hampered by a costly overemphasis on the importance of what is sometimes referred to as at-a-distance policing. This panoptic theory of policing is indebted to the notions of power, control and subjectification developed by Michel Foucault, a twentieth-century French post-structuralist philosopher, in works like *Discipline and Punish* (1977). The theory is situated prominently within the critical literature on contemporary policing. This has had serious consequences for the development of a more meaningful analysis of policing. Despite the extent of the panoptic writings, there nonetheless exists a considerable gap between the reality of contemporary policing and its portrayal in the literature. As a result, most critical evaluations of the goals of policing, and the techniques used to pursue them, are severely limited in their insights. They often gloss over, if not ignore, many of its harsh realities.

This chapter will look at the central issues regarding contemporary policing raised in the writings. It will measure the strength of the panoptic analysis by comparing it to some of the more prominent features of policing today. In so doing, the chapter will highlight the theory's limitations, as expressed in some very serious blind spots in its depiction of contemporary policing. It is marred by what I call techno-fetishism. The extent of these limitations indeed suggests that a substantively different approach to the study of policing is necessary.

Panoptic Themes

Three central assumptions shape most of the panoptic writings on contemporary policing. First, central policing practices today are done electronically and at a distance from the populations under surveillance; second, such electronic policing is a great equalizer, insofar as the entire population, regardless of class or racial background, can be caught in its web; and third, the state's role, to the extent that it has one, is narrowly circumscribed by the emergence of more local and autonomous forms of policing.

Ericson and Haggerty's *Policing the Risk Society* (1997) is an influential work in this body of literature and neatly captures all three of those assumptions. Similar to Foucault's *Discipline and Punish* (1977), for example, the idea of policing or governing at a distance is central to their notion of policing in a "risk society." Contemporary policing, according to Ericson and Haggerty, is focused on the production of knowledge about risk. From the threat of natural disasters to that of different individuals or organizations, the potential risks to social security — whether the risk is to the financial security of different institutions or to the careers or lives of individuals and organizations — are omnipresent in the contemporary world. Risk is not so much about moral wrongdoing as it is about *contingency*. It is often couched in terms of deviance. Potential risks reflect those individuals or events that deviate from societal expectations and consequently threaten the stability of different individual or institutional concerns. They represent uncertainties that cannot be easily absorbed into the order of things. Chance, uncertainty and difference — these are expressions of risk that should be segregated and monitored, not celebrated. Knowledge about such risks is essential to the proper functioning of institutions today, whether they be private or public.

It follows that "the main task of the police is to 'front load'... the system with relevant knowledge that can later be sorted and distributed to interested institutional audiences" (Ericson and Haggerty, 1997: 41). The police, in this respect, are a link in a chain constituted by "a wide range of risk professions and their forms of expert knowledge" (Ericson and Haggerty, 1997: 27). The police pursue what Ericson and Haggerty describe as "actuarial justice": the police produce and disseminate knowledge that serves as a form of insurance for institutions, enabling them to assess the prospects for, and ways of managing, deviations that might undermine their proper functioning.

As a link in the chain of risk expertise, the police deploy different technologies and communication formats to limit uncertainty. But since the risks identified constantly change and develop, showing how ephemeral our high-tech post-industrial world is, so "do the communication rules, formats, and technologies for dealing with them." Over the last thirty years we have witnessed "an expansion of regulatory systems" that develop "in accordance with the insurance logic of risk" (Ericson and Haggerty, 1997: 48–49). Policing thus becomes a perpetual form of "panoptic sorting" (Ericson and Haggerty, 1997: 40). Electronic surveillance is used to constantly classify, make predictable and thus render manageable the population. "Most of this work does not involve face-to-face communication with the person subject to police activity. The police officer serves as a 'faceless bureaucrat' or 'iconocrat.' This is *policing by human absence*" (Ericson and Haggerty: 1997: 45, emphasis added). Risk is thereby reduced, and chance and uncertainty tamed, by constantly monitoring the population, whether it be through criminal records or information gleaned from credit-card or health-care records.

This notion of "policing by human absence" runs throughout the writings. The sole change is simply the emphasis given to a particular technology used to police populations at a distance. Closed Circuit Television (CCTV), for example, garners a lot of attention. Coleman and Sim (2000) look at its introduction in Liverpool, while Bannister, Fyfe and Kearns (1998) trace its growth across the rest of the United Kingdom. What is constant through the studies of CCTV, however, is the notion of the way in which this form of technology "expands the capacity of visual monitoring in both space and time" (Norris and Armstrong, 1998: 5). Another writer, McCahill, makes this point:

> With the development of modern CCTV systems and telecommunications networks in public spaces the "direct supervision" of the subject population is no longer confined to specific institutional locales, nor does it require the physical co-presence of the observer. (1998: 44)

McCahill does note that continuous monitoring of populations is nearly impossible in public spaces, where people are free to go into or out of the area. The environment is not enclosed or controlled, nor are the people known to the observer. Nevertheless, McCahill and others clearly suggest that the electronic monitoring is more powerful and omnipresent than the bricks-and-mortar type described by Foucault. What makes it more powerful is the role of the camera:

> Since the camera is continually watching and has the ability, when coupled with a video-recorder, to enable the scrutiny of past, as well as contemporaneous events, it represents an extension of the architecture of disciplinary power encapsulated in Bentham's nineteenth century design for a new model prison with its central observation tower, allowing the guards to see everything without ever being seen themselves. (1998: 5)

Policing here is thus represented by the electronic gaze. It can efficiently monitor risk without any contact with subject populations. CCTV allows watchers to "zoom in to reveal the smallest details and monitor every nuance of their [the subjects'] facial expressions and gestures for clues to their intentions" (Norris and Armstrong, 1998: 5). Moreover, the spatial dynamic of CCTV policing is not simply a matter of several cameras being used at the same time. It is also the capacity of these cameras to rapidly transmit data and images of risk populations and "deviant identities" over long distances (McCahill, 1998: 45). This is also the case for the so-called "hot files" kept by criminal law-enforcement agencies in the United States; the hot files are filtered through centralized communication networks (D. Gordon, 1987). The greater the reach of electronic population surveillance, the less likely the contact between the monitors and the monitored.

This at-a-distance policing, whether through CCTV or other forms of electronic surveillance, contributes to a form of governance premised on what Ericson and Haggerty, borrowing from Foucault, refer to as biopower. "Biopower is the power of biography, of constructing biographical profiles of human populations for risk management and security provision," they explain (1997: 91). The concern is not with controlling people through forms of repression, but in dividing groups into particular risk categories. "Biopower makes people up, literally. The risk classification and management of populations is aimed at literally fabricating people into the social body" (1997: 95). Populations are fabricated according to their prospects for deviance and the forms of deviance they present. The result of biopower, Ericson and Haggerty argue, is the encouragement of people "to construct their own self-regulated courses of action" (1997: 95).

As people become aware of both their constitution as a potential risk factor and the increasing pervasiveness of electronic surveillance in their lives, they assume responsibility for the constraints that electronic policing is trying to impose on their behaviour. As Norris and Armstrong (1998: 6) suggest, surveillance thus "involves not only being watched but watching over one's self." Always under the electronic gaze, subject to constant monitoring and risk assessment, people will conduct themselves accordingly, careful not to alarm potential observers. In this way biopower contributes to the production of "docile bodies" (Norris and Armstrong, 1998: 7).[1]

This represents a more subtle and efficient use of power and control than previously known, a potent expression of the shift from criminal to the actuarial justice of a regulatory society (Ericson and Haggerty, 1997: 48 ff.; McCahill, 1998: 53). In the place of formal criminal prosecution reactively pursued by the state is a more diffuse form of power that produces compliant subjects through the construction of risk knowledge.

But who are these docile bodies constructed through the art of modern surveillance and risk management? Who is subject to the electronic gaze? For Ericson and Haggerty, risk management and electronic surveillance are equalizing in their effects. The affluent are just as policed as anyone else:

> The affluent are subjected to the state's taxation, education, licensing, social security and health surveillance systems, as well as a plethora of private corporate systems concerned with credit, financial securities, frequent flyer points and so on. Indeed, it is by no

means clear that marginal populations are the ones most subject to surveillance. (Ericson and Haggarty, 1997: 41)

Some commentators have noted the support closed-circuit television receives from business associations involved in projects to redevelop city centres, whose aim is to remove the homeless, panhandlers and adolescents who hang out there. They have also suggested, though, it is not limited to those targets alone (Coleman and Sim 2000: Norris and Armstrong, 1998: Bannister, Fyfe and Kearns, 1998). With CCTV's growth anyone who enters a public space in city centres or elsewhere is now likely subject to the electronic gaze. The monitoring may not simply be an issue involving the use of public space. In fact, we have arrived at the point that we are almost under constant surveillance the moment we step outside the home. The gaze of the electronic panopticon is total; it effuses a power throughout society in which all subjects, regardless of social class, racial or gender background are bound up, hopelessly embedded in the web of risk management.

In fact, for Ericson and Haggerty the most important class differences in risk society are established by risk profiling itself. Classes are the product of calculating risk probabilities. In each area of risk, a class of risk is determined and regulated, and thereby brought into being as a social reality (Ericson and Haggerty, 1997: 120). Thus class differences are not an expression of the form that wealth creation takes in capitalist society, or even of people's consumptive opportunities. Instead these differences are created when technological developments and the classificatory demands of efficient risk management intersect.

It is a staple of this literature, furthermore, that the extension of the all-pervasive reach facilitated through modern forms of surveillance is seen to correspond to the declining importance of the role of the state in contemporary policing. According to Ericson and Haggerty (1997: 49), to the extent that police work organized through the state does have a role, it is influenced by the knowledge needs of other institutions involved in risk management. The police, in this respect, form only one small, often subordinate, link in the complex chain of policing today. As knowledge workers, they respond to and provide information to other institutions. These are mainly private ones, ranging from insurance companies to provincial motor-vehicle offices. The police produce and distribute information that is severely circumscribed by what private institutions want to know (Ericson and Haggerty, 1997: 25).

Indeed, for the panoptic writers the state in contemporary society is generally seen as fragmented and decentralized rather than unified (Ericson and Haggerty, 1997: 52; Coleman and Sim, 2000: 630). Our attention is drawn to more "autonomous forms of expertise and localized technologies and mechanisms of rule" (Coleman and Sim, 2000: 624). Power, and its concomitant forms of social control, is diffused throughout society and reproduced by means of many local sites and institutions. CCTV is one example, as are personal credit records and insurance profiles. CCTV has spread in certain jurisdictions because of its use by private institutions, especially businesses. In fact, private interests often initiated its use by the public police. According to Coleman and Sim (2000: 626), "the private sector has played a central role in constructing definitions of risk and danger in the city and who should be targeted." Thus more local or autonomous sites of policing express the private character of contemporary policing (see also Ericson and Haggerty, 1997: 52). To focus our attention on the public police or on a state power that is strategically directing policing activity would simply lead us to miss the most central facets of policing today.

For Ericson and Haggerty and O'Malley and Palmer, this new fragmented model is reflected in the emergence of community policing. The fragmented state "ceases to be the directive core attracting to itself a monopoly of functions, and, instead, begins to shed or share many activities and responsibilities" (O'Malley and Palmer, 1996: 141). Community policing is based on the notion of public or community "responsibilization" (O'Malley and Palmer, 1996: 144). Local interests, reflecting community concerns, take the lead in developing and implementing policing strategies with the publicly funded force. Ericson and Haggerty have taken the argument even further, suggesting that community policing not only gives a role to the local community in developing policing strategies, but also "reconfigures the community into communications about risk in every conceivable aspect of life" (1997: 70). The idea of community here shifts: it is not "prediscursive" but is instead defined through the complex interaction of the police and community institutions as they communicate information with one another. Communities are thus formed (discursively for Ericson and Haggerty) in the process of their "responsibilization." The state recedes in importance over much of our public and private lives.

The withdrawal of the state in political importance expressed here mirrors the discourse surrounding neoliberalism, whose advocates or opponents respectively celebrate or mourn the decline of the state. The language of "responsibilization" discussed above with respect to O'Malley and Palmer, for instance, echoes the neoliberal mantra: private individuals or community agents can no longer depend on the state for such services as policing. Instead, they must take responsibility for policing themselves. Likewise, McCahill (1998: 54) argues that the shift to risk society must "be understood in terms of its relation... to the emergence over the last two decades of neoliberal political programmes," with the result that the individual is given the responsibility for managing risk. For some writers in the panopticon school, the emergence of more localized sites of power is as much a response to neoliberal restructuring as it is to the evolutionary growth of electronic techniques of surveillance. Neoliberal restructuring and modern technology intersect to spread the power of social control ever outward. One might even argue that the writers envisage a neoliberalism with startling efficiency: at the core of this theory of contemporary policing, as discussed above, are the notions of biopower and self-regulation. In other words, people have taken up the neoliberal call to "responsibilization" with stunning gusto. The political task facing supporters of neoliberalism, including ending people's supposed reliance on the state, and thus engendering greater self-responsibility and reliance on the private sector, is replaced by self-regulating and docile bodies.

Rethinking the Electronic Panopticon:
At a Distance or In Your Face?

It is presently fashionable among many critical theorists to suggest that policing is primarily done at a distance, targets everyone equally regardless of class or race, and is pursued largely through localized sites of power rather than the state. If we look a little more closely at contemporary policing, however, we find a significant discrepancy between its reality and its portrayal in the panopticon literature. This implies, in turn, that an alternative analysis is necessary. Such an analysis can more accurately account for the dynamics of contemporary policing as they are experienced by its targets. To get to that point, however, we need to look at the central tenets of Ericson and Haggerty and others. Such a study will demonstrate the limits to their analysis and highlight for us the actual character of policing today.

One way of measuring the usefulness of the panopticon theory is to compare it to the practices of community and zero-tolerance policing, which have had considerable influence on policing strategies in Canada, the United States and Britain over the last decade or more. Community policing, for instance, has become a guiding philosophy of policing in Canada. It has been promoted by the Royal Canadian Mounted Police (RCMP) and the Ontario Provincial Police (OPP), as well as numerous municipal police forces (Clairmont, 1991: 467ff.; Eck and Rosenbaum, 1994: 3). For Ericson and Haggerty, as we have seen, community policing is considered an essential feature of policing the risk society.

Zero-tolerance forms of policing have also been promoted in many jurisdictions, including those that promote community policing. Even though community policing is often seen differently from that of zero-tolerance, the difference is minimal. They both are premised on putting more police officers onto the streets, targeting specific neighbourhoods and focusing proactively on low-level public-order issues like vagrancy, panhandling, loitering and so on. In fact, perhaps the clearest difference between them is that community policing, as the name suggests, places greater emphasis on community participation in all aspects — from strategy, to focus, to implementation.

The reality, however, seldom comes close to matching the theory. The distinction between the two forms is superficial; drawing too fine a distinction does not help us understand contemporary policing any better. William Bratton, the former police chief of New York City, on the one hand, refers to the policing strategy adopted in the early 1990s by New York as community policing (Bratton, 1998). On the other hand many commentators view the strategy as a classic example of zero-tolerance policing (Greene, 1999: 171; Parenti, 1999: 72 ff.). It may be that Bratton's choice of terms was intended to provide political gloss to his controversial policing strategy, but the easy substitution of one label for the other, given the character of the policing under his leadership, is suggestive. Moreover, for Wilson and Kelling (1982), whose theory has influenced Bratton and is seen as a cornerstone of zero tolerance (Greene, 1999: 172; Parenti, 1999: 71), part of the responsibility regarding the fight against crime and disorder should include maintaining greater dialogue with neighbourhood residents — even if this is not formalized in public-police liaison committees in the way it is with some community-policing initiatives. Clearly, the idea of a dialogue between the community and police has become an important mantra in many jurisdictions. It is invoked to improve the police's image, thereby muddying the differences between community and zero-tolerance policing even further. Even Pollard, who argues that zero-tolerance strategies tend to be more explicitly harsh towards the targets than community-policing ones, suggests that the distinction is really only one of nominal gradations along the same policing continuum (1998: 46).

Underlying both community and zero-tolerance policing, then, is a similar orientation. One central facet of this orientation, as Crowther (1998) notes, is "they all rely heavily on a visible presence of police officers." Indeed, this is stated explicitly by the broken-windows theorists Wilson and Kelling (1982), whose writings have influenced contemporary policing practices, especially zero-tolerance ones (Parenti, 1999: 71; Greene, 1999: 172). Greater police presence on the streets is the premise of their strategy of targeting signs of social disorder. The visible presence of police on the streets and in communities has clearly not declined or simply been eclipsed by modern surveillance. In the U.S., for example, the 1994 Violent Crimes and Law Enforcement Act doled out $8.8 billion in federal government grants to local law-enforcement agencies to hire 100,000 additional police officers and to upgrade weapons arsenals (Parenti, 1999: 65). The 1991 Safe Streets law had already expanded New York City's police force by 7,000 officers (Greene, 1999: 173).

Canada has not witnessed such a dramatic increase. It would be misleading though to suggest that electronic surveillance has replaced the visible presence of police on the streets. For example, the ratio of police officers to the population in fact declined through the 1990s until 1998, when it began to rise again slightly. The decrease was most noticeable, however, in the senior ranks, "which has allowed the police forces to maintain the same level of constables 'on the street'" (Canadian Centre for Justice Statistics, 1998: 4–5). Further, the aim of an initiative like the City of Toronto's target-policing program is to specifically assign more police officers directly to the streets in so-called crime hot spots. The program is known as Community Action Policing. It was first implemented in the summer of 1999 and regularized the next year. For the initial program, the City spent $1.8 million to place 680 additional officers on the street in each of the eleven weeks it was run (Toronto Police Services, 1999). Although there is not a large increase in the number of officers assigned to the streets in Canada, certain targeted neighbourhoods are actually now experiencing greater police presence.

The physical presence of police on the streets and in specific neighbourhoods cannot be ignored. In the case of community policing, for instance, the emphasis on community participation is a pretext to place more officers in specific areas and better penetrate the communities with which police have had poor relations. According to P. Gordon, the strategy in Britain is to try to win legitimacy from specific sectors of communities and thus mobilize support for harsher forms of policing (1987: 139). With respect to Canada, community participation is little more than rhetoric and "may be a diversionary device to defuse potential criticism from the community" (Leighton, 1991: 507). The police themselves see the promotion of community involvement as an important source of public legitimization, even though they actively negate meaningful participation from the community in shaping policing practices (Fischer, 2000: 33, 173). Community-policing liaison committees rarely have anything more than a symbolic role, as police ensure that their own autonomy is not compromised by public participation. They control the financial resources directed towards such programs or take over the committees themselves (P. Gordon, 1987: 130–31, 137; Fischer, 2000: 199; see also Murphy, 1993: 20). In contrast to Ericson and Haggerty, Fischer has defined the community police officer as "a traditional 'police officer' with the mission and instruments to do traditional police work according to the traditional principles and practices" (2000: 199). Other critics of community policing have clearly noted its implications for greater social control (P. Gordon, 1987: 133, 141; Leighton, 1991: 510; Clairmont, 1991: 470). Under the guise of broadening public participation and offering greater accountability to communities, the police have effectively extended their physical presence in, and control over, certain communities. Any form of dialogue with certain community members consists of gathering low-level intelligence (P. Gordon, 1987: 134; Fischer, 2000: 173). As one member of a Black community in Britain has commented, "The police use this local 'bobby' approach to gather intelligence among the Black community with a view to busting them later" (P. Gordon 1987: 135).

Such strategies of social control are also a central feature of what is perhaps the more blatantly aggressive approach of zero-tolerance policing. In New York City, which many observers tout as the epitome of the zero-tolerance approach, Bratton "unleashed patrol officers to stop and search citizens who were violating the most minor laws on the books, to run warrant checks on them, or just to bring them in for questioning about criminal activity in their neighbourhood" (Greene, 1999: 171, 175). According to Pollard, regardless of the nature of the reforms brought about in different jurisdictions under the guise of zero tolerance, "the *emotion* underlying them seems to be concentrated on aggression: on ruthlessness in dealing with low-level criminality and disorderliness" (1998: 44). The aggressive focus here on low-level criminality and public order is partly rooted in the theory of "broken windows," posited by Wilson and Kelling: criminality and disorderliness are inextricably linked. Unless checked, they argue, signs of disorder such as graffiti, panhandling or minor vandalism will evolve into more serious forms of criminality, since disorderly people will think they can get away with it (Wilson and Kelling, 1982: see also Bratton, 1998). As crime became a hot-button political issue in the 1980s and 1990s in the U.S. and Canada, this more aggressive style of policing spread in influence (Parenti, 1999: 45.[2]

It should be noted, though, that concerns over public order have also been an explicit focus of community policing. Whatever the rhetoric, in actual practice community policing is no more concerned with violent crimes or higher-level criminality than zero-tolerance policing (Fischer, 2000: 123; Leighton, 1991: 510; Murphy, 1993: 23). A proactive focus on public order is thus the hallmark of policing today. This concern translates into a more visible and assertive police presence on the streets. The physical presence of police on the streets and in neighbourhoods is also accompanied by an increase in militarization. The goal of seeking public order does not always involve the heaviest forms of weaponry now available; however, the militarization of police forces in some jurisdictions is striking, reinforcing the fact that the operation of police power is not as subtle as theorists of the electronic surveillance suggest.

Interestingly, Ericson and Haggerty have noted this new feature of contemporary policing. But they attribute this trend to the adoption of military technologies used for data gathering and surveillance. They do not deny the possibility of militarization as a result of more directly coercive forms of technology, such as deadly weaponry. Their emphasis, however, is clearly on what they see as:

> The most distinctive attribute of the contemporary military establishment, its technoscientific structure as part of the information age.... The military influence on police work does not necessarily arrive donned in helmets and jackboots but can appear clad in the more reassuring attire of lab-coat or business suit. (1999: 234, 246)

Yet one of the most salient trends in policing today, as detailed by Parenti, is the growth across the U.S. of paramilitary tactical units or Special Weapons and Tactics (SWAT) teams. These were originally developed in response to inner-city riots and political violence in the 1960s. By the 1990s, he observes, these paramilitary units, armed with the latest in high-tech weaponry,[3] were being used increasingly for everyday policing. Parenti has described their role in some cities and the result:

> Paramilitary police units are increasingly called out to execute petty warrants, conduct traffic stops and round up non-violent suspects.... The paramilitary policing units militarize the regular police by osmosis as the weaponry, training and tactics of the police special forces are gradually passed on to the regular police. (1999: 124, 131)

And with the weaponry and training, he argues, comes a "militaristic set of social relations" (1999: 133). The fight against crime, the defence of public order, takes on the characteristic of a war, where certain communities literally live under armed occupation.

The scholarly literature offers us little information on the level of militarization in Canada. Police budgets generally do not disclose detailed information on spending priorities, especially if they relate to weaponry. Reports in the popular media, however, do give us some limited insight into this trend. Although militarization does not appear to have spread nearly as rapidly in Canada as it has in the U.S., some reports do suggest that tactical units have become more common since the 1980s in Canada as well. Almost every Canadian police force with more than a hundred officers now has one. There are at least sixty-five tactical squads across the country, twenty-six belonging to the RCMP alone.

The most recent growth in militarization can likely be attributed to an increase in political protest, particularly the global-justice movement. But the role of tactical units had been steadily increasing even earlier. Furthermore, an RCMP coordinator of the National Emergency Response Team has reportedly encouraged police divisions to expand the mandate of their tactical teams. In Edmonton, members of the SWAT team has been used for more routine policing, including traffic stops and responding to domestic calls (Pugilese, 1998).

The militarization of Canadian police forces has also notably occurred in response to Aboriginal land-claims struggles. After the Oka crisis in 1990, for example, the Sûreté du Québec (SQ) spent $2.4 million on three armoured tanks (Waganese, 1991:4). Shortly after the Gufstafsen Lake standoff in British Columbia in 1995, the RCMP began creating a permanent fleet of armoured tanks. The RCMP set aside $8.5 million for this venture, apparently to avoid having to borrow from the military for future standoffs (*Toronto Star*, 1997: A12).

What is also interesting to note here is the proliferation in Canada of so-called non-lethal weapons, particularly in the 1990s. These included pepper spray, electroshock taser guns, bean-bag guns and plastic bullets; they are often promoted by police as an alternative to deadly force. However, some of these weapons have been implicated in the deaths of Canadians.

- There have been at least seven deaths since the mid-1990s that involved the use of pepper spray to subdue a victim.[4]
- At least one death has resulted from a plastic bullet, after the victim was shot in the head.
- At least one death resulted from a bean-bag gun, where the bean bag was lodged inside the victim's body causing severe blood loss (Teel, 1997: 24–25).

Interestingly, representatives at a leading non-lethal research institution in the U.S. have acknowledged that there really is no such thing as a non-lethal weapon (Wright, 2001: 10). In Victoria, B.C., the sergeant responsible for organizing the Victoria police's taser trial in the late 1990s stated candidly that tasers are not an alternative to deadly force (Schuster, 2001: 27). Some police officials, then, do not share the view that such weapons are an alternative to deadly force. Perhaps they see them simply as additions to an increasingly sophisticated weapons arsenal in which control over subjects is the first and most important priority.

This may shed light on interesting statistics on the context in which pepper spray was deployed in Toronto in the 1990s. According to the City's Police Discipline Review Committee, the increased use of pepper spray in the 1990s occurred at the same time as the use of firearms increased (Rankin, 1998: B5). In Toronto, then, pepper spray is not a substitute for guns. In other words, it represents the extension of deadly force.

The aggressive focus on low-level disorder and militarization has also contributed to a context in which violence and brutality are becoming more common features of contemporary policing. The panoptic literature, however, make little mention of police brutality, emphasizing instead on policing at a distance:

> One searches high and low in Foucauldian texts for police officers themselves to appear and play a part in the exercise of power or the disciplinary project. For them, the police idea is emptied of the humiliations administered both on the street and in the police station, the thud of the truncheon and the gratuitous use of "discretionary" force. (Neocleous, 2000: x)

Whenever the police extend their reach over certain communities, tales of brutality increase. In the U.S., for example, a survey of SWAT encounters found a 34 percent increase in that the use of deadly force between 1995 and 1998. Pugilese's report and other newspaper accounts have detailed a series of killings (both intentional and accidental) and shockingly botched raids by Canadian SWAT teams (Parenti, 1999: 127; Pugilese, 1998). Statistics on police-related shooting deaths in Canada are collected very spottily by police and government offices outside Ontario. A cursory glance at newspaper accounts, however, suggests that, shooting deaths of civilians by Canadian police increased in at least five provinces — British Columbia, Alberta, Saskatchewan, Ontario and Québec — from the 1980s to the 1990s. The number of shooting deaths in fact almost doubled in Toronto and Montreal over that period.[5]

But this represents only the most extreme example of the violence of contemporary policing. Behind it lies daily forms of humiliation and aggression. In New York City, civil-rights claims regarding police brutality increased by 75 percent in the first four years (1994 to 1998) of the implementation of Bratton's zero-tolerance strategies. Another telltale sign: Amnesty International has reported that police brutality and unjustifiable use of force is a widespread problem (Greene, 1999: 176). New York, in turn, has paid out more than $100 million in damages as a result of police violence. As the aggressive focus on disorderliness and low-level criminality spread to other urban centres in the U.S., so too did the rapid increase of stories detailing police misconduct and brutality (Parenti, 1999: 83–85).

As with police shootings, it is hard to trace police brutality through official data. In Canada, much of the officially recorded information is spotty and does not attempt to examine the issue in any meaningful way. This problem is exacerbated in situations where governments abolish even the public-complaint agencies that have some limited civilian oversight. This was the case in Ontario, where the government shut down the Office of the Police Complaints Commissioner in the mid-1990s, replacing it with the Ontario Civilian Commission on Police Services. Under the old system, individuals could lodge a complaint at regional offices of the Complaints Commissioner; under the new system, complaints must initially be lodged and dealt with by the police stations out of which the officer involved works. Without meaningful civilian oversight to address concerns about police practices, one can assume that many potential complaints go unrecorded.[6] Official statistics may very well be just the tip of the iceberg then, not reflecting many of the harsh realities of a militarized policing aggressively bent on stamping out disorderliness.

In addition, statistics generally do not reflect the more systematic practices of abuse exercised by police against specifically targeted groups — forms of abuse that have become widespread enough that they are given labels, sometimes by the victims, as a form of shorthand. A reference to the label enables other victims or potential targets to figure out the rest of the story without need of further explanation. In Toronto, for example, many people living on the downtown streets, particularly squeegeers, refer to the "Cherry Beach Special": police take individuals to Cherry Beach, an abandoned industrial area on the city's waterfront, and beat them up (Esmonde, 1999: 133).

A deadlier version of this is the "Starlight Tours" in Saskatoon. "Starlight Tours" came to public light in early 2000 after a young Aboriginal man,

Darrel Knight, filed a formal complaint against the Saskatoon police. The police dumped him outside the city on a winter night after taking his coat. The bodies of two Aboriginal men were found partially clad in the same area where Knight allegedly was dropped off. They had frozen to death. Knight's complaint, together with the discovery of the two bodies, precipitated a wave of complaints from Saskatoon's Aboriginal community about similar forms of police abuse.[7]

In many communities today, the omnipresence of policing is expressed less by the cold, distant gaze of the camera or the personal records kept by different institutions than it is by the police officer working the beat who surveys the landscape for signs of disorder. The expression of power is translated through the hostile gaze or brute force of police officers. People do not experience power at work in an abstract manner as it weaves through communities and thereby produces self-regulating docile bodies.

Forms of electronic surveillance should not be ignored. However, their importance in terms of contemporary policing has clearly been overstated. Even the spread of CCTV is not as ubiquitous as some writers suggest. Much of the literature on CCTV focuses on its growth in the U.K. In a major urban centre like Toronto, for example, CCTV's use in public spaces has been more uneven. Responsibility over funding video surveillance has sparked debates between Toronto police and city officials. Plans to introduce it into certain so-called crime areas have also not taken off — or been implemented very haphazardly — suggesting it is not considered a high priority compared to other well-funded programs such as "targeted policing."[8]

More problematic, though, is that electronic surveillance has been overstated at the expense of considering more directly coercive expressions of policing. This point is in fact acknowledged by Coleman and Sim, who wrote about the introduction of CCTV in Liverpool, England. Noting the "militarization of street life," they conclude that the focus on at-a-distance policing "is theoretically and politically compromised by its failure to deal with the materiality of violence and coercion in securing compliance" (Coleman and Sim, 2000: 634). Likewise, Gill has noted: "there do come times when 'government'... will provide a better description of policing than governance.... Some people still enjoy and employ greater rights than others to kick down people's doors!" (1998: 302). Given the very direct and confrontational nature of contemporary policing, then, electronic surveillance might best be understood as playing a complementary role, with CCTV and "hot files" enhancing the efficiency of street police to monitor and intervene in communities.

Contemporary Policing: The Great Equalizer?

Who are the targets of contemporary policing? It is time to ask this important question. Are all groups experiencing aggressive public-order policing to the same degree? The Cherry Beach Special and Starlight Tours are clearly not

meted out equally across society. In its purposefully visible, often very aggressive and violent form, policing is targeted towards specific communities and
groups of people. Policing, is far from being class-, race- or gender-neutral.

A report written on targeted policing in Toronto, which was based on
interviews with its targets, for example, shows that the program is focused
on areas with a high degree of poverty and large concentration of people of
colour and new immigrants. This campaign to quell perceived disorderliness
was directed towards the poor, homeless, people of colour, immigrants and
sex-trade workers, according to the Committee to Stop Targeted Policing
(2000: 7).

Research on zero-tolerance and community policing practised in other
areas demonstrates a similar focus. Indeed, Wilson and Kelling are as explicit
on this aspect of policing in their theory of broken windows as they are on
the need for a greater, more visible presence of police on the streets. "'The
unchecked panhandler is, in effect, the first broken window,' they argue"
(1982: 34). Vagrancy, especially when accompanied by soliciting for money,
is clearly the disorder Wilson and Kelling are seeking to address. Indeed, it
has become a focal point for much of contemporary policing. When Rudolph
Guiliani was elected mayor of New York City, he and William Bratton, his
new chief of police, spoke often about reclaiming the streets from crime.
But the first targets of their "pacification program" were squeegeers and the
homeless, with sex-trade workers not far behind. These people were literally
forced off the streets; the homeless, to find refuge in the bowels of the city's
subway system. They were no longer able to ply their trade or look for spare
change without risking an aggressive police response.[9]

A similar focus of zero-tolerance policing developed in Britain during
the recessions of the 1980s and 1990s and the concomitant escalation of
poverty rates, especially amongst youth: "At times of major economic and
social upheaval the authorities have always tended to favour some form of
zero tolerance intervention in order to maintain social order" (Burke 1998b:
87).

Community policing has shown a similar focus on poverty, especially
panhandlers. According to Clairmont, community policing has been used
in Canada to recommend tenant evictions, reflecting the extent to which
contemporary policing has been able to insert itself into some neighbourhoods (1991: 480–81). This observation corresponds to the field work
Fischer has done on policing and the police-community liaison committees.
As we have seen, these committees are largely symbolic, at most used by
police to gather low-level intelligence. Interestingly, however, the committee members primarily reflected the business interests in the communities
they were supposed to be representing. According to Fischer, the police
apparently never saw the homogeneous character of these committees as
problematic. In fact they were quite clear about excluding the "undesirables"
from the community. Undesirables, they felt, were not "productive" to the

community: therefore they could not be considered legitimate members of the community. Such people were to be removed, not consulted (Fischer, 2000).

The focus on poverty and public order also goes along with the racialization of policing. According to Parenti, people of colour have been disproportionately made the victims of aggressive public-order policing, especially of its most militaristic and violent features. Much of this targeting has been nominally conducted under the rubric of the war on drugs, where entire communities come under virtual police occupation. Parenti cites the example of Operation Hammer, which took place in the deindustrialized ghettos of south L.A. in the early 1900s. Some 14,000 people — mostly young Black men — were arrested during a massive paramilitary occupation (1999: 58). However, Operation Hammer was just one egregious example; the targeting of Black communities or Black drivers outside of their communities has been a staple of other police anti-drug programs across the U.S. (Parenti, 1999: chapter 6; Wortley, undated: 5).

Operation Hammer is a form of racial profiling — the selective police interventions in neighbourhoods or on roadways based on the racial background of the person being stopped. It is very much a feature of policing in Canada as well as the U.S. The issue served as background to a controversy in Toronto a few years ago. It broke out after the *Toronto Star* published data collected by police that showed that being Black was a significant determinant of a person's likelihood to be stopped or arrested by police.[10] The *Toronto Star's* report, however, was really just an update on police practices that have been previously experienced and documented for some time.

The Commission on Systemic Racism in the Criminal Justice System in Ontario, which published its findings in 1995, reported that Black men are almost twice as likely to be stopped by police in Toronto than their white counterparts. Approximately 43 percent of all Black male respondents to the inquiry reported being stopped by police over a two-year period. The inquiry also found that police stops of Black people — whether in cars, on sidewalks or at shopping malls — were often intrusive, intimidating and not based on any criminal violation. They were not based on any violations of criminal law. The individuals in question perceived the interventions as related to their race and the desire of police to display their authority over Black people (Ontario, 1995: 353, 356).

Some Black individuals have dubbed such incidents as driving-while-being-black violations (Wortley, undated: 1). The discriminatory police attention towards Black people extends to detention patterns: Blacks in Toronto are much likelier than suspects from other backgrounds to be detained by police in the first instance; to be detained for longer periods of time; and to receive stricter bail conditions upon release (Wortley and Kellough, 1998). The effects of these experiences might explain the results of a recent City of Toronto study of youth in neighbourhoods with large Black and immigrant populations. It found that the second most commonly cited perceived threat to personal safety is the police (Smith, 2003: A21).

Commissions of inquiry in Manitoba and Alberta have documented a similar pattern of policing, this time directed against Aboriginal people. Noting the over-representation of Aboriginals in the province's jails, the Manitoba commission acknowledged this to be the end point of a long line of systemic racism (Manitoba, 1991: 85 ff.). Both commissions found that it is far more common for Aboriginals than other groups to be stopped in their cars or on the streets by police and questioned about their activities. But, as the Manitoba commission argued, even when charges were laid during a given stop, they were seldom pursued by police. Like the police stops of Blacks in Toronto, criminal law violations are not necessarily the principal reason Aboriginals were so frequently stopped by police. In fact, Aboriginals reported that police stops were not usually precipitated by any legal infraction in the first place.[11]

Given the amount of police attention they receive, it is not surprising to find that people of colour and Aboriginals have in turn experienced a disproportionate amount of the more aggressive forms of contemporary policing. The hyper-militarized and deadly SWAT interventions in the U.S., as detailed by Parenti, are most likely to occur in African-American neighbourhoods. In Canada, complaints flooded in from Saskatoon's Aboriginal community after Darrel Knight's story came to light. The sheer number of complaints suggested that there had been more incidents of Starlight Tours than those few that made news headlines. The victims of the escalated police killings discussed above, particularly in urban centres such as Montreal, Toronto, Ottawa and Saskatoon, are disproportionately Black or Aboriginal men. As Pedicelli has argued with respect to Montreal and Toronto, "they were killed under questionable circumstances."[12]

The special focus accorded to Black and Aboriginal communities suggests, then, that policing is deeply racialized. So too are notions of disorderliness, the focus of much of policing today, and criminality, which as we have seen is intimately connected to and derives from disorderliness (a point I will return to in the next chapter). According to Ontario's Commission on Systemic Racism, "The police single out Black men to display their authority and because they perceive the Black men as warranting more scrutiny than other people" (Ontario, 1995: 357).

Considering the findings of both the Manitoba and Alberta's studies on the relationship between Aboriginals and the judicial system, as well as the institutionalized violence expressed in such treatment as Starlight Tours, we can conclude the police display a similar attitude towards Aboriginals. Individuals are stopped and questioned in the police's campaign against disorderliness and potential criminality precisely because they are Black or Aboriginal. Members of these groups are what Skolnick (1966) has referred to as "symbolic assailants": criminal suspects until they prove they are not.

Policing, then, is premised on the criminalization of entire classes of people based on their socio-economic location, together with their race and gender. This process is intensified under zero-tolerance and community-policing initiatives (Crowther, 1998: 75).

Retreat of the State?

One of the most striking characteristics of the panoptic literature is the general downplaying of the role of the state in both policing and political processes in our society. The studies echo much of the mainstream literature on neoliberalism. There is a consensus among commentators that the role of the state today, in response to financial restraints and the internationalization of markets, has been greatly diminished. In response, sociologist Alan Sears argues that even though capitalist states have been engaged in restructuring for the past decade or more, it has not resulted in a reduction in state power. Instead, state power is being mobilized in different ways (Sears, 1999: 95).

One of these ways has clearly been in the areas of policing and criminal law. The present period of political and economic deregulation and unfettered expressions of the market "appears to require... a *more intensive* use of the criminal law as a tool of sovereignty in the penetration of public order" (De Lint, 1999). As we have seen, the police play a central role in pursuing this task.

In the U.S., for example, a series of judicial decisions and crime bills, spanning the past thirty-odd years, have significantly empowered the state and police at the expense of suspects and criminal defendants. The "get-tough-on-crime" legislation has granted broader rights to the police for purposes of search and seizure of property, as well as arrest and detention. The new laws have been backed up by increased funding to hire more police officers and buy high-powered, state-of-the-art weaponry:

> [T]he story is one of rapidly and insidiously escalating police power; the opening of a new stage in the development of an American-style, democratic police state. (Parenti, 1999: 72)

The U.S. appears to be on the cutting edge of activating state power in policing and criminal law enforcement, but it is not alone. The consolidation of neoliberal restructuring in the U.K. under Margaret Thatcher in the 1980s was accompanied by tough anti-crime legislation and the strengthening of police powers (Bonefeld, 1993: 140, 155–60). We have seen similar legislation in Canada: Ontario brought in The Safe Streets Act in 1999 and Ottawa introduced broad anti-gang laws in June 2001.[13] The anti-terrorism legislation adopted in the aftermath of September 11, 2001, went even further in promoting the law-and-order agenda and providing the tools to police bodies to pursue it. The recent anti-terrorism legislation has granted new powers to the police with regard to arresting suspected terrorists on a preventative basis and holding them for up to seventy-two hours without laying charges. Both measures did not exist in law before — with the exception of the War Measures Act, invoked in the fall of 1970 by the Trudeau government in response to the FLQ crisis.

In determining suspicion of involvement in, or contribution to, a terrorist group, courts "may consider among other factors whether the accused uses a name, word, symbol, or other representation that identifies or is associated with the terrorist group" (quoted in Galati, 2002). The definition of suspicion is not only extremely broad; it also smacks of racial profiling, given that many terrorist organizations use Islamic or Sikh religious symbols or Arab or Tamil cultural symbols. Even though the anti-terrorism legislation was passed in the wake of September 11, at least one critic has argued that "the manner in which the terrorist theme has been woven into the fabric of our criminal law will ensure the permanence of most of these provisions" (Trotter, 2001: 239). As far as policing and law enforcement are concerned, the government has steadily changed its role. The role has become broader and more coercive than it ever was before.

It is true that funding for police services (in terms of constant dollars adjusted for inflation) declined from the early to mid-1990s. So did the ratio of officers to the population. It is also true that private security has become a more regular feature in the lives of many individuals today, particularly poor people and people of colour. These developments, however, do not spell a decline in importance of the state and public police officers. In the five years that the funding in constant dollars decreased, the most it did so in any given year was by 1.75 percent. Since 1997, the funding has steadily increased by an average rate greater than that in constant dollars. If we calculate in terms of *current* dollars, the funding has increased since at least the mid-1980s (Canadian Centre for Justice Statistics, 2002: 15).

In a major urban centre like Toronto, police spending is easily the largest part of the City's budget. The police budget here increased in current dollars by 19 percent from 1996 to 2001 alone.[14] At the same time, the presence of officers on the streets has stayed fairly constant. In certain neighbourhoods it has in fact increased.

A similar growth pattern is seen in the industry of private security. However, we must consider this trend in the context of the discussion above: the increase in the number of private security guards has not occurred at the expense of state power and the role of public police in exercising that power. Private security guards, if anything, complement police officers. For one thing, private security guards simply do not have the legal power and weaponry to enforce their power as police do. The public police have much greater powers of search, arrest and detention than private security guards. The latter have the same legal power to arrest or detain someone as that of a regular citizen.

Security guards are generally employed to guard a particular space — a store or a housing complex, for example — whereas police officers working a beat can be deployed much more broadly in a community and thus gain a greater sense of its overall make up and rhythms. The greater powers and broader deployment accord the police an ability for proactive insertion into people's lives on streets, in cars, in parks and elsewhere in a neighbourhood. They can also target individuals in a combination of these spaces. The role of private security guards, then, might best be seen as an early warning system: it removes some of the grunt work for officers. In this respect, private policing represents a reinforcement of state-funded policing.

It is worth noting here that police officers in Canada earn, on average, more than double what private security guards make. They must also meet certain training requirements to get hired. With the exception of British Columbia and Newfoundland, there is no such requirement for security guards. This suggests that the state is still very interested in having a trained, organized and well-paid police force it can rely on to maintain public order and whose powers and authority are clear to the public. Again, this does not mean that security guards are irrelevant to the lives of the poor or people of colour. On the contrary, it suggests that emphasizing the role of private security forces, as much of the policing-as-surveillance literature does, is a serious mistake. An over-emphasis comes at the expense of analyzing the power of the state. The mistake is indeed serious given the ominous presence of that power, especially as it is exercised through police, in many people's lives today (Canadian Centre for Justice Statistics, 1997).

Panoptic Theory's Techno-fetishism

Most of the panoptic literature has several limitations: it ignores the phenomenon contemporary policing has acquired, and it fails to consider class, race or gender in its analysis. It likewise falls short of examining the central role played by the state. Without taking the above features into account, the studies cannot properly ascertain or begin to understand the social dynamics policing expresses today. In this respect, surveillance theories are marked by a fetishistic view of their object of study.[15] In a classically fetishized understanding of the social phenomenon under observation, the relation between people becomes a relation between things: a relation between electronic forms of surveillance and self-regulating docile bodies. The focus on technologies and at-a-distance policing, in other words, takes the place of a clearer analysis of social relations that lie at the heart of policing.

For this reason we do not get a sense of the class, racial or gendered basis of policing, or of the violence and humiliations meted out to people in very specific neighbourhoods. It follows that we have no hope of answering deeper questions as to the larger role of policing today. Why, for instance, is so much emphasis placed on the need for direct physical intervention in specific communities. To maintain order? And what precisely is the order being defended by the state in its fight against what is essentially low-level disorderliness? In order to address these questions, a theory of policing that is attentive to the social relations — to the relations between active human agents shaping their world — is required. We need a theory, then, that situates questions of state power and its relation to issues of class at the core of its analysis. It must also have at its core an anti-racist and feminist understanding of the class relations that fundamentally shape our society. With its main focus on technologies that facilitate the working of an abstract and decentralized form of power, the panoptic literature clearly is in no position to accomplish this. It is to the development of such a theory that we turn in the next chapter.

Notes

1. Norris and Armstrong borrow the concept of "docile bodies" from Foucault (1977: 135 ff.).

2. See Sears' useful comments on the rise of law-and-order rhetoric and harsher forms of policing in Canada (1999: 104–106). Zero-tolerance policing, it should be stressed, became a law-and-order trend in North America in the 1980s and 1990s, spreading from one policing jurisdiction to another like stylish designer clothes that everyone just has to have, and eventually made its way into schools. Its philosophy, as implied in this chapter, informs community policing. Its popularity among police and law-and-order advocates derives not simply from its calls for placing greater numbers of police in poorer communities, or into schools. It also comes from its philosophical intolerance for even the smallest sign of disorder — public drunkenness, begging, graffiti, loud noise, etc. According to the theoretical logic, if left unchecked, it will lead straight to dangerous crime and the breakdown of communities. This is akin to the gateway drug theory, where pot smoking is a virtual life sentence to heroin addiction. Such a philosophical stance, however weak analytically (not everyone becomes a violent offender, while violent offenders may have many common characteristics in their histories), nevertheless presents police with an intellectual opening to defend their aggressive presence in communities and target people and behaviours whose threat to public safety is questionable.

3. Along with the increased use of SWAT units and "non-lethal" weapons, militarization has also involved stronger fire power, including in some cases automatic weapons that can hit targets from greater distances with greater force and accuracy and fire off more rounds than more traditional handguns. Recently Toronto police have begun to use controversial hollow-point bullets, which are designed to collapse and ricochet inside the target's body rather than exit, causing extensive internal damage. Some suggest that the Toronto police's increasing use of dark colours for cars and outfits is an attempt to present a more imposing or intimidating image of police officers. Such a change in public image also reflects the trend towards militarization.

4. See Gregoire (2001: A1); Dougherty (2000: A5); Jeffs (1996: B3); Boyle (1995: A19).

5. This assessment is based on news items on police shootings appearing in major Canadian newspapers cited in the *Canadian News Index* for the years 1980–2002, and Pedicelli (1998).

6. See Landau's (1996) study on public perceptions of the police complaints system.
7. See *Vancouver Province* (2000: A27); *Calgary Herald* (2000: B10). See also Kossick (2000).
8. See, for example, Quinn (2002: B1, B3).
9. See, for example, Parenti (1999: 77) and Burke (1998a: 17).
10. Rankin, Quinn, Shephard, Simmie and Duncanson (2002: A1).
11. Manitoba (1991: 595); Alberta (1991: 2–5ff).
12. Pedicelli (1998: 63–77; 125–30). Again, this assessment is made based on the news items appearing in major Canadian newspapers cited in the Canadian News Index for the years 1980–2003, where the race of the victim is identified.
13. See Stuart on the significance of Bill C-24, passed by the federal government in June 2001 (2001).
14. Toronto Police Services (1984, 1986, 1992, 1996, 2001); Toronto Police Accountability Coalition (2002).
15. See Marx (1977: 163) on commodity fetishism. His theory of the "mystical" appearance of commodities in capitalist society, obscuring the social relations underlying them, provides a useful conceptual device for understanding the current literature's presentation of policing as primarily electronic.

2. Producing Capitalist Order: Police, Class, Race and Gender

That much of policing today is very direct and aggressive suggests that police targets are not as submissive as writers have portrayed them. If surveillance methods can transform people into self-regulating docile bodies, then why would the police, often carrying an arsenal of weapons, need to go into certain neighbourhoods? Such a strategy reflects resistance on the part of the residents to the state's attempt to impose forms of order on them, not their self-regulation.

Policing must be understood, then, in terms of people's agency, not docility. This is not to imply that people act completely outside of any constraints, however. Power structures like the state and police do shape people's behaviour in important ways. But the order they seek to impose is not automatic and never final; it is mediated by processes of struggle. To properly understand contemporary policing, then, we need a more nuanced theory of power, particularly of state power, through which much of policing is organized. In this theory the structures and struggles should not be seen as external to one another. By focusing on the struggles surrounding policing, we can shed light on the kind of social order being pursued by the state and resisted by the targets of policing.

This chapter will briefly explore the Open Marxist theories of state power, which, in their refusal to artificially separate structure from struggle, provide a useful spring board to look at the historical role of police in capitalist societies.[1] The study of policing in this chapter will also make good use of the work of the Marxist writer Mark Neocleous. His work on the development of modern policing helps to clarify some of the dynamics in contemporary policing discussed in the previous chapter. This enables us to situate the dynamics in a broader context: the role policing has played historically in capitalist societies. However, I will deepen these theories of state power in general, and Neocleous's theory of policing in particular, by analyzing the way in which state power and policing interact with the processes of racialization and gendering. Although both are integral to the mobilization of state and police power, they receive scant attention in the writings of Neocleous and Marxists in general. This is a significant limitation in the works that must be addressed.

State Power and Class Struggle

In the Open Marxist theories of the capitalist state, state power is understood to both shape and be shaped by human practice. Structure and struggle are connected internally to one another. The state does not exist independently of struggle or human actions, nor is the struggle outside the realm of capital or the state. This creates a useful perspective for understanding the history of modern policing, as well as the development of contemporary law-and-order policing. We will look at the latter in the next chapter.

Policing is closely linked with the struggles of working people against the wage-labour relation. It is shaped by such struggle, and it in turn affects the struggle. This framework thus provides a more nuanced understanding of both past and current developments of policing. It avoids reducing policing to either a mechanically understood repressive function or to the aspirations of specific institutional actors. As the condition — or "form," as these Marxists might articulate it — of capitalist state power is struggle, so too is that of policing. Like the state, policing takes on a general form in capitalist society. This form expresses the class dynamics of capitalist accumulation.

We will look more closely at policing in a moment. First, let us briefly look at how Open Marxists analyze the state. One of the central theorists in this group is Werner Bonefeld. His theory is based on the internal relationship between structure and class struggle. Bonefeld argues that the capitalist state is the political form, or mode of existence, of the contradictory nature of capital: capital's dependence on wage labour (Bonefeld, 1993: 15). To survive in the marketplace, capital must revolutionize the productive power of labour to make greater profits and accumulate more capital. Profit, is based on the ability of capital to limit "necessary labour" in order to produce more "surplus labour," i.e., surplus value.[2]

Such strategies are affected by the ability of workers to struggle for better wages, fairer health and safety conditions, or control over the labour process and length of the working day. There may even be a struggle against the central relationship between wages and labour. Labour exists contradictorily "in and against capital"; it is both the source of wealth and a barrier to its creation (Bonefeld, 1993: 17). Capitalist accumulation, therefore, is a process in which capital must struggle to constitute labour on a basis necessary for the reproduction of social relations. In other words, labour's "disruptive power to resist managerial strategies to set [it] in motion" must be contained within the limits of the capitalist form (Bonefeld, 1993: 40). Indeed, the existence of a class of wage labourers from the onset is not "an accomplished fact" (1993: 24–25). It must be formed, or recomposed, again and again. The existence of wage labour is a product of struggle, and it is through this struggle that the capitalist state form develops.

According to Bonefeld, the capitalist state is not created simply because the top brass of the civil service consists of wealthy individuals who act in the interests of their class.[3] Nor is it formed by its own internal logic — reflecting the dynamics of accumulation — which exists before human struggles occur.[4] Instead, the state develops in and through the historical movement of the class struggle. It assumes a specific form that expresses politically the contradictory nature of capitalist social relations, just as the production process expresses the relations economically. The disruptive presence of "labour in and against capital," is the "material constitution of the state form" (Bonefeld, 1993: 50). The contradiction of capital and the struggles deriving from it both shape and are, in turn, shaped by the development of the state.

The formation of a class of wage labourers is both the historical basis for the state to develop and the result of its development. The working class did not present itself to capital ready-made. It was in response to workers' struggles against the wage form that the state arrogated to itself, among other powers contributing to the social conditions necessary for capitalist accumulation, the power to decompose class relations on the basis of the market.[5] Through the imposition of capitalist law, in which the right of property was enforced over society, the state established the contradictory and unequal relationship between capital and labour as a legally bounded market relationship between formally free and equal property owners.[6] In so doing, the state effectively "imposes the rationality and equality of the right of property over society in the attempt to contain the social antagonism of capital and labour by the force of law" (Bonefeld, 1993: 47). The establishment of property rights in law for capitalists is crucial. It means that whoever owns property (in the broad sense of the word) can protect it legally.

If working people try to take over or threaten its property, for example, owners have legal recourse to prevent such a threat. Part of the state's role is to keep this from happening, and thereby do owners safeguard their means of production and their ability to make profits and accumulate wealth. As guarantor of the right of property, then, the state is a "distinct moment in the class antagonism between capital and labour, a moment within which the contradictory unity of surplus value production exists as a political relation, complementing the economic" (Bonefeld, 1993: 50). In this respect, Bonefeld notes, the state is engaged in class struggle through its historic role of enforcing capitalist reproduction.

But the imposition of capitalist law is not the only means by which the state enforces the reproduction of capitalist social relations. According to Bonefeld, the state also regulates the reproduction of the working class through its forms of administration. This point is developed by Neocleous

(1996), who argues that the political administration of the working class must be made central to our understanding of capitalist state power. Like Foucault, Neocleous bases his theory on the way in which individuals have historically become the objects of political administration and how such mechanisms operate to constitute subjectivities. But Foucault conflates the state and law with repression. Thus, in developing his positive theory of power, he refuses to question the central role played by the state in the constitution of subjectivities. For Neocleous, however, the working of power expressed in forms of political administration cannot be separated from our understanding of the capitalist state and the material dynamics it expresses. Foucault's failure to theorize state power means that he does not address the material constitution of the state's form. Not surprisingly, we find the limitations to his work compounded by "his deep structuralist neglect of the question of agency" (Neocleous, 1996: 58). Foucault treats objects of administration simply as "docile bodies" (Foucault, 1977: 135 ff.). He refuses to answer the crucial question: Who has the power? He also refuses to ask why that power is being exercised (Neocleous, 1996: 58). The disciplinary society Foucault writes about is rooted in the class antagonisms around the contradictory process of capitalist accumulation that have, historically, forced the emergence of a set of administrative mechanisms whose purpose is "to mediate class struggle and subsume it under the auspices of state power." Political administration, he argues, "is a product of class struggle and yet also polices that struggle" (Neocleous, 1996: viii).

For Neocleous, the development of state administrative mechanisms is crucial to the establishment of bourgeois society. But Neocleous's recognition of the importance of administration within the context of state power means he does not adopt Foucault's artificial distinction between juridico-legal and administrative power as two historically separate forms of power, where the state and law, with their focus according to Foucault merely on the repression of subjects, are seen as historically outmoded. Law and administration both exist, often in interrelated fashion, along the same continuum of state power. Law cannot be said to be simply repressive in its operation. Legal documents that mark people's citizenship are "a policing mechanism of the most modern kind." However, they do not "merely register citizens, they also help *constitute* them *as* citizens" (Neocleous, 1996: 89). Legal power can provide a basis by which the working class is made an object of administration. By taking legal form as citizens, "human individuals could become both *subjects of rights* and *objects of administration*, a process rooted in the constitutive power of the state and its role in fashioning and policing bourgeois society" (Neocleous, 1996: 89).

In its historical struggle with the state for rights — to vote, get welfare or form unions — the working class is transformed into and constituted as a collective object of administration. Struggles that threaten to go beyond the capitalist state are in turn subsumed by it, and the working class is reconstituted on a suitable basis for capitalist accumulation. In the case of England, the making of the working class "was *simultaneously its incorporation*" into the state (Neocleous, 1996: 90). But the other moment of its formation was the remaking of the state. Structure and struggle are understood by Neocleous as internal rather than external to one another: "Structures are a mode of class antagonism and thus both the result and the premise of class struggle" (Neocleous, 1996: 105). As an active historical agent, the working class in its struggles

> forced the emergence of new state structures — of political admin-istration — and through these a reordering, far more fundamental than that forced by the bourgeoisie in its struggle, of the relation between state and civil society. (Neocleous, 1996: 105)

In Britain, working-class struggles against poverty and unemployment, for instance, during the nineteenth and early twentieth centuries led to new legislation of the New Poor Laws and other social benefit schemes. These were in turn used by the state to consolidate a class of wage labourers. The British state, on the one hand, organized a centralized welfare system. On the other, it used this system to set up a more centralized approach to monitor the poor. Benefit payments were harder to get and workhouse conditions harsher than what had been offered previously. They increased dependency on wage labour for more workers (Neocleous, 1996: 157 ff.).

Race, Gender and State Power

Neocleous's emphasis on the role of citizenship highlights an important omission in Marxist scholarship: its race- and gender-blind character. Certain people, because they have been racialized or gendered in a specific way, have been excluded from full citizenship rights. But the very process of racialization and gendering has in fact been central to capitalist accumula-tion and state formation, particularly in a white settler state like Canada. To understand the power dynamics, then, we must also pay careful attention to the way in which that power is both raced and gendered.

For Satzewich and Wotherspoon (1993), for instance, the development of industrial capitalism and the capitalist state in Canada was bound up with the appropriating of Aboriginal land by means of military conquest and treaties, and the subsequent attempts to force Aboriginals into wage labour. Traditional forms of Aboriginal social organization proved useful to European colonizers during the period of the fur trade, and such social relations and the land used by Aboriginals for traditional subsistence were given some legal protection by Britain in the Royal Proclamation of 1763. This traditional form of social organization eventually proved a barrier to capitalist development as the fur trade declined. It was at this point that a more systematic and racialized domination of Aboriginal peoples began.

But Aboriginals have not simply been objects of conquest; they have also resisted the policies of the Canadian state. Land expropriation, as historians have noted, has at times been met with armed struggle.

One of the better-known examples was the Métis-led national liberation struggle during the 1860s to the 1880s. The defeat of this struggle cleared the way for capitalist expansion west of Ontario. A century later, the revolts at Oka, Gufstafsen Lake and Burnt Church remind us of the continued importance of armed resistance to defend the land and natural resources for Aboriginals.

Aboriginal resistance has also taken more subtle forms. Aboriginal wage labour was crucial to capitalist expansion in many parts of the country from the late nineteenth century to the Second World War. Wage labour in turn became a very important source of income for Aboriginals during that same period. However, Aboriginals consistently resisted becoming solely dependent on it for survival. They have held on to traditional forms of subsistence, such as hunting, fishing and trapping. Indeed, for many Aboriginals, working was a means of supplementing traditional forms of subsistence (Simmons, 1999; High, 1996).

Thus the Canadian state has been shaped by Aboriginal struggle: it sought to contain that struggle in order to recast the groups on a basis conducive to capitalist development. In the twentieth century, the struggle has led to a steady increase in the level of militarization in the effort to eliminate resistance to land expropriation. In the nineteenth century, the Royal Northwest Mounted Police (a forerunner to the RCMP), was created explicitly to deal with unrest in the then Northwest Territories. This trend has continued to this day with respect to the SQ after Oka and the RCMP after Gufstafsen Lake.[7]

On the other hand, the Canadian state has also established, through the Indian Act (1876) and successive Indian Affairs ministries "a totalitarian 'cradle-to-grave' set of rules, regulations and directives to manage Native lives" (Stasiulis and Jhappan, 1995: 114). The Canadian government granted "special status" and reserve land to Aboriginal nations, but it did so in such a way as to undermine Aboriginal self-sufficiency and provide an opportunity for closer surveillance of their communities. The Indian Act was premised upon the racist ideological notion that Aboriginals were uncivilized and in need of guardianship by white people. Through it, the government arrogated to itself total political authority over the reserves. It imposed the band-council governing system to replace traditional governing structures. (To this day the Minister of Indian Affairs has the authority to overturn decisions of band councils.)

Special "Indian Agents" were charged with closely monitoring reserve communities and using the Pass Laws to inhibit Aboriginal movement off the reserves (Stasiulis and Jhappan, 1995: 115). But from the late nineteenth century to the Second World War, many people were working at jobs off the reserves in many parts of the country. The Pass Laws aimed to keep the Aboriginals from pursuing traditional forms of subsistence off reserve land — even if that land could not support an entire community, as was usually the case.[8] At the same time, gift-giving festivals that promoted economic redistribution and traditional Aboriginal leadership structures, such as the Potlatch, were outlawed from 1880 to 1951 (Stasiulis and Jhappan, 1995: 115). Moral training was also pursued: wives of missionaries trained Aboriginal women and girls in housekeeping and cooking. Children were forcibly removed from their homes and placed in white residential schools.

Such policies were geared towards what the state and missionaries saw as the civilizing of Aboriginals. They were to be made, in other words, more like white Europeans. But, as Satzewich and Wotherspoon argue, to be civilized for Aboriginal peoples meant something specific; these policies emerged within the context of capitalist social relations. The State's "aim was not simply to transform Indian people into Christian 'Europeans,' but into Christian Europeans... who would work for someone else for wages" (Satzewich and Wotherspoon, 1993: 29).

The fact that Aboriginals have never totally acquiesced to the "civilizing" process has meant that they have never been fully assimilated; they remain, to borrow a phrase from Bannerji, "an ambiguous presence" in the Canadian state (2000: 91) and therefore in need of close monitoring. Their constitutionally granted special status thus highlights their struggle for self-determination and the desire of the state to contain that struggle and turn them into administrative entities. The racist and gendered practices to control Aboriginal peoples have become deeply embedded in the institutions of the Canadian state both at federal and provincial levels. As such, it is impossible to discuss state power in Canada without accounting for this fact.

Immigration policy is also another area in which the racialized and gendered character of state power is clearly expressed. For nearly a century after the formation of the country, the Canadian state pursued an official "white Canada" policy (Jakubowski, 1999: 98; Stasiulis and Jhappan, 1995: 98). With respect to immigration, emphasis was placed on the preferred white immigrant, who was considered to be of "superior stock" (Jakubowski, 1999: 100) and would be able to promote British values (Stasiulis and Jhappan, 1995: 98). But this policy was complicated by the labour demands of rapid industrial expansion.

By the 1880s Canada was recruiting immigrants who departed from the ideal British type. As Stasiulis and Jhappan argue: "Non-European would-be immigrants would be excluded unless their cheap labour was needed, in which case they would be granted lesser access to settlers' and citizens' rights" (1995: 98). At a time when immigrants of colour were entering Canada to meet the labour needs of a rapidly expanding economy, race became an important issue in immigration policies. From the 1880s onwards a series of explicitly racist laws were passed: they targeted Chinese, South Asian and Black workers, making it more difficult for them (or their families) to get into the country. The laws also limited their legal rights once they had entered. The laws were adopted in a context of growing anti-immigrant backlash among white workers, especially in the west. But, significantly, these policies did not stop the inflow of immigrants. As McNally (2002: 137) argues with respect to current immigration policy in Canada, the United States and Europe, that the state and employers indeed wanted the immigrant labour, they just wanted it on their own terms: "frightened, oppressed, vulnerable" (2002: 137).

Most of the writing on immigration policy notes the concern federal authorities had about the country's ability to assimilate non-British, particularly non-European, immigrants. But they clearly also sought to promote the visibly and culturally different character of these immigrants as workers best suited to the most poorly paid and dangerous forms of work. The aim of assimilation, in this respect, was partial. In order to maintain the new immigrants' status as a cheap and highly exploitable form of wage labour, it was crucial to emphasize their non-white character and systematically deny them citizenship rights (Stasiulis and Jhappan, 1995: 112). Assimilation did not extend much beyond the need to fill the demand for a cheap and reliable labour force to build the railroads, open mines, etc.

Such a policy is not without its contradictions for state policy-makers, however. Brutal forms of exploitation are not met simply with obedience on the part of immigrant workers; they are, rather, fiercely contested. The fear policy-makers invoked by this challenge was compounded by the presence of the non-British, not-fully assimilated immigrant Other, whose place in the nation posed a constant threat to the health and well- being of "white Canada" and its British values. Thus the presence of the not-fully compliant or partially assimilated immigrant labourers required several state measures to control them as a reliable class of wage labourers. By the turn of the century, the state was engaged in greater policing and the systematic medical inspection of new immigrants; by the 1930s it began using deportations more frequently as a weapon against both radicals and the unemployed — with some immigrants being both those things (Stasiulis and Jhappan, 1995: 116; Sears, 1990).

Although changes to immigration legislation in the 1960s, such as the adoption of the points system in 1967, ended official racial discrimination, "issues of race remain just below the surface of current concerns about immigration" (Satzewich and Zong, 1996: 279). International immigration offices are selectively located: there are a few in under-developed countries of the Global South. According to Jakubowski, their location suggests a continued preference for white European immigrants (1999: 11). The wide discretion given to officers under the points system still allows for potentially discriminatory decisions. For many immigrants of colour who are allowed to enter, though, such as Filippina women, citizenship rights are strictly curtailed through a "temporary status" residency provision and the requirement that they live with their employer. They can only enter Canada to work as domestics. Their precarious legal situation leaves them extremely dependent on their employer and thus open to greater exploitation (Arat-Koç, 1999a: 148).

Recent changes to refugee legislation are also very racialized. Humanitarian concerns are being downplayed by the state, and refugees are being turned into "simply another category of immigrants to be managed" (Jakubowski, 1999: 119). The "Safe Country" provision — in which status can be denied to refugees who arrived in Canada via a third country that was prepared to grant status (similar to the "Continuous Journey" stipulation of 1908) — will significantly reduce the number of refugees. Most come from the Third World, from where it is nearly impossible to travel by direct air routes to Canada.

> The ultimate effect of the legislation, then, without ever mentioning the word race, is to control a particular dimension of the refugee population — developing world refugees, the majority of whom the government classifies as visible minorities. (Jakubowski, 1999: 120)

Since September 11, 2001, the situation has only worsened for immigrants and refugees, especially those of Middle Eastern background. But, again, as McNally (2002: 137) points out, the aim is not to stop the inflow of immigrants or refugees. The aim is to control it in such a way as benefits employers. Immigration policy today is just as much a tool of labour-force management as it was a hundred years ago.

For Bannerji, the ongoing racialized control exacted by the state over immigrants, refugees and people of colour is also deeply rooted in the politics of official multiculturalism: "We demanded some genuine reforms," she remarks, "and instead we got 'multiculturalism.'… [As] the state came deeper into our lives — extending its political, economic and moral regulation, its police violence and surveillance — we simultaneously officialized ourselves" (2000: 89–90). According to Bannerji, multiculturalism is a contemporary example of the way the state has both been shaped by the struggles of immigrants, and in turn reshaped those very same struggles. It has absorbed or co-opted them. In so doing the state effaces people's varied histories, languages and cultures, reducing them to more abstract and easier-to-manage categories such as "visible minority," "immigrant," "ethnic" or "new Canadian." In the process, it is able to gloss over historically embedded power relations that mark peoples' lives, thus neutralizing this experience in official discourse (Bannerji, 2000: 96).

At the same time, such categories express people's difference from English and French Canada. The term "visible minority," for example, suggests that some people are more visible than others, and it is towards this "peculiarity" that the state draws our attention. But it can only mark this peculiarity by measuring it against an average, a mode of appearance that is itself made *invisible* by the state's determination of it as the norm. What is the norm then? It is the concept of "whiteness" that is rooted in colonialist history and the policies that attend the aspirations for building a nation based on British values. It is the pivot around which categories like "visible minority" or "ethnic" constellate.[9] Together, the concepts of whiteness and other terms form a binary relationship: you are either black or white, visible or invisible, ethnic or native. Multiculturalism, then, highlights the distance from the norm. Such groups are at the margins of Canadian society, politically marking them for special attention.

Unfortunately, there are few extensive studies on the racial and gendered character of state power in Canada. The task requires more serious and systematic attention than can be provided here. How we view state power, however, is crucial to how we look at policing. Class formation in capitalist societies does not occur separately from the historical processes of racialization and gendering (see McNally, 2002; Kelley, 1997; and Clarke, 1991) Classes are always raced and gendered. Since the state, as we have seen, is both presupposition and the result of class struggle, constituted by and in turn constituting classes in motion, then its power must be understood as materialized specifically through the processes of racialization and gendering. Such a comprehensive view of state power will allow us to develop a much richer understanding of policing and its particular role in society.

Policing and Class Struggle

In *The Fabrication of Social Order*, Neocleous argues that a central feature of state power is the police. The state has a constitutive power over the working class, expressed through a range of mechanisms he refers to as political administration. The police in their day-to-day interactions with the public need to be understood as exercising that power of political administration. In its historical development in the first half of the nineteenth century, the modern police came "to play a crucial role in the fabrication of a new order of bourgeois rule." This has remained its main task (2000: 65).

Neocleous is not the first Marxist commentator to link the development of modern police with the development of capitalist society. But much of previous Marxist analysis suffers from functionalist limitations, viewing police simply as a repressive institution charged with guarding private property. A good example is provided by Harring's (1993) analysis of the historical development of the modern police in the United States. He traces their origin to the role police played in repressing strikes in the last third of the nineteenth century.[10] The police "were solidly in the hands of local commercial and industrial elites, who often administered them directly through the police commissions on which they sat" (1993: 551). Functionalist views such as Harring's tend to mistakenly rely on the class background of the individuals who oversee police and who make policy decisions to explain police behaviour. The police, however, cannot be seen as central to the creation of bourgeois order simply because they have been controlled by elites or because they have put down strikes or riots. If we accepted this, how would we explain policing in contemporary Toronto? No members of the commercial or industrial elite sit on the police services board, nor have there recently been riots and mass working-class upheaval.

Clearly the manner in which police exercise power is not simply a matter of the class background of the specific individuals in charge or the presence of more explosive forms of unrest. (In the latter instance, the army can be called in). The issue for Neocleous is the *form* policing takes, as a feature of state power and political administration, in capitalist society. As we will see, in its day-to-day functioning, policing is aimed not merely at the repression of the working class but at the "fabrication of order." This order is more than the simple absence of upheaval. Policing has evolved historically into the key means by which the state produces the working class and responds to its day-to-day struggles against the social order.

To explain how police developed in capitalist society, Neocleous draws our attention to its historical focus on the poor.

> So central was the question of poverty in discussions surrounding the emergence and development of the police forces in nineteenth century Europe, that it would be no exaggeration to say that the forces were for the most part seen as an extension for the emerging machinery for managing the poor. (2000: 67)

In Britain, for instance, the leading administrators of the new poor law and the police force were in fact engaged in a symbiotic relationship with one another, exchanging ideas and information. The degree to which this was the case was expressed in official reports written by both institutions, at the heart of which were conscious attempts to dissociate poverty from indigence or pauperism and criminality. The goal was to separate the respectable from the unrespectable poor. Poverty was to be left alone, as it was not considered a social problem. Indigence was the problem because it was linked to crime. The indigent were defined as those unrespectable poor individuals who refused or failed to gain subsistence through the wage and thus participate in the market.[11]

What is especially important for Neocleous here is not only the common focus on the poor and the distinction between poverty and indigence, but their emergence (which is not a coincidence) within the context of the constitution of new industrial capitalist order. To develop successfully, it required the creation of a working class conducive to that order. That process — the creation of a class of wage labourers, workers separated from the ownership of the means of production and therefore dependent on the wage for subsistence — entailed "a massive police operation." Thus, grounded in an obsessive focus on pauperism and the poor:

> the ultimate aim of the police project was the commodification of labour through the consolidation of the wage form. As such, the project of social police has historically been central to the function of political administration in fashioning the market. (Neocleous, 2000: 69)

The aim of the New Poor Laws, Neocleous argues, was to enforce the dependence on paid work for subsistence. They did this by limiting relief outside the workhouse to only the most destitute and by making the conditions in the workhouse worse than those found in the most exploitative jobs. In so doing, it separated the indigent, or the paupers, from the rest of the poor, bringing them under the domain of the Poor Laws. In turn, it reinforced the notion that, "as the labouring class the poor were expected to obtain subsistence through the market and the wage" (Neocleous, 2000: 69). Relief was thus not geared towards ending poverty; it fashioned out of the poor a class of wage labourers.

The new police had a very similar function. As Neocleous argues, "the contribution of the new police was to coercively close off any access to any means of subsistence other than the wage" (2000: 70). In the eighteenth century, workers were still often partly remunerated in kind. Under the customary system of ancient entitlements, it was understood that coal workers could appropriate some of the coal they handled; or dock workers, the commodities that were spilt. As a result, workers were not fully bound to their salaries. Private property was still somewhat "indeterminate in character," not yet fully consolidated in the hands of capital.

In order to make workers completely dependent on a wage and hence the market to survive, employers sought to recast these non-monetary forms of payment as crimes and bring them under the domain of criminal law. (This also meant the sanctity of private property was extended.) The customary rights of labour were deeply entrenched, however, and led to strong resistance. A massive police operation was required. For the new police theorist Patrick Colquhoun, a primary goal of police was to "break workers' notion that the appropriation of goods on which they laboured was 'sanctioned by custom'" (Neocleous, 2000: 73). Police were organized by Patrick Colquhoun to oversee and regularly inspect labourers at their workplaces to physically ensure they could no longer appropriate goods (see also McMullan, 1998 on Colquhoun). Complementing this strategy, the marine police on the River Thames in London were even given the responsibility of setting workers' pay.

> The net effect of the first preventative police system was thus not just a *defense* of property, but the creation of a social order founded

> on private property via the consolidation of the money wage and commodification of labour. (Neocleous, 2000: 74)

This preventative aim helps to clarify the historical focus of policing on the streets. Early in the mandate of the new police, a series of laws were enacted that provided officers with a broad range of legal powers to control the streets and target specific persons and forms of behaviour. The various laws were used against any persons in public spaces or obstructing walkways whom the police deemed to be suspicious: specifically beggars, sex-trade workers and people selling various items or simply sleeping. These laws included the Vagrancy Act (1824), the Highways Act (1835) and the Metropolitan Police Act (1839), which provided officers with a broad range of legal powers to control the streets and target specific persons and forms of behaviour.

For Neocleous, this reflected the state's effort to criminalize a range of activities, which centred on the street, "the proletarian public sphere" (2000: 75). Such activities were recreational or provided people with the chance to eke out a living outside the formal market. Street policing, in other words, extended the strategy to eliminate alternatives to the paid job:

> The attack on the non-monetary form of the wage and its trans-formation into a fully-fledged money form meant criminalizing a range of traditional working-class activities... a project designed to stamp the authority of private property over the living conditions of the majority of the population and confirm the power of capital as the new master. (Neocleous, 2000: 76)

Like workplaces, the streets and other public spaces would be ordered by police to facilitate the subordination of the labouring class to the demands of capitalist accumulation.

Similar strategies were also adopted in Canadian cities with the development of municipal police forces in the nineteenth century. Empowered by city bylaws and anti-vagrancy statutes, Canadian police systematically targeted the same kinds of behaviour that Neocleous describes with respect to Britain. Public drunkenness, disorderly conduct, gaming, prostitution and begging were overwhelmingly the principal targets of police attention. Vagrancy statutes and public order charges such as "disturbing the peace" gave police a wide scope of proactive opportunities to target people they felt were likely to breach public order. Like in Britain, the Canadian state criminalized a range of street-based working-class activities that were carried out either for pleasure or as an alternative to gainful employment (Boritch and Hagan, 1987; Marquis, 1994). To this day, the police still focus on a range of public-order offences and thus the criminalization of a series of activities centred on the street. Even the police's own statistics suggest public-order offences rather than criminal law violations garner most of the police's attention (Canadian Centre for Justice Statistics, 2001).

The degree to which policing has been concerned about the constitution of the wage-labour relation is also expressed by the way the state has historically understood crime. Up to the present, the solution to crime has been work. Official documents in Britain, Neocleous notes, have repeatedly stressed that crimes against property (such as theft) are met more severely by the state than crimes against persons, because they make survival possible outside the formal job market. This helps explain the new police's identification of crime with indigence rather than poverty. Poverty, Colquhoun stressed, is the condition that forces workers to rely on a wage to survive. Indigence, on the other hand, is the state of the able-bodied poor attempting to avoid such reliance. This is why the able-bodied claimant was prescribed such harsh treatment under the New Poor Laws, and indigence is conflated with criminality. The pauper is either engaged in or potentially pursuing activities in order to eke out a living beyond the formal market and the discipline of gainful employment. Hence, for the state and moral reformers whatever instills a good work ethic diminishes crime (Neocleous, 2000: 76–77).

Even today, a person who holds a job is far more likely to be released from state custody than an unemployed person. Work has supposedly shaped character, making the individual trustworthy and able to stay out of trouble. The person who works and so avoids idleness is thought to be less likely to fall prey to moral vices. For how else, in the eyes of the state, could one obtain an income outside of work? Thus all those activities historically targeted by the state and moral reformers are ones that offer alterations to working or distractions from it: begging, gaming, prostitution, the consumption of alcohol and other intoxicants, and the display of idleness. Here lies the focus of police work.

The creation of a criminal class, then, has historically been important to the making of the working class. The state and police have facilitated the formation of the latter by playing up the division between the respectable poor, who are willing to enter the market, and those who don't. The benefits claimant, the beggar, the sex-trade worker all represent a threat to private property, the failure to accept the capital-labour relation. The harsh punishments serve as a constant reminder to the rest of the working class about the consequences of not respecting the order of things. But the more intense the criminalization of one section of the working class is in contrast to the other, the more likely the criminalization will be projected onto the entire class (Neocleous, 2000: 82). The categories begin to blend together.

This is an important point to note in considering the historical evolution of policing and notions of criminality. Individuals can move from one segment of the working class into the other — from a benefits claimant at one moment to a gainfully employed worker the next. Thus the risk is ever present that all workers might be infected with moral vices and criminal behaviour.

In this respect the entire working class, in the eyes of the state, is viewed as potentially criminal. This observation helps us make sense of the fact that police, in their putative fight against crime, seldom actually target individuals engaged in criminal activity but, instead, are told to look for a set of appearances and behaviours. In his study of the early development of municipal police forces in Canada, Marquis (1994) notes that police viewed criminality more as a lifestyle than a particular act. In looking for a lifestyle it is much harder for police to discern the individual person violating a specific criminal or public-order offence from the rest of the class to which they belong. The same point is made by Ericson in his field research on police patrol work. Police routinely are looking not for particular legal infractions but for "things and people out of order" in a particular locale. Typically, they stop young men of lower socio-economic backgrounds on the assumption they may be committing a number of violations (Ericson, 1982: 78–79). Police here are not targeting individuals or specific actions as much as they are a class. Indeed, the extent to which criminal behaviour is in fact linked to the working class is demonstrated by the way crimes commited by capital, which result in a much higher cost in human, financial and ecological terms, are pursued a lot less earnestly than are crimes against property (Neocleous, 2000: 82–84).

Another significant point about the history of policing is that, as the criminalization of the working class extended in its scope, so too did the original police mandate in Britain, as well as Canada. The early police forces monitored workplaces and streets and worked closely with the institutions set up by the New Poor Laws. They also took responsibility for health and hygiene matters in cities (in some cases for clearing refuse), inspection of drinking establishments, and sheltering and providing emergency services to transients and the homeless (Neocleous, 2000: 84–90; Marquis, 1994: 32). These responsibilities were understood as part of the broader project of ordering all facets of working-class life. Much of the work that social workers and health inspectors do today, then, was traditionally done by the police, in the absence of other state agencies to carry out the tasks. Thus the narrowing of the contemporary role of the police should not be seen as a narrowing of *policing* per se, but as the evolution of a more specialized division of labour, which occurred over the twentieth century. Indeed, the policing-inspired disciplinary role of social workers assigned to welfare casework has in fact become more prominent under neoliberalism in Canada (see, for example, Riches, 1989: 117). Police still maintain a close working relationship with other institutions representing public order, such as various social-work and welfare agencies, as they did with the institutions of the New Poor Laws in the nineteenth century (Neocleous, 2000: 93).

What should be clear by now is how broad the police mandate is and how little in actual fact it has to do with criminal-law enforcement. This aspect of policing is worth stressing here, given the pervasive belief in Canada, promoted by the media, politicians of all stripes and police themselves, that the police are first and foremost crime-fighters. The criminalization of the working class, and its most impoverished sections in particular, entails control over very specific forms of behaviour that rarely fall under the purview of criminal law. As both Boritch and Hagan (1987: 316) and Marquis (1994: 32) note with respect to nineteenth- and early twentieth-century Canada, police directed very few of their energies towards fighting criminal-law violations. The overwhelming majority of arrests were for public order matters rather than offences against persons or property.

As noted above, Ericson's field research on Canadian police uncovers a similar pattern: police regularly initiate encounters with individuals who seldom have anything to do with any perceived violations. The focus of the police, Ericson argues, is public order and the perceived threats to it, the "suspicious persons/circumstances" police go looking for on the beat (Ericson, 1982: 79). There is in fact:

> a mass of research on the police which has shown that criminal law enforcement is something that most police officers do with the frequency located somewhere between virtually never and very rarely. (Neocleous, 2000: 93)

For example, most calls for police assistance are "service" requests, while less than 10 percent of police time is actually devoted to traditional criminal-law concerns (Neocleous, 2000: 93). It would therefore be a serious mistake to suggest, as many do, that police, as the frontline in an ongoing war on crime, merely enforce the law. The so-called "thin blue line" is a buffer not from a world of lawlessness, but from one of state-defined disorder.

The historical prominence given to order in the police agenda is also demonstrated by the way in which law is in fact subordinated to this end. The relationship of law to order is expressed in a few important ways. They relate to both the law's role for police as one means of combating disorder, and to the way in which its use intersects with the discretionary power allotted to officers. As most commentators note, police power is shaped by the central role that discretion plays in the work. Discretion affords the officers a range of alternatives not only about which situations to respond to, but also about how to respond. So police tend to focus on specific matters, such as signs of public disorder, rather than on other matters, such as white-collar crime. They can employ a variety of means to fabricate order in a given situation: laying criminal charges, invoking city bylaws (which entail fines), issuing warnings about the use of criminal charges or bylaws, conducting stop-and-searches, showing aggression and intimidation, or any combination thereof. The police toolkit is varied. Criminal law is but one of the tools employed. Indeed, research suggests that police seldom even resort to the criminal law to restore order (Neocleous, 2000: 93).

Significantly, even the law, when utilized, is used very flexibly by police. It is manipulated to assist them in achieving the desired outcome in a given situation (Ericson, 1982: 14). This is perhaps best exemplified by such open-ended discretionary powers existing in Canadian law like "reasonable suspicion" or "breach of peace." Although they are not criminal offences per se, they are designed to give the police the leeway in managing particular situations. Individuals can be held for up to twenty-four hours for a breach of peace. The phrase is vague enough that it can be imposed in a number of different contexts to restore order (see Esmonde, 2002a).

When it comes to arrest, police have a great deal of discretionary power over a suspect. They have the power to decide whether to conduct a strip search; whether to allow the suspect to contact a lawyer; whether to keep someone in custody for the maximum twenty-four hours before their release or before they are brought before a justice of the peace: and whether to recommend pre-trial custody to a justice of the peace. In short they can greatly influence the pre-text treatment of suspects.[12]

There are procedural guidelines police must consider when dealing with the public, but the discretionary authority described here suggests that "the power resides almost entirely with the state and is exercised through the body of the police" (Neocleous, 2000: 101). Even judicial rulings in cases in which the police have been found to have acted outside their legally constituted mandate can be used by police to reinforce the role of discretion and the flexible use of law in policing. In Canada, for example, a judicial decision clearly delineating the procedural guidelines for strip searches has been used by Toronto police to expand their power to conduct a broad use of strip searches. Toronto police have established a form on which they can summarily check off all the procedural rules demanded by the court during a strip search to "demonstrate" proper procedure, whether or not it has been followed.

In this regard, police power, deriving from the authority of the state, is organized so that it faces only limited constraint by any rule of law. Instead, law is a tactic used and shaped by police, and subordinated to the end goal of producing order. The law is not used to govern police too closely. This view may seem to fly in the face of conventional wisdom concerning the much vaunted rule of law in liberal democracies; it is worth entertaining, if we see the police as an administrative form of state power rather than a mere legal arm. Indeed, as a social practice, policing operates on a different — and *much less* abstract — level than does the law. This very fact makes it difficult to regulate policing, to the extent that the state wishes to do so. It is accorded wide room to manoeuver:

- The police can use the law flexibly as a means to produce public order.
- Officers are rarely charged with or found guilty of misconduct in situations where there is strong evidence that they acted in a manner that much of the public would consider inappropriate.

- On rare occasions when officers are found guilty of an offence, they typically receive lenient sentences.
- Civilian bodies have limited oversight of police budgets or practices.

A wide range of options and a great deal of power, in other words, has historically been vested in the state, and its police agents, in the pursuit of order. Police are less "a form of juridical power" than "street-level" state officials who exercise a form of political administration (Neocleous, 2000: 102). Police are front and centre not in a war on crime but in the state's effort to contain and manage the struggles of the working classes.

Policing, Race and Gender

Like its theorization of the state, the Open Marxist theory of policing does not address policing's racialized and gendered dynamic. This is a serious gap, given, as we noted in the first chapter, how intense this dynamic is. Any theory of policing must be able to account for the role that race and gender play in police work.

As we have seen, capitalist state power is itself systematically racialized and gendered. Class composition and re-composition in capitalist society are embedded within, and thus inseparable from, the historical processes of racialization and gendering. The state's efforts to contain struggles from below and administer the working class (efforts in class re-composition) are invariably intertwined within these dynamics. Given its role in "street-level administration," as Neocleous puts it, we can see how policing is intimately bound up with these processes. Situating police within the context of state administration highlights the way in which these dynamics are rooted in the heart of policing itself, rather than simply a feature of individual racist or sexist police officers. If the police, in its struggle for order, focuses most of its attention on working class and poorer communities, and if women, people of colour, immigrants and Aboriginals in Canada, facing systemic discrimination, are disproportionately represented in these groups, they are likely to receive a disproportionate amount of police attention. But the police do not merely respond to these groups after they have been classed, racialized or gendered in a particular way. The location and experiences of these oppressed groups are not static; they emerge out of the ongoing struggles for better wages, citizenship status, equality, land and so on, and the state's efforts to contain these struggles. The police are part of this process. By targeting these groups because of their social location, police reinforce their marginalized status. The policing of women, people of colour, immigrants and Aboriginals is therefore both a precondition and result of their location.

These groups, as we have seen, are also the unassimilable. Their labour and land might be central to the building of Canada, yet the need to keep to them vulnerable and highly exploitable precludes the possibility of full assimilation into the nation. This precarious relationship to the Canadian nation is compounded by their struggles against oppression and land expropriation. As Bannerji has so succinctly stated: "We remain an ambiguous presence, our existence a question mark in the side of the nation" (2000: 91). This ambiguity highlights the uncertainty as to how they fit into the order of white Canada, as it is formed along class, racial and gender hierarchies, but also to the potential ruptures that visibly lie at the heart of that order.

Thus the criminalization of the working class and the poor in Canada has a virulent side for women, people of colour, immigrants and Aboriginals. Skolnick's (1966) argument that in the United States young male African Americans are "symbolic assailants" pertains to groups in Canada as well (it can be extended to the experiences of immigrants and Aboriginals). Symbolic assailants are criminals until proven otherwise. It is not simply that they meet some of the characteristics of the criminal, but that they have come to define the criminal. Hence the inordinate amount of attention, documented time and again in Canada, that police give to the young Black or Aboriginal male drivers. It is not the actions they perform, but merely their presence that signals criminality.

These observations also help us to make sense of why researchers find that Black Canadians of higher status are still much more likely than whites from a similar socio-economic background to be stopped by police. While higher-income Blacks are less likely to be stopped by police than lower-income Blacks, that likelihood declines much less for them than it does for higher-income whites (Ontario, 1995: 335). Such targeting shows how deeply rooted the anxiety, on the part of the state and its administrators, is over the presence and perceived dangers of Blacks. Despite some socio-economic advancements, they face great difficulty being fully assimilated into a country whose history was shaped by a racial hierarchy centred on the idealization of whiteness and British values.

At the heart of the criminalization of women, people of colour, immigrants and Aboriginals also lies an anxiety that extends beyond the mere uncertainty as to how they fit into the Canada nation. The fear of their negative impact on social order shapes state policy and police practices towards these groups. Central to racist psychology is, on the one hand, the attempt to attain whiteness and respectability by intensifying "the internal psychic repression that is part of industrial capitalism — the subordination of desires for recreation, drink, festivity, sex and social celebration to employers' demands for a sober, industrious and disciplined workforce"; and, on the other, the projection of these very same desires onto other social groups who themselves have not achieved whiteness and respectability (McNally, 2002: 122). In post-Civil War America, for example, the Irish, in their efforts to attain whiteness and respectability:

> projected onto Blacks the very characteristics they strove to repress

in themselves. The more they undertook to discipline themselves, the more they came to hate African-Americans (as fantastic repositories of the very desires and behaviours they hoped to control in themselves). (McNally, 2002: 122)

Racist projection expresses both the aspiration to fulfill the (very bodily) desires sacrificed in order to achieve respectability and the distancing of oneself from those very desires and the primitive or uncivilized Other who has come to embody them.

A central dynamic of racism is thus the fear whites harbour of their desires being known and of being identified with the uncivilized Other. This manifests itself in an anxiety around the body itself: its smell, its dirt, its different "physical productions" (Neocleous, 2000: 86; McNally, 2002: 123). The more the imperial reach of Europe and its settler states stretched over various non-white peoples (and likely the more the labour of these peoples was relied on at home), the more intense this fear of the Other, the "body-peoples," became (McNally, 2002: 123). In this context, which also includes bourgeois anxieties about white "body-peoples," there developed extremely compulsive attitudes towards cleansing the body and the surrounding physical environment (McNally, 2002: 123). "Social technologies" like the fork or handkerchief were increasingly employed to "mediate between the physical productions of the body and interactions with others" (Neocleous, 2000: 86). By seeking to sanitize interactions with such people or eradicating physical traces of bodily expression by which one could be identified with them, these behaviours serve as a means of social differentiation, as Neocleous (2000: 86) suggests. They are also aimed at mitigating the threat of contamination the uncivilized Others pose to bourgeois society.

Not surprisingly, we find that the new police were very occupied with issues of sanitation and cleanliness. It was during the period of the new police that "the metaphors of pollution and moral contagion became the standard form of expression of social commentary" (Neocleous, 2000: 85). For social reformers and new police theorists, there was a very clear, intimate connection between property, order and cleanliness, on the one hand, and poverty, dirt, disease and crime on the other. While they were concerned with sanitation in heavily populated working-class areas, the dirt and refuse also denoted something about the class that lived in those conditions. Identification was made between the state of the working class and the sanitary condition of the neighbourhoods, expressed in the usage of words like "refuse" or "offal," which referred to both "the sewage waste that constituted the sanitary problem and the human waste that constituted the social problem" (Neocleous, 2000: 86). Police jargon today is still marked by the identification of the poor/potential criminal with dirt and refuse through terms like "scum" or "pukes" (Neocleous, 2000: 87; Ericson, 1982: 79). Prone to disorder and criminality, the workers, through the "miasmas" they exhaled as much as through the dirty and unsanitary conditions in which they lived, were identified as the most dangerous agents of infection to bourgeois order. Thus the task of police was to clean the streets not only physically but morally as well. Sanitation strategies tried to instill discipline and order in working-class lives through rituals designed to enhance cleanliness and health (thereby creating, it was hoped, a more reliable labour force) and reduce the perceived possibilities that people might transmit contagions to the rest of bourgeois society. Valverde (1991) offers a similar history of the movement for moral reform, and its relationship to issues of working-class cleanliness and order, in Canada in the late nineteenth and early twentieth centuries.

Neocleous identifies the new police's focus on sanitation with a concern with the working class more generally, without citing any racial or gender dynamic to it; and, indeed, McNally (2002: 123) notes that the anxieties surrounding bodies and cleanliness in bourgeois culture are often extended to the entire working class. Nevertheless, he is clear that such anxieties were very much racialized and gendered. It would be short-sighted to ignore the way in which a racially and gendered-influenced concern over bodies, sanitation and moral contagion, and the threat they pose to bourgeois civilization, have shaped policing practices. We have observed this already with respect to the state's practice of medical inspections and close monitoring of immigrants developed early in the twentieth century. It is also expressed in police's targeting of women's sexuality. According to McNally, the fear of bodies, dirt and moral contagion has been deeply bound up with fears over the physical powers of the working class and colonized women and overwhelming sexual insatiabilities. Their role in particularly physical labour (such as in the mines, or in hunting and agriculture for many Aboriginal women) and their sexuality were seen by early social reformers and the bourgeoisie as exhibiting a potentially destabilizing force over the supposedly natural bourgeois order, at the apex of which is the western bourgeois male (McNally, 2002: 124). Their proclivity towards sexual promiscuity has been identified by state officials with the flouting of necessary paternal authority figures in their lives. Thus, on the one hand, the state made a concerted effort, particularly with respect to Aboriginals in Canada, to remove women from more exacting forms of physical labour and to feminize and domesticate them (McNally, 2002: 124; Satzewich and Wotherspoon, 1993: 117ff.) and, on the other, to closely police their sexual activities. The latter point partly explains the systematic targeting by police of sex-trade workers in Canada, often through vagrancy statutes,[13] as well as the targeting of supposedly promiscuous women via the Female Refugee Act until 1960 (Sangster, 2002) and truancy laws until the 1970s (Reitsma-Street, 2000: 223). While truancy laws have been repealed in Canada, similar police practices aimed at imposing paternal authority over "truant" women continue today through "failure to comply" offences, which are disproportionately applied against young women.

Their land and labour were desperately needed, but they stood outside the white ideal and were never fully obeisant to domination. Working-class women, the colonized and immigrant workers thus do not fit so neatly into Canada's bourgeois order. Their uneasy presence remains a cause of anxiety, a potential rupture (both physically and socially) within the order of things. Following Bannerji (2000: 91), they are a "question mark in the side of the nation," a reminder, perhaps, of the potentially transitory nature of bourgeois society. Their presence, then, demands careful scrutiny and the constant reminder, expressed through the mobilization of state and police power, of their place in the bourgeois order and of who retains authority in their lives.

Conclusion

The focus of contemporary policing on public order is not new. As we have seen, this has historically been the central focus of policing. But the order being sought, and resisted, is fairly particular. Police power has been mobilized to criminalize a series of street-based activities that either provide people with an opportunity to survive outside market relations or serve as distractions from waged work. In the process, policing has worked to *constitute* a class of labourers dependent on the wage for subsistence and thereby a bourgeois order rooted in the authority of private property and the subordination of working people to the imperatives of capital accumulation. Rather than focusing on fighting crime or some abstract notion of order imposed at a distance, policing, as part of the state strategy for administering the working class, is historically a very confrontational strategy and driven by a moral discourse on the importance of work and the discipline of the wage in shaping a person's character. These processes are also shaped by the racialized and gendered character of a capitalist white settler society such as Canada. The assertion of authority over women, the colonized and immigrant communities by relentlessly targeting any signs of irreverence toward state-defined modes of appropriate behaviour is given high policing priority.

Situated within this historical context, the meaning and significance of the dynamics of contemporary policing, especially under the banner of law and order, are illuminated much more clearly. It is to law-and-order policing, then, as it has emerged in much of the so-called advanced capitalist world since the 1980s that we now return.

Notes

1. See the three-volume series, *Open Marxism* (1992 [Bonefeld, Gunn and Psychopedis], 1992 [Bonefeld, Gunn and Psychopedis], 1995 [Bonefeld, Gunn, Psychopedis and Holloway]), where most of the heterodox Marxists, though not all, can be found.
2. "Necessary labour" is the amount of time in a work day it takes a worker to produce as much value in the work process as the employer pays her in wages and benefits (i.e., an amount equal to her labour power). Any work done beyond

that time is "surplus labour" and represents profit for the employer.
3. Functionalists in the tradition of Ralph Miliband argue this interpretation.
4. Claus Offe and Alain Lipietz promote the capital logic and regulation school approaches, respectively.
5. See Bonefeld (1993: 46).
6. See Bonefeld on the constitution of money as an abstract social equivalent, mediating inequality between those owners with property and those without.
7. The Oka Revolt began in the spring of 1990 in Québec. The local Oka municipal government (situated outside Montreal) sought to appropriate land containing burial grounds from the Mohawk community of Kanehsatake in order to build an extension for a country club golf course. Members of the Mohawk Warrior Society took up arms to defend the land. A gun battle ensued after the Sûreté du Québec (SQ) officers invaded the land, and an SQ officer was killed. An armed standoff ensured between the SQ and the Mohawk Warriors. The SQ was eventually replaced by the Canadian army later in the summer. The armed standoff ended in the fall of 1990, approximately six months after it began. The golf course was never built.

    The Gustafsen standoff began in June of 1995. It involved an occupation of sacred sundance lands at TS'Peten by members of the Shuswap Nation. The land had been leased to an American rancher. Four hundred paramilitary RCMP officers were mobilized, armed with machine guns, armoured vehicles and land mines. The RCMP and B.C. government engaged in a massive disinformation campaign portraying the indigenous defenders as violently irrational and without legitimate claim to their land. The standoff ended in September, and thirteen Shuswap Nation members were subsequently sentenced to jail for defending their land.
8. On Aboriginals and wage labour, see Laliberte and Satzewich (1999); Simmons (1999); High (1996); Knight (1996) and Elias (1988).
9. See Bannerji (2000: 106 ff.) for a discussion of white supremacy as an ideology for imperialist domination. See also Howard Adams (1989).
10. See also Jock Young (1979: 13–16) on the functionalism of what he refers to as the left idealism that emerged in criminology in the 1960s and 1970s.
11. The use of "indigence" here is based on Mark Neocleous's study of the writings of nineteenth-century police theorists like Patrick Colquhoun and the designers of the New Poor Laws (2000: 52–54, 68–70). While "indigence" has been used to refer to the aged and infirm, who cannot physically obtain their own means of subsistence, it was also used by police theorists and designers of the New Poor Laws, along with "pauperism," to demarcate the able-bodied employed poor from the able-bodied poor who avoided work. Neocleous cites the use of the term as an important expression of the move beyond undifferentiated notions of poverty in the early nineteenth century as the British state was actively trying to establish a labour market. In some of these writings, Neocleous argues (2000: 55) that "'Indigence' is merely coda for the attempt to avoid wage labour, to refuse exploitation." It is in this respect that the term is employed in this book.
12. See Neocleous, 2000: 100 and Wortley and Kellough, 1998, for illustrations of the police's influence over the pre-trial release of suspects from custody.
13. Sex-trade work also represents, as noted above, a potential means of subsistence outside the formal wage economy.

3. Contemporary Law-and-Order Policies: Policing, Class Struggle and Neoliberal Restructuring

This chapter offers a political-economic analysis of law-and-order policing in the 1980s and 1990s as it emerged in Britain, the United States and especially Canada. Employing the same theoretical framework as Chapter 2, we will outline of the central role the police have played in neoliberal restructuring.

Law-and-order policing, as we will see, has little to do with fighting crime. Instead, its main aim is to transform the working class into a cheaper and more flexible labour force. Translating the goal into reality entails the adoption of anti-vagrancy laws, as well as zero-tolerance and community policing, because they serve to eliminate alternatives to paid work. Thus law-and- order policing is one component of a broader state strategy that has a twofold aim: lowering expectations with regard to wages and job security and forcing people to take the worst jobs in order to survive.

As a result, it has become increasingly difficult to avoid having a paid job. The alternatives in the past — unemployment insurance claims, welfare benefits and panhandling — no longer guarantee survival over the long term. They spell the opposite in fact: they mean living below the poverty line. Opportunities to opt out of market relations (the formal job market), even on a temporary basis, have gradually dried up. Opting out to study has likewise become prohibitive.

This chapter will also show that law-and-order policies are not simply the coincidental product of various right-wing governments. Indeed, they have been implemented by governments of the moderate left. Rather, these coercive policies are part and parcel of capitalist states in the neoliberal era. In turn, it will become clear that neoliberal restructuring has not resulted in less government, as is fashionable to argue in some circles today, but a different role for the government, one that is often more coercive than it was before.

We will begin with a brief look at the Open Marxist theory of capitalist crisis, followed by an examination of the rise and fall of the Keynesian welfare state in advanced capitalist countries, and the emergence of monetarism and neoliberal state policy in response the political and economic crises of the 1970s. Law-and-order policing is integral to this project of political-economic transformation.

The Welfare State Bites the Bullet

Since the 1970s governments in advanced capitalist countries have undergone significant changes. These came about in reaction to the global economic crisis, which began in the 1970s, and the escalation of class struggle accompanying the initial efforts to manage the economic downturn.

The Keynesian State Form

Following the Open Marxist analysis of the capital-labour relation and its relation to state power explored in the second chapter, we note that as the contradiction of capital appears in the disruptive presence of labour in and against capital, economic crises are rooted in capital's inability to integrate labour into the capital relation on the basis necessary for accumulation. Capital's ability to constitute labour in a manner necessary to maintain capitalism is called into question. Crises are not caused by the state. While the state is a moment in the class antagonism between capital and labour, the contradictions of capital do not confront it directly but get reproduced by the state as fiscal, monetary or social crises through its different efforts to manage them (Bonefeld, 1993: 3).

Keynesian policies[1] developed in response to the disruptive potential of labour. They were partly based on the global strength of the American and Canadian economies at the end of the Second World War. It took several years for Europe and Asia to recover from the devastation of the war. In the absence of serious competition, the North American economy, already technologically more advanced, was able to bolster its competitive strength and long-term profitability. The policies were fostered, too, by a recognition of the strength of the working class in terms of organization. In Canada, for example, a significant strike wave occurred during the 1940s. The period also saw a rapid growth in industrial unionism.[2]

In Western Europe and Japan, meanwhile, Communist-led trade unions gained in strength, providing an incentive for companies to promote collaboration. Meanwhile, the war had wiped out weak industries, and into this vacuum came industries with more advanced American production methods. Large pools of labour reserves kept excessive wage increases in check. The internationally coordinated monetary regime under the leadership of the U.S. economy and the dollar provided a firm foundation for the strong renewal of accumulation and the introduction of Keynesianism.

"Keynesianism," Bonefeld (1993: 69) suggests, "was an attempt to integrate labour into the capital relation on the basis of full employment growth policies and institutionalized forms of redistribution of wealth." The organized working class won, among other things, the right to bargain collectively and a commitment to monetary policies conducive to low levels of unemployment. It also won a significant increase in wages via various entitlements from the state such as unemployment and welfare benefits, health care and pension programs. Capital and the state, absorbing working-class struggle through the formalized administration of the union movement, achieved greater social peace with the working class. This helped guarantee that wage increases were kept at the same level (or below) as increases in productivity. It also established the ability to contribute to "the partial nationalization of social reproduction" of the working population, and thus to a healthy and stable workforce, by means of more standardized social policies (Sears, 1999: 92).

All of these new measures helped to establish the welfare state. In Canada, a series of social-welfare measures laid the foundation for this welfare state: universal health care, introduced under the Health Care Act; unemployment insurance benefits; and old-age pensions available to all seniors at the age of sixty-five. Still other measures improved the health and safety of workers. For example, workers injured at a job site could file for benefits under the Workers' Compensation Program. Labour laws were revised to regulate working conditions under the provincial employee standards acts, which contained important definitions of a working week, a working day, overtime, and vacation pay. As a result, paid work increased in value beyond the actual pay cheques. Unionized workers were more amply rewarded than non-unionized workers, given the new fringe benefits: private pension plans (funded by the joint contributions of employers or employees or by one group), medical and dental plans, paid sick days, etc. (Up until recently, employers would calculate an additional 15 percent over the hourly wage to finance these benefits.)

All of these things, together with the spread of U.S. technologies and production methods and the coordination of the international economy under U.S. leadership (Bonefeld, 1993: 70–71, see also Clarke, 1988: 244 ff.), helped contribute to a period of historic levels of economic growth for most advanced capitalist economies, sustained by unprecedented secular profit rates and productivity increases, leading to the long-term prosperity, and thus stability, of capitalist economies.[3]

It should be noted that welfare states varied a great deal in strength. Their influence in shaping the postwar experiences of working-class people was thus different even in advanced capitalist countries. As Esping-Andersen (1990) shows, Scandinavian countries developed much stronger welfare states than those in Western Europe or North America, particularly the United States. In Scandinavian countries, the state-funded social programs contributed to what Esping-Anderson refers to as a partial de-commodification of labour power. On the other hand, in the United States, the role of the free market in the labour market was far less mitigated by the state even though the standard of living rose steadily for a significant portion of the working class.

At the same time, we should be careful to avoid the pitfalls of theoretical approaches to the study of capitalist orders, such as those made by the Regulation School. They tend to relegate struggle to a phenomenon caused by the objective laws of capitalist development. They also overstate the degree of political and economic stability of the postwar period, as well as the degree to which labour was integrated into capital relation.[4] Access to the benefits of the welfare state were limited. Specific groups in Canada, including women, people of colour, Aboriginals, gays and lesbians, and Francophones, were in many different ways excluded partially or totally from these gains (Sears, 2003).

Meanwhile, the period witnessed a certain degree of mobilization, sometimes fairly militant on the part of union activists. It ranged from the asbestos strike in Québec in the late 1940s to the emergence of a rank-and-file rebellion across the country by mainly younger trade unionists in the mid-1960s. They directed their protest against management's authoritarian control of the shop floor and the often cozy relationship between managers and union leaders.[5] There was clearly an overall political and economic coherence to the capital-labour relation during the postwar years, involving several quid pro quos (returns on favours) between owners and workers. Their relationship, however, was never smooth, and gains to the latter were certainly never distributed evenly.

Emergence of the Crisis

By the late 1960s cracks in the Keynesian foundation of many of the advanced capitalist economies began to appear. The mechanisms designed to keep capital's tendency to overaccumulation from expressing itself and thus to ensure long-term profitability had run their course. Overaccumulation of capital, driven by "the unfettered development of the productive power of labour" (Bonefeld, 1993: 72), continued to worsen, contributing to a decline in the rate of profit. This increased the dependence on relatively cheap and easily accessible credit to sustain economic growth and thus contributed to growing inflation. In other words, the conditions that had paved the way for the period of unprecedented economic growth now led to structural imbalances in the advanced capitalist economies. The boom times — expressed in the growing markets for capital and consumer goods, high profits and easy access to cheap credit — had encouraged employers to invest in production (in technologies, tools and machinery) at a rate at which, eventually, they could no longer be employed profitably. The growth in the productive capacity of capital had far outpaced the growth of the market, putting downward pressure on prices and profits. The Keynesian regime of cheap credit enabled capital to sustain accumulation despite the weakened profits without restructuring or triggering a recession. The cost was increasing inflation and mounting debt.

In such a situation labour's disruptive power has to be contained. Labour must be integrated into the capital relation in a manner conducive to the renewal of healthier accumulation through rising profit rates, in order for capital to pay for credit previously borrowed as well as to continue to invest in more efficient means of production. Capital and the state can recompose the working class into a cheaper and more efficient labour force — reducing "necessary labour" — by doing such things as limiting wage gains or even decreasing real wages, pursuing and inflationary devaluation of wages, introducing new technologies or socially reorganizing the workplace in order to increase labour's productivity. But the disruptive power of labour, expressed in rising industrial militancy in several advanced capitalist countries, undermined initial efforts by capital and the state to respond to the growing structural imbalances in the economy through what Bonefeld (1993: 90) refers to as policies of "austerity by consent."

In 1969, the Canadian government tried voluntary income-and-price restraints through the Price and Incomes Commission, to halt the growing inflationary spiral (Haythorne, 1973). The commission met failure largely due to the "militant non-compliance of labour": workers refused to limit wage demands in the face of an inflationary assault on wages. Facing an election in 1972, the Trudeau government was not willing to prioritize an attack on inflation over keeping unemployment low (Wolfe, 1984: 63). As Roberts and Bullen (1984: 131) have noted, "One-quarter of all work stoppages since 1900 occurred between 1971 and 1975." The government's hesitant pursuit of monetary restraint compounded the situation caused by numerous strikes. Inflation continued to spiral. Canada's international competitive position worsened, according to the Department of Finance, because labour costs were growing out of proportion with those of its main trading partners (Wolfe, 1984: 69).

By the mid-1970s, governments in much of the advanced capitalist world began to abandon Keynesian policies and take more coercive measures against what they viewed as a dangerously rebellious working class. The increase in the money supply and the extension of credit and state loans, central to the Keynesian fiscal strategy in the face of severe profit squeeze, only fuelled the inflationary spiral further. The strategy of substituting easy access to credit and creating demand by means of an inflationary fiscal policy for the kind of restructuring necessary to increase profits could not go on indefinitely. Overaccumulation and thus weak profit rates would only worsen. International financial pressures, in the form of growing debts and increasing balance-of-payments problems, would bear on those states that continued to pursue inflationary policies.

In the fall of 1975, the Canadian government opted to pursue a "gradualist strategy of monetary restraint to bring inflation under control through steady decreases in the rate of growth of the money supply" (Wolfe, 1984: 71). The same strategy was adopted by other countries. This new policy was called monetarism: it is the practice of controlling the supply of money as the chief method of stabilizing the economy. According to Bonefeld, it represented an attempt to reform social relations on the basis of market exchange (1993: 88). The tight money policy also aimed to adjust the balance between labour and capital. Capital, in other words, was forced to reassert over workers its right to manage. The failure to do so under a regime of tight money policy and high interest rates would lead to its redundancy.

In Canada, this policy was coupled with Trudeau's Anti-Inflation Program. While the program nominally targeted both unions and business, Trudeau's focus was the former. Indeed, Trudeau mostly blamed workers' expectations for the faltering economy: "In this struggle," he proclaimed, "we must accomplish nothing less than a wrenching adjustment of our expectations — an adjustment of our national lifestyle to our means."[6]

If workers were not so inclined to abide by Trudeau's new policies, the full force of the state would ensure they did. In 1975 the Anti-Inflation Program was adopted; in 1982, the Public Sector Compensation and Restraint Act. Up until the present, in effect, the state has used an increasingly heavy hand to force workers' compliance to a process of capitalist restructuring. The ultimate goal has been a cheaper and more flexible labour force. Federal and provincial governments have jailed union leaders and rolled back wage gains won through collective bargaining. Increasingly, they have resorted to suspending collective bargaining, designating public-sector workers as essential, and passing back-to-work legislation with strict penalties for those who fail to comply. In many cases, the penalties have been draconian: striking workers who disobeyed the new law faced the loss of seniority, and crippling fines were levied against a union, its executive, and its locals. Clearly, this strategy has amounted to a systematic attack on the postwar accord between organized labour, capital and the state.[7] The labour movement, however, has put forward little meaningful coordinated resistance to this major step backward in industrial relations (Palmer, 1992: 345).

At the same time, monetarist policies were taking their toll on workers across the advanced capitalist world. In Canada, high interest rates and a restrictive money-supply policy contributed to a big increase in unemployment rates by the late 1970s. During the recession of the early 1980s, interest rates reached 20 percent, a swath of uncompetitive capital was wiped out and the official unemployment figures hit 13 percent (Wolfe, 1984: 74). The "pragmatic" monetarist policy of the Bank of Canada, based on the steady reduction of increases to the money supply, had given way to an unplanned and much sharper reduction in the supply of money. Interest rates in Canada soared to defend the dollar in the face of rising interest rates in the U.S., and the subsequent movement of international money holdings from Canada to the U.S. (Drainville, 1995).

As a result of monetarism, organized working-class resistance to restructuring faltered, especially since unions were already reeling from the coercive measures enacted by different levels of government. By the 1982 recession, the strike rate had dropped sharply from its height in the 1970s.

Indeed, a growing number of workplace struggles were initiated as employer lockouts. "Emboldened by the many ways in which the downturn tipped the scales of class struggle in their favour," Palmer observed, "employers pushed concessionary contracts down unionists' throats" (1992: 347). Even when the unemployment rate began to decline in 1986, the percentage of wage settlements below the rate of inflation had risen to 87 percent. As Palmer dryly notes, it was "an indication that the softening of hard times was benefiting employers more than workers" (1992: 350) Despite the continued weakness of working-class movements through the 1980s and 1990s, the Canadian government stuck with its monetarist policy: the policy shifted its focus from money supply to price stability and the direct targeting of the yearly rate of increase in the Consumer Price Index (CPI) (Drainville, 1995: 32).

Neoliberalism and the Continuation of Class Struggle from Above

High unemployment rates and coercive anti-union policies provided companies in advanced capitalist countries with a firmer position from which to assert their control over the workplace. Monetarism has aimed at forcing employers to reassert their right to manage, while providing them with more appropriate conditions to launch workplace offensives. It also wiped out redundant businesses, thus creating higher rates of unemployment. A former adviser to Margaret Thatcher has described the British government's attack on inflation in the early 1980s through the Medium Term Financial Strategy this way: "What was engineered, in Marxist terms — was a crisis in capitalism which re-created a reserve army of labour, and has allowed the capitalists to make high profits ever since."[8] Unemployment and regressive anti-union policies set the stage for a radical attack on the postwar labour-capital relationship and working-class expectations. In effect, monetarism has entailed the undermining of the institutional mechanisms of the Keynesian era — collective bargaining rights, class collaboration, material concessions to workers, all of which had promoted the integration of the working class into the capital relation. Workers' consumption, and thus reproduction, is no longer tied to a social wage provided by a strong welfare state or membership in a class, but to their willingness to be a productive individual in the market. Underlying this is the clear attempt to reimpose the market on people by clamping down on alternatives to wage labour.

By the early 1980s the capitalist offensive led to the introduction of lean production methods. Lean production aimed to secure significant increases both in productivity and profits — to reverse the decline in profit rates that had occurred since the late 1960s. According to Sears (1999: 95ff.) lean production has three main features: the introduction of new technologies, the elimination of waste associated with older production methods, and the remaking of workplace culture. Let us look at each feature in more detail.

First, the introduction of new technologies, which were resisted by unions in the 1970s, were designed to speed up production and reduce the workforce without lowering profit rates. New and more efficient technologies have forced workers, whose work pace is set by the rhythm of the technology, to work more efficiently and produce the same amount of value for employers in even less time than before. This represents a significant reduction in labour time and costs.

The second feature has to do with eliminating waste associated with older mass-production methods. Lean production emphasizes these changes: just-in-time delivery, modular production chains and the breaking down of more regimented job classifications for a workforce that is more flexible in size and is expected to change from task to task (multi-tasking).

The third feature is the remaking of workplace culture, which involves "management by stress." Stress derives from the accelerated pace of work, ever-rising expectations of productivity increases and the continuous threat of layoffs. Stress is reinforced by the growing differentiation of the working class in terms of wages and job security, and as employers turn more and more to non-standard types of labour: contract, part-time, permanent part-time, etc. These are usually non-union and provide little to no job security, or few or no benefits. The goal is to create a labour force that is cheaper, flexible and more productive.

But the restructuring of the working class in this manner, even with the defeat of the wave of strikes by the early 1980s, is not automatic. It involves a dramatic readjustment of expectations and work experience. The restructuring of the state along neoliberal lines has been geared towards this end. We can compare the neoliberal cultural revolution to the Industrial Revolution in its early stages. A working class was created in the U.K. and its expectations were similarly altered. As we saw in the previous chapter, labour power was made into a commodity to be bought and sold on the market by the state's efforts to forcefully deny working people any alternative opportunity for subsistence. Customary entitlements and expectations that had shaped the experience of labourers and peasants in pre-capitalist England had to be systematically destroyed because they were incompatible with capitalist market relations. This represented a significant change to the moral economy of pre-capitalist England.

Similarly, employers and state officials began to view the welfare state as a significant impediment to the imposing of lean production and the restructuring of the working class (Sears, 2003: 12; Albo, 1994: 145). Its labour market had "rigidities" in the form of union rights and the opportunities for workers to earn an income outside the workplace.

Known for its strong advocacy of free trade, for example, the Canadian government's MacDonald Commission, which published its findings in 1985, also advocated the systematic dismantling of the welfare state, identifying it as a barrier to the readjustment of the unemployed's expectations and willingness to take jobs with lower pay, few benefits and little job security (Bradford, 2000: 68). These developments marked a dramatic narrowing of the "parameters of citizenship" established with the welfare state and its social entitlements (Sears, 2003: 10).

As Sears (1999: 100) argues, the state has "sought to increase the compulsion to work and reduce incomes at the lower end by dramatically diminishing alternatives to the wage for subsistence. This strategy requires the destruction of any sense of entitlement built up through the period of the broad welfare state." As the unemployed might be inclined to avoid poorly paid jobs, states have responded by slashing benefits to unemployment and welfare programs, increasing eligibility requirements and launching an ideological assault on benefit recipients.

In the 1980s, the federal government in Canada began cutting its direct spending on social programs and its social transfers to the provinces. It also reorganized the criteria for getting social assistance (Russell, 2000: 39). The result has been twofold: the amount a recipient can receive for unemployment benefits has dropped considerably over a twenty-year period. To receive payments, recipients have to attend job-training programs. These programs, however, do not provide any of the particular hard skills that are touted as crucial for success in today's labour market. Instead, they stress the importance of assuming greater responsibility for one's lack of work and making more effort to find whatever work is available.[9] These conditions apply only for those who meet today's Employment Insurance eligibility requirements. In 1989, 87 percent of unemployed Canadians qualified for unemployment benefits. By 1996 that number had dropped dramatically to 42 percent (Gabriel, 2001: 136).

A similar, if not harsher, trend has taken place with respect to welfare benefits. Before the federal government axed the Canada Assistance Plan in 1996 and replaced it with the Canada Health and Social Transfer, mandatory work programs connected to welfare programs were prohibited by federal law, though this did not prevent entirely "workfare-style experimentation" (Peck, 2001: 218). Since 1996, not only have the transfers decreased substantially: the conditions imposed by the federal government on the provinces have also been eliminated, opening the door for workfare. Thus, while welfare benefits have decreased dramatically, in most cases falling well below minimum wage levels, at least seven provinces have now made mandatory participation in employment programs an eligibility requirement. As an Alberta Tory social services minister stated bluntly, welfare "has to be uncomfortable enough that people will try to find an alternative way of living" (quoted in Peck, 2001: 218). This, not politicians' and the media's oft-repeated refrain that governments have lived beyond their means, is the central aim of governments' cuts to and reorganization of benefits programs.

Despite sharp cuts to welfare in Ontario under the Harris government, administrative costs have remained high as a result of attempts to implement workfare. The costs have had to cover the hiring of more welfare spies, officially called Eligibility Review Officers (Mosher, 2002: 47), and Andersen Consulting to find more ways of throwing people off the rolls. One Ontario welfare official, interviewed by Peck, made this comment on the Tory's costly welfare strategy: "I don't think costs even enter the equation. It's more [concerned with] having people behave properly" (quoted in Peck, 2001: 244). This also suggests, contrary to commonly espoused opinions in both academia and popular media, that the restructuring of the state in recent years "does not simply require the reduction of state power." Rather, as Sears (2003: 12) argues, "The 'free' market is not produced by the elimination of the state, but rather the mobilization of state power to reduce barriers to commodification." Social programs are being actively used to reorganize the labour force in a manner suitable to lean production.

Of course, this strategy has been accompanied by an ideological assault on benefits recipients. Governments and mainstream media have pushed the idea that those on welfare or unemployment benefits are lazy, undeserving and starving the government and public of much-needed funds; and that most recipients are cheating the system or generally criminally inclined. But the problem for the state and other neoliberal boosters, to be clear, is not the poor per se. Like the nineteenth-century moral reformers and those administering the New Poor Laws, poverty in and of itself is not a concern. Indeed, if we recall from the previous chapter, nineteenth-century officials saw poverty as the appropriate condition of the working class, for it would compel people to seek a wage for subsistence.

This attitude clearly informs welfare reform today. What cannot be tolerated is indigence: the condition of the able-bodied poor collecting social assistance or avoiding wage labour. It does not matter what kinds of jobs exist in today's labour market; we never hear government officials or reporters talk about how badly paid, insecure or alienating such jobs may be. Instead, we get stories of the slothful and vice-ridden character of welfare recipients or panhandlers, and how work, often couched in very moralist terms, is the only appropriate thing to improve their character. As the Ontario Tories argued in their Common Sense Revolution manifesto, "the best social assistance program ever created is a real job" (quoted in Peck, 2001: 236).

The result of neoliberal restructuring in Canada, as elsewhere, has been an increase in non-standard or flexible employment and a corresponding decline in income and wages for significant sections of the working class. "Despite the decline in official unemployment," Burke and Shields (2000: 98) note, "levels of economic marginalization continue to climb." This marginalization gets expressed in the increasing prominence since the 1980s of what they refer to as "vulnerable forms of work such as part-time, contract and other types of 'flexible' and inherently volatile employment" (Burke and Shields, 2000: 105). By 1998, well over one-third of the adult labour force in Canada was stuck in such flexible or insecure work (Burke and Shields, 2000: 112). While wages for most full-time and more secure work stagnated through the 1990s, the wages for "vulnerable" work have remained significantly less. In 1998, the median wage for workers under the age of thirty in vulnerable work was only twelve dollars an hour, and workers in this type of employment can only expect very marginal increases in their wages as they get older (Burke and Shields, 2000: 112).

The restructuring of work also disproportionately affects youth, women and people of colour (Gabriel, 2001; Galabuzi, 2001). Not only do they suffer much higher rates of unemployment than older, non-racialized men, but when they do find work it is often of the most "vulnerable" and lowest paying kind. In 1998, for instance, the average pre-tax income of racialized workers in Canada was 24 percent less than that of non-racialized workers. Not surprisingly, then, over 35 percent of racialized individuals live under the poverty line according to Statistics Canada, compared to 17.6 percent of the general population (Galabuzi, 2001: 17). They also face a much higher incidence of poorly paid non-standard work (Gabriel, 2000: 146). Because they are stuck in jobs where they are less likely to be unionized, they are also disproportionately affected by changes to labour standards that clearly favour employers. Such changes include frozen minimum wages, the granting of greater flexibility to employers to impose overtime, significant reductions to health and safety standards, and cuts to the staffing levels of the inspectors who are supposed to impose minimum requirements in this area on employers.

The Rise of Law and Order

It is in the context described above that we must situate the emergence of law-and-order policing. Law-and-order policing is not simply a policy whim of right-wing governments, who fear a rise in crime or at least play on such fears for electoral gain. This is not to deny that politicians and police have made recourse to law-and-order themes — to a supposed increase in crime and rise in lawlessness, especially among youth and youth of colour — in order to win votes or public support for more funding for policing, or that they have been successful in doing so. The emergence of law-and-order policing in several advanced capitalist states since, in some cases, the late 1970s, at a time when governments and capital have been pursuing agendas of fairly deep-rooted restructuring, suggests it represents more than opportunism. In Canada the government's own records indicate that overall recorded crime rates, particularly for violent person-to-person crime, were declining through the 1990s, when many of the law-and-order policies were adopted, although, interestingly, arrests for public-order offences like mischief or disturbing the peace increased (Canadian Centre For Justice Statistics, 2001). To be properly understood, then, law-and-order policing needs to be seen as part of the form of the neoliberal state. It is one end of a continuum of policies, including cuts to social programs and the attack on workers' rights, designed to impose a specific wage form on the working class, particularly those at the lower end of the labour market.

Law-and-order policing does not necessarily mark a fundamental break from the general historical role of policing in capitalist societies, as outlined in the second chapter. However, the stress placed on it by neoliberal states may speak to a certain urgency that was not as strongly manifested during the postwar period. The rise of various law-and-order policing strategies in Britain, the United States and Canada, for example, is an expression of this urgency, as is the alarming increase in police militarization in many North American policing jurisdictions.

The state's efforts to administer the working class, we noted in the second chapter, involve the imposition of disciplinary norms geared at promoting certain forms of behaviour and expectations. Various areas of policy-making are used to this end, including welfare, education and policing. Strategies for administering the working class shift over time according to the rhythm of class relations and the dynamics of the capitalist economy. Following Sears (2003: 86), there was a general optimism among reformers and state policy-makers during the Keynesian welfare state, influenced no doubt by the struggles from below during the 1930s and 1940s, that the masses could be elevated and molded via state intervention "into a productive and harmonious citizenry" that exhibited greater forms of self-regulation. This optimism contrasted sharply with attitudes towards the working class, especially its poorest sections and immigrants, in the nineteenth and early twentieth centuries, where the prevailing opinion was that social or cultural elevation was not possible. The optimism during the period of the Keynesian welfare state was translated by incorporating of greater layers of the working class into the state and its citizenship rights. This was achieved, Sears notes, by extending social benefits and educational opportunities that were aimed at producing a healthy and compliant working class.

Policing in this period was no doubt shaped by the mood of reformers and state policy-makers. The location of crime and disorder in broader social environments, rather than simply with individual responsibility, and the possibility of rehabilitation influenced attitudes towards criminality. The lower levels of unemployment and the increase in decent paying jobs meant a decline in indigence to be targeted (Parenti, 1999: 136; O'Malley and Palmer, 1996: 138).

The breakdown of the postwar order and the turn to neoliberalism mark a shift in the state's disciplinary strategies towards the working class. We have discussed how this shift has affected the organization of social programs. The impact on policing has been significant. For instance, while vagrancy as an offence in the Criminal Code was considerably de-fanged in the early 1970s, the more recent adoption of zero-tolerance and community policing strategies, as well as anti-panhandling and anti-vagrancy laws, has led to the de facto renewed criminalization of vagrancy and panhandling in Canada (Esmonde, 2002b; Schneiderman, 2002: 85), as we shall see in the next chapter. As the form by which capital and the state seek to integrate labour into the capital relation has changed, leading to changes in the organization of the state, so the focus of policing shifts, and intensifies, as well. The organization of law-and-order policing expresses the struggles around neoliberal attempts to restructure the working class.

Locating the Emergence of Law-and-Order Policing

A turn to a more aggressive style of policing occurred in Britain and the United States in the late 1960s and early 1970s, in response to rising industrial and political unrest (Hall, Crichter, Jefferson, Clarke and Roberts, 1978; Parenti, 1999). But the consolidation of a policing strategy designed to restructure the working class, rather than simply putting down flash points of urban upheaval, would come with the political shift from the Keynesian policies to monetarism and the neoliberal state. We should be careful not to conflate the policing of riots or industrial unrest with the arguably more important day-to-day function of law-and-order policing: the targeting of generally low-level forms of disorder to fabricate a working class suitable to the needs of capital in the period of lean production. At the same time, as Hall and his co-authors (1978) suggest in the case of Britain, the deployment of aggressive forms of policing to quell strikes and inner city turbulence in the early 1970s was accompanied by coercive legislation, like the Industrial Relations Act, or racist policy papers playing on themes of the Black "enemy within," like the 1973 White Paper on police-immigrant relations. These helped to legitimize the state's increasing reliance on force in communities, especially communities of colour, in the support of neoliberal restructuring.

By the late 1970s, when the British state, first under Labour and then Thatcher's Conservatives, had moved decisively to restructure class relations along monetarist lines, police in Britain had begun consistent, targeted interventions in poorer, often immigrant, neighbourhoods. They were the ones hardest hit by recession, unemployment and government cutbacks (Bonefeld, 1993: 156). The number-one tactic was the stop and search (Smith, 1986: 91). This tactic gives police broad discretionary power to stop people they deem to be suspicious and search them for evidence of illegal behaviour. It was used overwhelmingly against younger, poor and unemployed persons, especially in Black communities. The arbitrary stop and search was the main tactic of the Swamp '81 project, in which approximately one thousand young people (mainly Black) were targeted for police intervention in a supposed crackdown on crime. It was one of the major precursors to the Brixton riots (Greaves, 1986: 77).

During this period in Britain, zero-tolerance and community-policing practices began to be widely adopted. Both effectively take the spirit of a limited mandate program like Swamp '81 and apply it to the general approach of a police force with respect to specific communities.

Similarly, in the United States in the 1980s, as the neoliberal agenda forged ahead so did the spread of zero-tolerance policing strategies and the targeting of vagrancy and other low-level signs of disorder, influenced by the broken-windows theory, first advanced in 1982 by Wilson and Kelling. Along, too, came the development of a number of very aggressive police programs aimed usually at Black and Chicano neighbourhoods. As discussed in the first chapter, much of this policing has grown increasingly militaristic in character, typified by the spread of paramilitary forms of policing (Parenti, 1999: 112 ff.). One of the better-known examples is the Los Angeles Police Department's (LAPD) Operation Hammer. Likening it to the American war against the Vietnamese, Mike Davis (1992: 268) has described it as a police policy of "jacking up thousands of local teenagers at random like so many surprised peasants." A series of judicial decisions and laws were designed to increase police powers in the fight on crime. The Violent Crime Control and Law Enforcement Act of 1994 allocated billions of dollars of grants to police for weapons, new hirings and the pursuit of community-policing initiatives (Parenti, 1999: 49ff.).

Tied in with law-and-order policing has also been the "gang scare" and the concomitant war on drugs. Gang violence is indeed a reality for many people in communities hit hard by plant closures, unemployment and government cutbacks. According to Davis, however, the gang scare and its impact on more affluent neighbourhoods have been blown well out of proportion by police, politicians and acquiescent media and used as a pretext for more heavy-handed policing and targeting of Black and Chicano youth (1992: 268 ff.). As expressed with Operation Hammer, most anti-gang initiatives have seen the incarceration of record numbers of Black and Chicano youth. They have also allowed police to regularly stop and search thousands more, adding their names to their databases, without any intention of arrest. Also included in the law-and-order strategy in Los Angeles has been the imposition of curfews almost exclusively against Black and Chicano neighbourhoods, and the wide discretionary use, backed by the state's supreme court, of truancy laws. In effect, "Police now have virtually unlimited discretion, day or night, to target 'undesirables,' especially youth" (1992: 285).

In Canada, where neoliberal state restructuring was generally not pursued with the same vigour as it was in Britain and the U.S. until the 1990s, we see a similar rise of zero-tolerance and community-policing initiatives, modeled on practices in Britain and the U.S. There has also been the widespread adoption, municipally and provincially, of laws targeting panhandling in

Canadian cities since the 1990s. According to Collins and Blomley (2001: 3), by 1999 thirteen of Canada's sixteen largest municipalities had such laws.

Many of these restrictions come in the form of city bylaws that prohibit supposedly aggressive or intimidating begging. The bylaws usually target when and where people can panhandle. Panhandling at night or near bank machines is usually prohibited. There is a ban on panhandling in public areas twenty-four hours a day (National Anti-Poverty Organization, 1999: 8–9). The bylaws also usually come with steep penalties for offenders. In Vancouver a panhandler can be fined a minimum $100 up to a maximum of $2000. In Calgary the maximum fine is $10,000. A person unable to pay it can receive a jail sentence of up to a year. In Winnipeg panhandlers can receive six months in jail if they do not pay their fines. Meanwhile, in 1999 the Ontario government passed the Safe Streets Act (SSA), adding greater authority to the Ontario police mandate of targeting the poor and low-level signs of disorder. We will discuss this in more detail in the following chapter.

"Get a Job!": Policing and Work

Law-and-order policing strategies, together with the laws backing them up, emerged in Britain, the United States and Canada at the time governments began pursuing neoliberal restructuring. But it is not the timing alone that ties it to neoliberal restructuring. Law-and-order policing, with its emphasis on low levels of disorder, people of colour and the poor, also expresses the orientation of state power in a period of lean production and the monetarist recomposition of wage labour. Together with cuts to social programs and a tight monetary policy, it is central to the neoliberal state and its project of driving down wages and expectations at the lower end of the labour market. The restructuring of the welfare state and the destruction of the expectations and entitlements that came to shape working-class experience during the postwar compromise have involved dramatic changes to the lives of working people. They have involved the extension of the free market into greater areas of people's day-to-day existence. The imposition of market relations on working people today, in place of social entitlements, requires not the retreat of the state, but the mobilization of state power, just as the successful imposition of market relations in the early days of capitalism in England required the mobilization of state power to forcefully cut off alternatives to wage labour through the workhouse, targeting vagrancy and stamping out the system of ancient entitlements. Complementing the restructuring of social-benefits programs discussed above is a law-and-order policing that expresses many of the historical dynamics of policing described in the second chapter.

As Sears (1999: 105) has argued, "State disciplinary activities reinforce market discipline by visibly suppressing forms of deviant conduct which threaten the norms of commodity exchange." Bonefeld (1993: 140) likewise argues that the imposition of market-exchange relations on the working class "presupposed law-and-order policies, i.e., the law and order of money." The success of monetarism and neoliberal restructuring is contingent on law-and-order policing. As Bonefeld (1993: 158) puts it, law-and-order policing is "the other side of a policy of state austerity."

Thus, the retreat from the welfare state involved forms of industrial and political unrest that have often drawn sharp police responses in many advanced capitalist countries. In the case of the global justice movement, the reaction is still the same. Law-and-order policing cannot be reduced to such repression. To do so would lead observers to miss its key dynamics and its central place within neoliberal state power, namely, the production of a cheaper and more flexible class of wage labourers.

One area in which this is expressed, for example, is the policing of vagrancy and panhandling. We have noted above the added priority that governments and the police have given to vagrancy and panhandling in recent years under the banner of law and order. This is particularly the case when the persons in question are able bodied, as with squeegeers, who are the principal targets of the Safe Streets Act. Police and law-and-order advocates may suggest they are targeting criminals or criminal hot spots, as they have in Toronto under the Community Action Policing Program (also known as Targeted Policing) or in various policing jurisdictions where similar programs, usually as part of a zero-tolerance strategy, have been introduced. But the targets of such crusades are expressions of low-level public disorder: almost always the poor, panhandlers, squeegeers, youth hanging out in parks and sex-trade workers. They are poor and working-class people who are either seeking an income outside of the formal labour market or simply enjoying recreational pursuits rather than enduring the discipline of the wage (Committee to Stop Targeted Policing, 2000).

There may be a number of reasons why someone might choose to pan-handle, squeegee or sell sex for money. Sometimes the individuals are unable to find work that week, or they have a job that doesn't pay enough to meet all their living expenses. In the case of the sex trade, it is sometimes a matter of simply enjoying the work (Kelley, 1997: 73). However, it is often also the case that people are consciously avoiding paid work or looking for that second job. As Kelley (1997: 45) argues, when most of the higher-paying jobs have evaporated in working-class communities, especially communities of colour, people often turn to different strategies to avoid some of the more unfulfill-ing jobs. One response of African American youth to economic restructur-ing is to turn the pursuit of pleasure, leisure and creative expression, often involving highly skilled and labour-intensive efforts, into an opportunity for cash. Artistic endeavours like break-dancing and rapping, or sports like pick-up basketball have been performed on streets and in parks by African American youth for money. Here labour and leisure, or what Kelley refers to as "play," intersect in a creative, financially successful effort, at a time when corporations selling athletic gear or music are themselves marketing and seeking to make a profit out of the decaying inner city landscape and the creative expressions of "play" found within it. The contemporary use of forms of "play" is not new, though; it has a long history of working-class street performance aimed at generating income outside the formal labour market.

But for Kelly, despite the historical importance of the use of "play" in this manner, especially in African-American communities, it should not be misconstrued as emancipatory. Instead, he is simply noting the way in which it has come to provide "a range of strategies within capitalism... intended to enable working-class urban youth to avoid dead-end wage labour while devoting their energies to creative and pleasurable pursuits" (Kelly, 1997: 45).

Indeed, Kelley argues that "play" often reinforces hierarchical gender boundaries. Women have fewer opportunities for "play" because they have greater domestic responsibilities. They also have less access to public spaces, fiercely guarded by men, often because of the supposed dangers for women. Artistic, athletic and other forms of "play" or simply hanging out have historically been an important part of the construction of masculinity. Kelley argues that "play" may be even more important now for preserving the masculine identity. The workplace, long the central site for shaping of gender norms, may be less important today in African American communities because of the higher rates of unemployment for the men and the so-called feminization of much of the labour market (Kelley, 1997: 54–55; on the feminization of the labour market, see Bakker, 1996: 7).

In their study of policing in Britain, Hall and his co-authors also note a similar response to economic restructuring by working-class youth, especially in Black communities. The preference for street-based activities steadily increased as prospects for decent paying jobs with the possibility of upward mobility decreased through the 1970s. Likewise, O'Grady, Bright and Cohen (1998: 322), in their ethnographic study of squeegeers in Ontario, found that squeegeers quite explicitly considered their work on the street "to be preferable to most 'legitimate,' low wage employment." Earning an income off the streets, which is not without its difficulties and dangers, is often a more enticing option than poorly paid wage work, the conditions of which they have no control over. Thus, for O'Grady, Bright and Cohen (1998: 322) "working the streets... can be regarded as a form [of] resistance to low wage employment."

These street-based income-earning strategies, pursued in response to deteriorating opportunities at the lower end of the labour market, are fundamental to the shaping of law-and-order policing practices. These activities are being systematically targeted by police. As Kelley notes, Black youth have been arrested for disturbing the peace when break-dancing in public spaces to earn cash (1997: 53). It is hard to discern the danger of break-dancing in public — or for that matter panhandling, squeegeeing or hanging out with friends in public spaces. Despite policing claims to the contrary, little evidence has been given to prove they are a real threat to public safety. Yet they are all considered policing priorities today. The real danger to public order lies not in the acts in and of themselves, but in the possibility of participants earning an income from them. The order being defended, in other words, is very specific: the order of capital, which demands the complete subordination of labour to the wage form. Earning an income outside of the formal labour market, in this respect, is an affront to that order and as such intolerable.

The argument here provides a different take on law-and-order policing than that found in most critical studies, particularly those on policing in Canada. A common explanation for law-and-order policing views it as a bulwark for gentrification. Attempts to turn low-rent, poorer neighbourhoods into more upscale yuppie enclaves require the police to clean up the neighbourhood, removing the undesirables who hurt local businesses and jeopardize rising property rates. Another explanation advanced, sometimes in conjunction with the gentrification argument, is the fear-of-the-Other syndrome: the poor are an unsettling reminder, especially to the affluent, of the darker side of economic restructuring and the boom of the 1990s. Rather than deal with poverty in a socially constructive way, the affluent, neoliberal governments and police would rather sweep them under the carpet.

These arguments are insightful but do not fully explain law-and-order policing. It is indeed the case that gentrification has been a significant social force affecting the landscape of many urban centres in the United States, as well as Canada. Wealthy residents' associations, supported by local police, have sought to remove panhandlers and other visible signs of poverty from their neighbourhoods. But, how do we explain the fact that law-and-order policing is not limited to gentrified neighbourhoods? Toronto's Targeted Policing program, described in the first chapter, focused on several different working-class neighbourhoods and communities of colour, not all of which are serious sites of gentrification (Committee to Stop Targeted Policing, 2000). Similarly, in the United States zero-tolerance policing and the anti-gang initiatives that have been used as a pretext to target thousands of Black and Chicano youth who clearly have nothing to do with gangs, have not been limited to gentrified communities. It is the Black and Chicano communities, not affluent ones, which Parenti and Davis describe as being under military-style police occupation. Clearly neoliberal states have a broader interest in their policing initiatives than simply the promotion of gentrification.

At the same time, law-and-order policing is not so much about the targeting of a certain socio-economic condition embodied in an Other, such as poverty, as it is the targeting of forms of behaviour. It is useful here to recall again that for the New Poor Laws and the new police, working together to establish a capitalist labour market in nineteenth century Britain, their concern was not with poverty but indigence — the condition of the able-bodied poor who sought to avoid wage labour. As this same pattern is being expressed today in the neoliberal restructuring of the welfare state, so it is with law-and-order policing as well. The target of policing is not so much the poor but the contemporary indigent. It is much more acceptable to the state and police for someone to be poor if they are working or actively looking for work and not trying to live outside the labour market. As I have argued above, the poor being targeted under law-and-order policing are often seeking an income outside the wage form. At a place of legitimate employment, the poor are not at risk of being targeted by police.

This point becomes clearer if we note the way in which wage work, as we discussed in the second chapter, is intimately bound up in capitalist society with a person's moral standing. This is important to remember for our considerations of law-and-order policing. The poor on welfare or begging, we have noted, are derided as undeserving, dependent on hand-outs and lazy and the solution is always seen as wage work, which has historically been a sign in capitalist society of self-discipline and respectability. Thus this moralism surrounds not poverty but indigence, and it has become a deeply embedded feature of our society, such that signs of it are treated as automatic expressions of disorder that must be targeted, whether or not the police officer on patrol is consciously seeking to produce capitalist social relations. Indeed, so strong is the moralist concern surrounding indigence that, again as we saw in the preceding chapter, it is sometimes merely the potential for it that is targeted. Merely being poor can turn a person into a sign of potential disorder and criminality. Thus we find that sometimes, whatever the particular pretext police choose to employ (drugs, gangs, noise laws etc.), the targets of law-and-order policing, especially youth and people of colour, are simply hanging out with friends in parks or on the street (Committee To Stop Targeted Policing, 2000; Parenti, 1999: 80). When not at work, the poor in recreational as well as other pursuits represent potential disorder. Law-and-order policing in this respect cannot be reduced to attempting to remove the Other from sight.

The historical dynamic of criminalizing indigence and targeting potential signs of disorder is shaped today by neoliberal restructuring and the introduction of lean production methods. The era of lean production is guided by the ethos of the "lean person." As the flexible worker entails the willingness and ability to be more productive, work longer hours, multi-task and, if necessary, carry more than one job to make ends meet, so "the lean person is driven to maintain herself or himself at peak levels of fitness and generally organizes her or his life around lean principles, avoiding waste and dependence" (Sears, 1999: 103). Personal sacrifice and self-discipline, bound up with the willingness to work a lot harder for less pay is the norm expected from the state and employers today. The inability or refusal to live by this ethos speaks, in the eyes of the state and employers, to a person's weak moral and potentially criminal character.

At times the emphasis on this ethos can translate into real simmering anger towards poor people who are on the streets, rather than at work, panhandling or labouring for spare change or simply hanging out, particularly from police officers charged with being the front line against those with weak moral character and thus criminal inclination. It is not an accident that "Get off the streets and get a job, you pieces of shit" is one of the forms of verbal abuse directed at squeegeers by police (O'Grady and Bright, 2002: 27). Such comments express the way in which wage work is strongly imbued with moral connotations and how people's choice to seek alternatives, and not simply the condition of being poor, is an affront to respectability and the moral order. Kelley (1997: 53) notes how a similar disgust and anger, mixed with an unconcealed fear which betrays a deeply rooted racist stereotyping, has shaped popular images of African American male youth today. As large numbers of African American youth opt, in the face of chronically underfunded schools and bleak job prospects, to seek alternative sources of income or simply hang out or pursue "play" on the streets and in parks, they have been increasingly portrayed by police, politicians and media as out of control and a threat to order. It is in this context, he suggests, that terms like "wilding" have emerged to refer to the supposedly immoral and undisciplined behaviour of young African American males who do not have the disciplining experience of wage work in their lives. Kelley's observations also indicate how deeply racialized law-and-order policing is. The threat to order represented by being poor and not in work are magnified for people of colour and immigrants, an important point we will return to in Chapter 5.

Kelley's observations also point to the way in which youth in particular have been made a target of the anger, often cut with a real sense of fear, towards those out of work. Over the last two decades, in fact, youth, including young children, have been increasingly portrayed as a real danger that must be controlled (Sears, 2003: 199). Sears suggests that the separation of childhood from the world and responsibilities of adulthood during the period of the Keynesian welfare state is being broken down with the emergence of the neoliberal state. During the period of the Keynesian welfare state, social policy aimed to "incorporate children as citizens who were sufficiently disciplined and self-regulating. Children were confined to a separate realm, which suspended certain expectations and tolerated a level of non-instrumental activity that, in adults, would be categorized as lazy, dependent, rule-breaking and time-wasting" (Sears, 2003: 202). But as the neoliberal state moves to impose greater forms of independence and self-reliance on people (usually through the market and wage labour), the dependence of children and youth on adults and the state, which assumes a paternal character toward children through things like schooling and social programs, becomes less tolerable. Youth are expected to become more disciplined and self-reliant at a younger age, and the state is mobilizing its energies to ensure this happens through coercive means. Thus, in Ontario for instance, people under the age of eighteen are no longer eligible for welfare benefits, while youth are increasingly made the objects of law-and-order practices. As noted above, the principal targets of the Safe Streets Act are squeegeers, many of whom are youth. The zero-tolerance policing strategies discussed earlier have also been introduced into schools in Ontario by the Tory government and in parts of the United States, while truancy policies, a key strategy for the policing of the poor, especially women, in the nineteenth and first half of the twentieth centuries (see Chapter Two), have been increasingly utilized since the 1990s against youth who are not in school (Davis, 1992: 286; Parenti, 1999: 77). Meanwhile, an important plank of the Ontario Liberal Party's successful campaign in the 2003 provincial elections was raising the legal drop-out age to eighteen, extending the paternal authority of the government via the educational system over youth. Increasingly strict discipline, deference toward authority and self-reliance are the order of the day for children and youth under the neoliberal state.

Conclusion

An analysis which takes seriously the integral role of policing as a feature of a racialized and gendered state power that expresses the rhythms of class struggle enables us to move beyond narrow and simplistic explanations of law-and-order policing, which reduce it to an issue of gentrification or wiping poverty under the carpet, so to speak. Employing the theoretical approach to policing outlined in the previous chapter, then, we can situate the emergence of law-and-order policing centrally within the developments of neoliberalism. As "the other side of a policy of state austerity," as Bonefeld aptly refers to it, law-and-order policing is not some whimsical policy addition, that can be dropped without consequence, to the rest of the neoliberal regime. Rather, it is as important to neoliberalism as cuts to social spending. Just as the mobilization of state power was historically required to impose the capitalist market on people, so neoliberalism, with its emphasis on strengthening the role of market relations in people's lives after decades of Keynesian welfare state policy that mediated the impact of the market, requires the active support of the state. This comes in the form of restructuring of things like welfare and unemployment benefits, on the one hand, and law-and-order policing, on the other. In both cases the neoliberal state is actively seeking to produce a labour market that is cheap, flexible and vulnerable by breaking down possible alternatives to wage labour. Panhandling, performing and cleaning windshields for money, or in some cases even hanging out with friends on the street or in a park, have become the primary signs of disorder the state and police are worried about, as these activities potentially provide recourse to a life outside the formal labour market and the disciplining norms of the wage form. In the remaining chapters we will look in more detail at how this strategy is pursued, first through anti-vagrancy initiatives and then through the forms of policing of immigrant communities that are so central to neoliberal restructuring.

Notes

1. Keynesian policies or Keynesianism: the terms are named after John Maynard Keynes (1884–1946), a British economist whose theories greatly influenced the economic policies of many governments after the Second World War. His book *General Theory of Employment, Interest, and Money* is considered one of the most important theoretical works of the century. It was published in 1936 during the Great Depression, the worst crisis to affect Western countries since the Industrial Revolution. In it he argued that there was no self-correcting measure to lift an economy out of a depression. Because of boom-or-bust cycles inherent in capitalist economies, governments should not rely on private investment to maintain high employment levels or a flow of money in the economy. They should instead use their powers to spend money, vary taxes and control the money supply to cushion the effects. In a depression, a government should increase its spending to counteract the effect of the decrease in private spending; during a boom, it should decrease its spending to control speculation and inflation. His ideas radically affected the way in which capitalism worked in Western countries, leading to the adoption of the welfare state.

2. See Roberts and Bullen (1984: 112–18); Palmer (1992: 268 ff.).

3. In their essay, "The Rise and Fall of the Golden Age," Glyn et al. provide data on productivity growth and capital investment during the postwar period in the advanced capitalist world (Glyn, Hughes, Lipietz and Singh, 1990). Readers interested in the profit rates between 1947 to 1991 in Canada should consult Smith and Taylor (1996).

4. See, for example, Harvey (1990) or Lipietz (1987). For a concise critique, see Bonefeld (1993: 7–11).

5. See chapter 6 of Palmer, 1992.

6. Quoted in Roberts and Bullen (1984: 132).

7. See Panitch and Swartz (1988).

8. Quoted in Harvey (1999: xv).

9. The author has first-hand experience in the mandatory Employment Insurance jobs training program. See also Sears' (2003) very insightful analysis of the kind of skills employers are actually seeking from workers today.

4. Panhandling Bylaws and the Safe Streets Act: The Return of Vagrancy Law

In the last chapter we looked broadly at the development of law-and-order policing in Canada in the 1990s. Its development was discussed along the backdrop of the political and economic restructuring that took place starting in the 1980s. State power was partly directed at re-imposing money on social relations, a role for money that had been weakened by the adoption of Keynesian fiscal policies and the development of a welfare state in the postwar period. As a result the commodification of our social life has increased. Our access to things that previously we could claim as citizens and for which we did not wholly rely entirely on the market — health care, education, food or housing — depends more and more on the market, i.e., on money (Bonefeld and Holloway, 1995). The imposition of monetary relations on our social life has not only created new avenues for capital to pursue profits; it has also put greater stress on the need to find paid work, regardless of its quality. Law-and-order policing is central to this agenda.

Part of the agenda entails the renewal of vagrancy laws. The present chapter will look at this important aspect of contemporary law-and-order policing. Vagrancy laws have played an historical role in the state's efforts to produce a class of wage labourers. We will briefly examine the way in which vagrancy laws were historically linked to consolidating the capitalist order, at the heart of which is the subordination of the working class to the needs of capital. In the postwar period, the sharp edge of the vagrancy law was significantly blunted in Canada through a series of amendments. They removed vagrancy as a status offence from the law books. The offence was being poor yet able-bodied and avoiding work. It has re-emerged as a key point in the recent struggle to impose a new form of social order. While the vagrancy offence as such has not returned in the Criminal Code, it has returned in a de facto manner through anti-panhandling bylaws, as well as through other bylaws, provincial laws and police practices that now target specific forms of behaviour in the public spaces. One of the most prominent laws in this state arsenal is Ontario's Safe Streets Act (SSA).

Vagrancy Laws

Vagrancy law was at the heart of the historical development of the new police in Britain in the early nineteenth century (Neocleous, 2000: 67). Vagrants posed a potential threat to private property. As noted in Chapter Two, the consolidation of the authority of private property and capitalist order was not automatic. The vagrancy laws were intended to deal specifically with this matter. They were part of a broad array of laws aimed at criminalizing traditional street activities that provided recreational or material disincentives to finding "legitimate" work. Idleness was a defining vice of the vagrant. It led, and indeed was tantamount to, criminality. The idle were the people most likely to engage in criminal behaviour. Idleness itself was to become a crime.

The Vagrancy Act of 1824 was passed to address the growing concern over idleness. The new vagrancy law, however, defined a variety of street-based activities as illegal. It allowed police to target a broad group of people and street-based activities, including "suspicious characters, beggars, prostitutes and people selling and sleeping in public" (Neocleous, 2000: 75).

The law had another important feature that helped police exert such control over street life. It reversed the assumption of innocence so sacrosanct to British common law: the accused vagrants were presumed guilty, not innocent. The burden of proof rested on their shoulders. Such a startling reversal of the onus of proof enabled the police to clamp down on a variety of individuals, prohibit a variety of activities and impose order on street life.

Thus it was up to the accused to prove they were not vagrants. They had to show they were persons of good moral standing who respected the requisite parameters of moral discipline, who did not avoid working and who did not engage in any illicit activity. Such police power made it well nigh impossible to beg, sell items or hang around in public places, especially if the individual was deemed fit for work. The mere presence of such a person in a public area attracted police attention.

Similar laws were introduced in Europe during the early period of capitalist development, in the mid 1800s. In the United States, we find the same type of laws. They defined vagrant in very broad terms, giving police sweeping powers to target activities or people deemed disorderly:

> Late nineteenth- and early twentieth-century American vagrancy statutes were usually designed to separate the "worthy" poor from their less worthy counterparts. (Adler, 1989: 215)

The disorderly (the vagrants) were the unworthy poor. The unworthy poor were the able-bodied who supported themselves outside of work by begging, stealing, gaming or selling items illegally in public. State officials, including the police together with the moral reformers, feared the deleterious effect that liberal policies towards the poor would have. Just as their counterparts in nineteenth-century Britain argued, they claimed such policies "rewarded indolence and encouraged able-bodied men to become 'professional' tramps and full-time beggars." Vagrancy statutes were invoked to stop "the rise of a 'dangerous class' of wanderers, laggards and 'parasites'" (Adler, 1989: 216–17). In this way being able-bodied and without work was made into a crime.

Vagrancy Law in Canada

There are few studies of the vagrancy laws in Canada. However, a look at the statutes themselves suggests that vagrancy laws played a similar role in Canada to the one they played in the United States, Britain and continental Europe.

Vagrancy laws in Canada predate Confederation of 1867. The new Dominion of Canada passed the Vagrancy Act in 1869 as part of the government's consolidation of criminal law. (The Criminal Code was adopted in 1892). Modelled after British law, the intent of the Canadian statute was very clear, as these clauses from the Criminal Code of 1892 show:

> Every one is a loose, idle or disorderly person or vagrant who:
>
> (a) not having any visible means of maintaining himself lives without employment;
> (b) being able to work and thereby or by other means to maintain himself and family wilfully refuses or neglects to do so;...
> (d) without a certificate signed, within six months, by a priest, clergyman or minister of the Gospel, or two justices of the peace, residing in the municipality where the alms are being asked, that he or she is a deserving object of charity, wanders about and begs, or goes about from door to door, or places himself or herself in any street, highway, passage or public place to beg or receive alms;
> (e) loiters on any street, road, highway or public place, and obstructs passengers by standing across the footpath, or by using insulting language, or in any other way;
> (f) causes a disturbance in or near any street, road, highway or public place, by screaming, swearing or singing, or by being drunk, or by impeding or incommoding peaceable passengers;... (Canada, 55 Vict., c. 29, s. 207).

The target of these clauses is the indigent — the person who is "able to work and thereby... to maintain himself" but who "refuses or neglects to do so." And thus this law is a classic status offence: the person is targeted because of who they are. One's criminal status is based on one's identity rather than any particular act. Simply being "without employment" and with no "visible means of maintaining" oneself (read poor-looking) is cause for police intervention, arrest and a possible jail sentence of six months with hard labour. At the same time begging, which in itself poses very little threat to public safety, is criminalized, unless permitted by the proper authorities. Judging from the first two subsections, it is clear that an able-bodied person is unlikely to be given such permission. This is a very sweeping law, and the onus of proof is placed on the suspect — who has no visible means of employment or who is begging without a proper certificate — to prove they are not a vagrant. The way to avoid being targeted as a vagrant is not to be able-bodied, visibly poor and unemployed in public spaces, namely to find a legitimate source of income. The vagrancy statute is a clear means to create a class of wage labourers. It aimed to stamp out alternatives to holding a job or other reasons to avoid work.

The inclusion of subsections (e) and (f) are also worth noting. Causing a disturbance, loitering or being drunk in public — regardless of whether one's actions while drunk are actually a threat to public safety — define a person as a vagrant. The implication is clear: gainful employment signifies moral discipline; idleness or loitering or carousing in public signify the opposite. Such activities constitute disorderly behaviour under the law.

The vagrancy statute in effect enables police to target a wide range of activities in public spaces — loitering (hanging out), singing, swearing, drinking — whose impact on public safety on most occasions is negligible at best. The danger lies not so much in the activities themselves than the participants. They represent a potential danger because their attitudes challenge the expected behaviour and discipline demanded of the working class. Carefree or festive actions, which express pleasure or an escape from the drudgery (or danger) of wage work, are acceptable only within certain limits. They are more permissible, for instance, if they are not seen as undermining a person's work ethic; they do not create a thriving counter-culture outside of market relations; and if they are forms of pleasure that are commodified.

Subsections (e) and (f) also target the obstruction of pedestrian traffic, which, interestingly, figure in some of the contemporary anti-panhandling bylaws and the Safe Streets Act. Such clauses, in their deliberate vagueness, reinforce the idea that someone poor, able-bodied, without work and possibly begging on the streets is dangerous by ascribing an ipso facto criminal character to behaviour that is not necessarily a threat to public safety. After all, as lawmakers and police must surely be aware (then as now), someone hanging out with friends or looking for spare change will most likely block a pedestrian's way to a certain degree, particularly on a crowded sidewalk. The same conclusion can be drawn for someone selling newspapers, a Salvation Army volunteer soliciting donations or a police officer surveying the scene. They, too, occupy part of the sidewalk, but they are not the ones meant to be targeted under the vagrancy statute. Again, it is not the act of obstructing the sidewalk that is the issue in the vagrancy law, it is who is doing it and why.

How was the vagrancy law applied across the country? In the second half of the nineteenth century, in Halifax, it was primarily directed towards the able-bodied unemployed. "Most vagrants were of prime working age," according to J. Phillips. A disproportionate number of those charged belonged to Halifax's Black community. This was an example of the harsh reality of racism during capitalist development in Canada, where race intersects sharply with notions of public disorder and unemployment, leaving Blacks especially vulnerable to the systematic targeting of state and police (Phillips, 1990: 137).

In Calgary, charges rose significantly in the first two decades of the twentieth century, during the city's rapid industrial expansion. Those charged were individuals who rejected the values and work ethic expected of labourers in the western boom town (Bright, 1995). In Toronto, the law came in handy to deal with the so-called tramp problem. The tramp here is synonymous with the vagrant. They were likewise able-bodied individuals who might be found begging or reveling in public spaces rather than working. They thus failed to live up to bourgeois standards of sobriety, industry and discipline. According to J. Pitsula, who researched how Toronto police treated tramps in the late nineteenth century, the goal was to enforce "the work ethic on a population still influenced by the irregular rhythms of pre-industrial America" (1980: 117). The harsh treatment was intended as a warning to newly arrived immigrants from Eastern Europe, whose commitment to bourgeois order might be in question.[1]

Given its role in targeting the unemployed, it is perhaps not surprising that "the incidence of vagrancy fluctuated with economic conditions" (Phillips, 1990: 130). More charges were laid during economic downturns. The policing aim here may have been to assert control over the unemployed particularly when the rate of unemployment shot up, to prevent them from cultivating a culture and habits that would undermine bourgeois notions of industry and sobriety. Their influence on the rest of the labouring population would have made it more difficult to ensure today's unemployed are tomorrow's disciplined and reliable workforce. But the aim was likely also to force the unemployed to work during bad times when wages and working conditions got worse.

The general attitude among police, moral reformers and media was quite clear: jobs were always available for those willing to find them (Phillips, 1990: 143–45). Newspapers warned charities of the danger of giving to the "professional street beggars" because it would encourage them to refuse work. While there was some recognition that economic problems caused unemployment, the able-bodied unemployed were nonetheless typically seen as "lazy" and "shiftless." Not only did they face police harassment; they were sentenced to a workhouse or prison. Such a sentence was considered to be the means to instill the work ethic in them. As an official in Calgary remarked, the policing of vagrancy distinguished between those who performed steady industrious labour and "the shiftless, drunken and degenerate" who refused to do so.

According to Pitsula, to be eligible to receive charity in Toronto, the able-bodied unemployed had to perform meaningless but physically demanding labour tests. The enforcement of the vagrancy law, together with the administration of social benefits, thus delivered a clear message to the labouring class: "No one should have the illusion that he could live except by the sweat of his own brow" (Pitsula, 1980: 132). The sweat of one's brow, of course, would only be acceptable if produced through market relations.

Vagrancy Law and the Sex Trade
The targeting of prostitution was yet another feature of the vagrancy statute. Section 207 of the 1892 version of the law continues:

> [Every one is a loose, idle or disorderly person or vagrant who:]
>
> (i) being a common prostitute or night walker, wanders in the fields, public streets or highways, lanes or places of public meeting or gathering of people, and does not give a satisfactory account of herself;
> (j) is a keeper or inmate of a disorderly house, bawdy-house or house of ill fame, or house for the resort of prostitutes;
> (k) is in the habit of frequenting such houses and does not give a satisfactory account of himself or herself. (Canada, 55 Vict., c. 29, s. 207)

Until the amendments of 1972, vagrancy statutes were the most frequently used laws against prostitutes.[2] It is important to recall our discussion from the second chapter on the threat posed by working class and colonized women — "people of the body." Their physical exertions at work and their supposedly rapacious sexual urges were seen, in the bourgeois imagination, as a danger to the paternalistic bourgeois order. The prostitute was an embodiment of that fear; she was seen as "the conduit of infection [moral as well as physical] to respectable society" (Faraday, 1991: 16).

In the late nineteenth and early twentieth centuries, the targeting of prostitutes and women more generally under the vagrancy statute was related to a rising concern among police and moral reformers about women's participation in the work force. The fixed hours of a job allowed for more time for leisure activities than did other forms of women's work:

> Under the scrutiny of her family, or the keen eye of a mistress, a young woman was assumed to be safely anchored, but under a foreman's control for a mere sixty or seventy hours per week, or even less in periods of unemployment, the female worker seemed to be adrift in a sea of urban dangers and temptations. (Strange, 1988: 261)

Betraying the state's fear of the pursuit of play and pleasure, which was discussed in the last chapter, reformers and police felt that the absence of paternal authority, which ran along a continuum from the father to the husband to the employer, implied a vacuum that drew women into a world of vice and temptation. Strange argues that a strong sexual threat was attributed to women's leisure: without proper paternal supervision, women would be unable or unwilling to control their bodily desires. Reformers and police feared "that working women's taste for fun would divert them from their duties to their families, their employers, and later to their husbands and children" (Strange, 1988: 252).

This concern was amplified by the apparent phenomenon of "occasional prostitution." This consisted of women who may have from time to time traded sex for money, but did not live entirely from its proceeds (Strange, 1988: 264). Occasional prostitution represented a woman's pursuit of pleasure (or descent into vice in the eyes of the state and reformers) that undermined patriarchal familial relations; it might also have been perceived as weakening women's dependence on a wage income. Either way, it signified an unacceptable expression of women's insubordination to patriarchal authority, in the home to the workplace. The fear of part-time prostitution was probably exaggerated since police and moral reformers believed that a lone woman on the street was up to no good. There was a fine line in the eyes of the police and moral reformers between simply being in public on one's own and being guilty of illicit activity.

> Often it was not so much a young woman's behaviour as her location and the time of day or night that left her vulnerable to apprehension by police.... Arrest reports frequently mentioned that women were apprehended as moral offenders if they could not give a satisfactory justification for their presence at night on one of the city's streets without parental supervision or a respectable male escort. The assumption in virtually all cases of female juvenile delinquency or vagrancy was that the woman must have had an immoral purpose for appearing in public beyond normal work hours. (Strange, 1988: 267)

This amounts to another type of status offence under the vagrancy law: like the unemployed, working-class women in public spaces and absent of paternal authority were deemed criminal.

The policing of women under vagrancy law was not only gendered; it was also racialized, as Aboriginal women were a principal target. According to the historian Joan Sangster, who researched Aboriginal women's treatment by the criminal justice system from 1920–1960, Aboriginal women's criminalization resembled other women's, with a heavy emphasis on public-order offences. However, they were disproportionately targeted.

> For native women, crimes of public poverty and moral transgression
> always dominated over crimes against private property or the person.
> Vagrancy... dominated as the most significant charge for Native
> women in the 1920s (50%) and 1930s (31%). (Sangster, 1999: 37)

Legal authorities and moral reformers especially emphasized the absence of
paternal authority and a woman's descent into vice for Aboriginal women.

As "colonization permeated further north," Aboriginal women began
migrating to cities from reserves in search of work, intensifying this concern.
"Native women suspected of prostitution, or who engaged in sex for no money
and with no obvious moral regret, were especially vulnerable to incarceration"
(Sangster, 1999: 43). Aboriginal women represented the uncivilized Other
to the civilized, self-disciplined and morally respectable white Canadians.
They represented, as McNally might argue, the bodily desires long since
repressed by Europeans in their efforts to achieve bourgeois respectability,
inflated to the point of omnipresent threat as a source of moral contagion. As
Sangster puts it, Aboriginal women played the role "of the licentious 'wild
woman' symbolizing sexual excess and the need for conquest and control"
(1999: 44). The vagrancy statute, as well as other public-order laws such as
the Female Refuges Act, were central to this dynamic. The vagrancy law
at once constituted women absent of paternal authority as criminal, while
providing police with sweeping authority to arrest them.

The Declawing of Vagrancy Law

Commentators usually refer to the amendments of 1972 as the significant
changes made to the vagrancy statute, removing the status offence from the
legislation. But the process was initiated with the consolidation of criminal
law in 1953–54. A person was a vagrant who "(a) not having any apparent
means of support is found wandering abroad or trespassing and does not,
when required, justify his presence in the place where he is found," or "(b)
begs from door to door or in a public place." However, many of the toughest
components found in the 1896 version (subsections (a) to (f)) or added in the
years following 1896 were removed. If one follows the parliamentary debates
leading up to it, the reason for the amendments is quite clear. The general
consensus on the part of all three parties (Liberal, Progressive Conservative
and the Cooperative Commonwealth Federation) was that being jobless
and able-bodied should no longer be considered an offence (Canada, 2–3
Elizabeth: 2267–82, 3004).

In considering these changes, we should recall the discussion in the
previous chapter of the broader political and economic context of the
postwar period, which framed parliamentary debates on vagrancy law.
Vagrancy was likely less of a concern at a time of historic levels of economic
growth that featured higher employment rates and a steady improvement
in wages and working conditions for much of the working class. Further,
these changes were in part a product of struggles from below that dated back

to the Depression of the 1930s, in which the mobilization of the poor and unemployed had figured prominently. The postwar period, and the struggles helping to shape it, also influenced attitudes in the criminal justice system. There was a greater inclination to look beyond the individual offenders to societal forces shaping their behaviour and to recommend rehabilitation along with punishment rather than a big dose of the latter. A new attitude towards the poor emerged in this period, while poverty and unemployment themselves declined sharply. The removal of above sections (a) and (b) from the statute in 1972 was a culmination of a process begun in the 1950s.

What had remained unchanged in the 1950s, however, was the clause relating to prostitution, which was removed in 1972. As the Royal Commission on the Status of Women (1970) noted, the clause was aimed exclusively at women. Thus the main targets of vagrancy law had been women until the provision was repealed (Canada, 1970). A lone working-class woman who appeared in public places unaccompanied by the proper paternal authority was still suspect in the eyes of the state.

The removal of this section of the vagrancy statute in 1972, along with sections (a) and (b), significantly declawed it. The last vestiges of a status offence finally disappeared. However, prostitution still remained a target of public-order policing. The tool here was the "soliciting" law, which was replaced with the "communicating" law in 1985, as well as community-policing and zero-tolerance programs. In addition, women in the criminal justice system are still targeted by a type of modern-day truancy law in the form of "failure-to-comply" orders attached to bail conditions, which demand strict paternal oversight by fathers, husbands and police. Expressions of women's independence and sexuality still appear to cause considerable concern to authorities.

The Re-emergence of Vagrancy-style Laws

As noted in the preceding chapter, with the shift from Keynesianism and the broad welfare state to monetarism and state cutbacks in Canada in the 1980s and 1990s, following the economic crisis of the 1970s, came a shift in attitudes towards the poor, particularly the young and able-bodied. While the job market, especially for youth, has deteriorated, and social benefits have been cut back sharply, the common attitude among policy-makers and politicians has again been shaped by the view that the poor are lazy, need to take personal responsibility for themselves and should accept whatever work is available. Emerging out of this context is the renewal of policy that echoes vagrancy statutes of the past. Vagrancy itself has not re-emerged as a status offence in the Criminal Code. The federal government likely has not seen the need to enter this particular legal arena and rush into existence a classic vagrancy statute. For one thing, there has not been a significant demand for criminal legislation from jurisdictions (primarily the larger urban centres) affected by vagrancy, as municipalities and the Province of Ontario have themselves taken a lead on the issue thus far. But just as importantly, the provincial legislation and the municipal bylaws, and the police practices surrounding them have effectively criminalized vagrancy. Perhaps if poverty continues to increase and the labour market continues to worsen, the federal government may feel the need to intervene on the issue, but for now it is municipalities and the province of Ontario drafting legislation.

When squeegeeing grew in the 1990s in Ontario, for instance, and began to draw the attention of police, politicians and media, the then-federal cabinet minister responsible for the Greater Toronto Area, David Collenette, mused about changing the Criminal Code to deal with the problem. But he did not follow through when the Ontario government, eager to provide a solution, committed itself to the Safe Streets Act (Wanagas and Warmington, 1998: 7). The response of Canadian governments to the new undeserving poor is still developing, and will likely continue to develop over time in a manner that, in the eyes of the state, effectively meets its needs in a given context. Indeed, while the general patterns of neoliberalism frame public policy across Canada, including those related to poverty and crime, its implementation is not uniform, but shaped by such things as the ideological bent of political parties or the strength of social movements operating in different jurisdictions. Thus, while most major urban centres have bylaws against panhandling, only Ontario has provincial legislation like the Safe Streets Act, though British Columbia may be adopting its own version of the latter.

The Municipal Bylaws

The Safe Streets Act (SSA), along with the policy documents and lawmakers' comments surrounding its introduction, is the best example signaling the return of the vagrancy law. Another important form this has taken, however, is municipal bylaws targeting "disorderly" public behaviour, especially panhandling. Anti-panhandling bylaws do not carry the degree of authority that the SSA has, since transgressors cannot be forced to give identification or jailed under municipal bylaw offences. They do also vary in terms of their coerciveness. They are still important to look at, given how broadly some of them define panhandling and how they clearly express a concern not simply with panhandling but with indigence more generally. Policing of panhandlers grew in Canada in the 1990s as labour market restructuring undertaken in the 1980s led to the growth of poorly paid non-standard (part-time, casual, contract) employment.

Cutbacks to social services made it much more difficult to access programs like welfare, unemployment insurance or subsidized housing, or to live off the former two in cases where one did manage to get benefits. With poverty increasing and the number of beggars and poor people, especially youth, to be found on the streets of urban centres noticeably on the rise, policing philosophies like zero-tolerance and community policing, which emphasized the danger of public disorder expressed in begging or loitering, were adopted in departments across the country. Municipalities also began introducing tough anti-panhandling bylaws.

By the end of the 1990s more than a dozen of Canada's largest cities had passed bylaws targeting beggars. The bylaws imposed three general types of restrictions on panhandling. First, they restricted when a person may panhandle, usually limiting the hours to daytime. Second, they stipulated where it cannot occur, such as within certain distances from automated teller machines (ATMs), banks, transit stops or pay phones — all places where people are likely to have money handy. Third, they specified the manner by which someone may panhandle, which usually meant no "aggressive" or "obstructive" demands for money (Collins and Blomley, 2001: 6). Breaking the bylaws may bring unwanted police attention and fines. In some cities the fines could climb as high as several thousand dollars, which would be very difficult to pay if you are unemployed.

While the bylaws may aid in the gentrification of certain neighbour-hoods or remove unsettling reminders of the contradictions of economic and political restructuring, these explanations, as noted in the previous chapter, are insufficient and gloss over the way in which these laws are woven into the historical project of state and police power imposing market relations on people. The bylaws and police practices enforcing them come close, in some instances, to making it very difficult to beg and seek a living outside of market relations, as the vagrancy statute did. The bylaws obviously do not have the weight of criminal law and do not explicitly make it illegal to be able-bodied, poor and unemployed in public as the old vagrancy law did, but they can be crafted and supported by police in such a way as to have some similar effects as the classic vagrancy statute. A closer look at certain bylaws will clarify the point.

Bylaws and the "Dangerous" Beggar

It is important to note that a link between begging and criminality usually dominates discussions preceding implementation of anti-panhandling by-laws. This topic expresses the historical connection, in the eyes of the state, police and public, between unemployment and criminality. It reinforces the view that the unemployed on the streets are dangerous and untrustworthy, thus helping to justify targeting them. This view is evident in the specific case of the SSA, as we will see below.

The fact that many bylaws ban begging at night is suggestive here. Criminals are known to lurk at night in dark places ready to pounce on unsuspecting victims. Their identity is hidden by the darkness. Prohibiting begging at night is based on the belief that those who beg are dangerous and likely to use the night for criminal pursuits. Further, the prohibition may well make it difficult for those who beg in the day to be on the streets at night, regardless of what they are doing. It is possible that the police, already influenced by the broken-windows theory, may question or harass them. If you have been identified as a beggar in the daytime, and thus as a potential criminal, you will have to prove you are not looking for trouble after dark. At night the working class, away from the disciplining effect of work and engaged in an urban world oozing with vice and temptation, has historically been regarded as an object of fear, and contemporary anti-panhandling bylaws restricting activities at night share that inspiration (see Palmer, 2000).

Equally suggestive in the bylaws is the explicit prohibition of begging anywhere near locations where people may have money readily accessible, such as ATMs, bus stops and taxi stands. Certainly this provision intends to keep beggars away from areas where they may actually be more successful at making money. But it also assumes panhandlers are more likely to be thieves than other citizens (National Anti-Poverty Organization, 1999: 9). The manner in which someone is begging isn't considered; it is the act itself and the individual performing the act that are the issues. Simply being poor and trying to survive on the street implies a threat to public security.

Panhandling is also construed by police, politicians and media as an integral part of a broader context of criminality. The City of Vancouver's Urban Safety Commission, for instance, was established "to identify key issues affecting the safety and quality of life of Vancouver residents and visitors" (City of Vancouver, 1998a: 1). It was operating in the period preceding the adoption of Vancouver's panhandling bylaw. The Commission describes panhandling as a major threat to security in the city. The administrative reports written by the city manager on the proposed new bylaw emphasize the bylaw's importance because of the danger panhandling — which is not only "unsightly" but "intimidating" — poses to public safety (City of Vancouver, 1998b: 2).

Winnipeg likewise passed a panhandling bylaw in 1998. After the law was enacted, the City of Winnipeg issued a press release entitled, "Stronger Police Presence and New Programs Will Make Downtown Safer." It quotes a city councillor asserting "that criminal and disorderly conduct will not be tolerated.... This problem will be dealt with." The release includes this statement by the Chief of Police: "We're establishing a zero-tolerance policy... that means we will no longer tolerate intimidation, disorderly conduct, panhandling, or interference of any kind" (City of Winnipeg, 1998).

The following year, the Annual Report of the Winnipeg Police Service discussed its Downtown Safety Strategies. These strategies would "address minor offences and disorder issues that make people feel unsafe, such as aggressive panhandling, graffiti, and intoxicated persons" (Winnipeg Police Service, 1999).

It is useful to recall here Toronto's Targeted Policing campaign (or Community Action Policing), which was established in explicit response to supposed crime hot spots. It focused most of its energies on public-order issues like panhandling. In her field-work study of squeegeeing in Toronto, Esmonde argues that supporters of a bylaw prohibiting panhandling and squeegeeing — who also became advocates of the Safe Streets Act — took great pains to identify beggars and squeegeers as a danger to the public. They drew on "centuries-old narratives of the 'dangerous poor,' painting squeegeeing as a *threat to the safety of the City*" (Esmonde, 1999: 123; emphasis in original). Hermer finds a similar equation of panhandling with criminality and public danger in his study of the police and politicians' discourse surrounding the introduction of Oshawa's Public Nuisance bylaw. According to Hermer, the police claimed that Oshawa's downtown was so dangerous that people avoided it out of fear. Actual concrete incidents of people being harmed were not given, though police and the bylaw were quick to point to the danger of such things as panhandling and "gathering" in general (Hermer, 1997: 173).

Similarly, there is little evidence from other jurisdictions that demonstrates how panhandling is a threat to people, or that people have actually been harmed by beggars or people hanging out in public spaces. At best there is limited anecdotal evidence and unsubstantiated or greatly exaggerated claims by supporters of strong police-enforcement measures. In her study of squeegeeing in Toronto, Esmonde notes that despite efforts by police and councillors in Toronto to portray unemployed poor youth who are begging, squeegeeing or hanging out as out-of-control criminals ready to assault or steal from anyone who crosses their path, "the policy documents only vaguely explain why these 'enforcement measures' are necessary" (Esmonde, 1999: 119). Vocal supporters of a panhandling bylaw and the SSA, when pressed to provide examples of incidents they had initially described with suggestive verbs like "attack" or "harass," greatly exaggerated the dangers of the incident. In some cases "attack" described the following:

> windshields had been washed without permission. Similarly, complaints about being "harassed" by panhandlers usually meant nothing more than that several panhandlers had asked for money. (Esmonde, 1999: 125)

Observations like these suggest, again, that the act itself, or the people themselves begging or "gathering," are dangerous and criminal. While some of the discourse surrounding the bylaws and police practices may emphasize dangerous types of behaviour sometimes associated with panhandling or hanging out, the focus really amounts to the very acts themselves and the people participating in them. A closer look at some of the bylaws helps to illuminate this point.

A Closer Look at the Bylaws

Vancouver's and Winnipeg's first panhandling bylaws are especially useful to look at. Winnipeg's was one of the earlier bylaws, providing inspiration to other cities as well as being seen as a potential template. Because both cities' bylaws were fairly far-reaching, they also gained a lot of public attention. Both were eventually repealed and replaced when constitutional challenges were mounted against them. In the case of Winnipeg, a judge had suggested during the initial hearings that the city's proposed bylaw might be unconstitutional since it was so close to criminal law (the federal government being the only level with the authority to enact criminal law). The bylaws nonetheless provide us with a glimpse of what lawmakers and supporters were aspiring towards. Further, the second set of bylaws, which we will look at below, have similar aims to the first ones, even if they have been more carefully constructed.

The original versions were more open and explicit, and so worth our consideration here. Winnipeg's first bylaw contained a number of clauses that narrowly restricted a person's ability to beg in the city (City of Winnipeg, Bylaw No. 6555/95). It prohibited panhandling within ten metres of bus stops, bus shelters, ATMs, hospital entrances or bank entrances. It effectively restricted the area where beggars might be successful at making money. In a move clearly aimed at squeegeeing, the bylaw further prohibited any soliciting from drivers, whether they had stopped at a traffic light or parked their cars. This constituted a status-type offence since it made no attempt to distinguish between permissible or non-permissible forms of soliciting from cars. (The targeting of squeegeeing, usually performed by the young and able-bodied, is an important feature of the renewal of vagrancy laws in Canada that will be taken up in more detail when we discuss Ontario's SSA, which was in part designed explicitly to deal with squeegeeing). The Winnipeg bylaw also limited panhandling to daylight hours and states that the person could not follow anyone who has declined a request for money. Notably, the latter clause did not require a person to be begging in order to violate the law, leaving open the possibility that a panhandler could be arrested for walking down the street. Like most other panhandling bylaws, it also specifically exempted charities in its definition of panhandling, suggesting clearly that it was aimed at a particular class of people who were soliciting money.

Combined with the area near ATMs, liquor stores and bank machines, the bus-stop clause blocks off an even larger area of the city's downtown compared to that stipulated in Winnipeg's first bylaw. One critic, in fact, drew up a map to show how panhandling was outlawed on entire streets in the downtown (Supreme Court of British Columbia, 2002).

Most of the bylaws define panhandling as requesting or begging for donations by spoken or written word. Vancouver's original bylaw, however, also included "bodily gesture" in the definition. But the phrase "bodily gesture" itself was not defined, leaving a great deal of discretion to police to determine who was actually begging simply by standing, walking or sitting in a certain way. The bylaw also prohibited anyone from sitting or lying down while panhandling. Combine these two clauses together, being identifiably poor on the street, whether walking, standing or sitting, can potentially make someone a target under the bylaw.

Neither of the bylaws was an exact replica of the old vagrancy statute, of course; however, they embodied the same aim and went some distance in their effort to achieve it. The bylaws made clear who the real targets were by exempting acceptable forms of solicitation done by charities and narrowly circumscribing the opportunities for acquiring an income outside of capitalist market relations. Vancouver's first bylaw furthermore potentially made it a status offence to appear on the streets if one was unemployed and visibly poor.

Oshawa's Public Nuisance bylaw, on the other hand, has received little public attention from proponents or detractors outside of Oshawa. It was just as strong as Vancouver's and Winnipeg's. It was introduced at a time when politicians and police were raising concerns about the downtown turning into a dangerous area taken over by youth hanging out, begging and generally causing trouble. The bylaw is aimed at promoting the social hygiene of the city by removing expressions of social disorder and moral pollutants before they spread. This fear was palpable in policy documents, police statements and newspaper accounts about the decline of Oshawa's city centre.

The fear resulted in a very heavy-handed bylaw. For instance, to beg is defined as "to go from place to place or to remain stationary and, while there, to solicit donations for oneself or for another person" (City of Oshawa, Bylaw 72–94). Soliciting for charities is exempted. The definition is quite broad, since it fails to stipulate how the soliciting is performed — in written or oral form. Presumably someone could be deemed to be soliciting through other, perhaps less obvious, means as well. Police, in other words, are handed a great deal of discretion to decide who is begging and who is not (Hermer, 1997).

The actual prohibitions in the bylaw, furthermore, are themselves very sweeping. Part Two includes the prohibitions against specific "Public Nuisances." With respect to begging, for example, it states, "It shall constitute an offence for a PERSON to BEG, either from door to door, or on any HIGHWAY or in any other public place." Besides mimicking a section included in the old vagrancy statute of 1892 — prohibiting begging "from door to door" — the bylaw makes it illegal to beg, period. The bylaw is equally sweeping regarding other nuisances. It targets, for instance, "gathering" of three or more persons on any street, walkway or in any other public space that "might obstruct a free passageway for PEDESTRIANS or vehicular traffic." A similar clause on "Interference" also targets activities deemed to be interfering with roadways and sidewalks. These clauses echo the provision in the vagrancy statute that prohibited the obstruction of pedestrian traffic. Given that charities are excluded from the bylaw's prohibitions, it is assumed that they would not cause interference on sidewalks, at least not the kind that matters.

Like the first Vancouver bylaw, the Oshawa one also comes close to making the appearance of being poor and able-bodied a status offence. Oshawa police, according to Hermer, have acknowledged that in fact the bylaw has a similar effect to criminal law. It has the added benefit, in their view, of not tying up criminal courts. Its sweeping prohibitions backed with their efforts to uphold it are enough to solve any problems of public disorder perceived to be plaguing the city. However sweeping its definition of begging or its prohibitions are, though, the targets are very specific. Responding to concerns that the bylaw might encourage police to overextend their reach, a downtown beat officer replied, "[W]e know who the troublemakers are" (quoted by Hermer, 1997: 178). The troublemakers, following discussions leading up to the bylaw's adoption and the wording of the bylaw itself, are primarily youth who are begging or hanging out in public spaces. It is their presence on the streets that will be targeted. It is not an exaggeration to suggest, considering its provisions and the discussions, that the bylaw is concerned as much with who is soliciting or "gathering" as it is with the acts themselves.

Other bylaws are also fairly restrictive and make it difficult to either beg or appear on the streets if one is visibly poor. The City of Hamilton's panhandling bylaw, for instance, appears in the City's municipal code as an amendment to The Streets Bylaw. It targets "aggressive panhandling" (City of Hamilton, Bylaw No. 97-162). This is defined in three ways:

1. approaching, speaking to or following a person to solicit money in such a manner as would cause a reasonable person to fear bodily harm or harm to property in the person's immediate possession [13.1(a)]
2. "following a person after a person has made a negative response" [13.1(c)]
3. panhandling "in such a manner so as to intentionally block, obstruct or interfere with the safe passage of pedestrians or vehicles" [13.1(d)]

This is indeed a broad definition of the term "aggressive": it derives from the common belief that panhandlers are dangerous.

For starters, what constitutes a "reasonable person"? That question is important, when considering the re-emergence of vagrancy laws. It is likely a panhandler or visibly poor person is not going to be considered reasonable enough to determine if their actions are aggressive or not. But how reasonable is someone else's judgment, when panhandlers are being actively identified by police and politicians, and through bylaws like this one, as potential threats to public safety? We have already seen how the threat the poor and beggars posed to public safety in Toronto was exaggerated. After all, as a number of observers argue, actions that could be deemed a threat to someone's personal safety constitute only a very small portion of panhandling. This suggests that the issue (if indeed there is an issue) is not panhandling but certain other forms of behaviour that usually do not accompany panhandling.[3] Moreover, there are already laws that deal with aggressive behaviour, such as assault, uttering threats and so on. Nevertheless, the City of Hamilton, like dozens of other municipalities, adopted a bylaw specifically targeting panhandling. The use of the adjective "aggressive" both links panhandling with danger and criminality and gives the bylaw the appearance of targeting conduct associated with panhandling, rather than the activity itself.

The other components of the definition of "aggressive" noted above also play on this theme of criminality and provide police with a good deal of discretionary power. Like the original Winnipeg bylaw, section 13.1(c) prohibits a panhandler from following a person who has refused his or her request and makes it possible for the police to charge a panhandler who is simply walking down the street. Subsection (d) is equally sweeping and targets something that may have little to do with aggression or harassment. It is difficult to panhandle on a sidewalk, especially during the busiest hours, without obstructing passersby, if only in a limited way. This fact was obviously uppermost on the minds of those who drafted the bylaw. Consider also the ban on soliciting drivers in this subsection: it is clearly aimed at squeegeeing. In case anyone has missed the point, another clause reads: "No person shall congregate and sit or stand so as to obstruct the free passage of either pedestrian or vehicular traffic on any streets or sidewalks regulated by this Bylaw."

Interestingly, while the bylaw is entitled "Panhandling," this clause makes no mention of panhandling or soliciting. But since the clause appears in a bylaw on panhandling, it is reasonable to presume the lawmakers and police had the visibly poor and unemployed — people who are the most likely to panhandle — in mind. Simply being on a sidewalk, then, could potentially make such a person a policing target.

The Calgary bylaw is perhaps less restrictive than ones already mentioned. Its definition of panhandling is narrower: it is "the personal, verbal and direct solicitation" (City of Calgary, Bylaw No. 3M99). But the identification of panhandlers with criminality is still present. Panhandling within ten metres of ATMs, bank entrances and transit stops is prohibited, as is panhandling at night. Squeegeeing is likewise treated as a status offence, as any soliciting from occupants of motor vehicles is restricted. The clause regarding the obstruction of pedestrians, found in almost all other bylaws, is present here as well. At first glance the Calgary bylaw appears to have less teeth to it than its counterparts, but it does effectively circumscribe the legal way to beg and brand those who do as quasi-criminals.

Let us now consider the second versions of the Vancouver and Winnipeg bylaws. Both focus on "obstructive solicitation" without mentioning the term panhandling per se (City of Vancouver, Bylaw 8309, City of Winnipeg,

Bylaw 7700/2000). They are also more carefully worded. The new Vancouver bylaw was challenged in court on the grounds of constitutionality just like the earlier law was. This time, however, the B.C. Supreme Court ruled it was constitutional. In their decision the judges argued that "it is directed at the consequences of a specified conduct [begging that causes an obstruction] as opposed to the conduct itself" (B.C. Supreme Court Decisions, par. 134). In other words, it "does not engage any absolute prohibition of panhandling other than in the vicinity of ATMs" (B.C. Supreme Court, par. 139).

Nonetheless, the potential impact of the new bylaws is the same as the earlier ones, even if the wording is not as explicit. The term "solicit" has a very similar meaning to the term "panhandle," used in the previous legislation. The definition of solicitation includes bodily gestures, as well as verbal and written communication. Obstruction is also defined broadly enough in both bylaws to provide police with plenty of discretion in this respect. As the Vancouver bylaw states, obstruction is that which "impedes the convenient passage of any pedestrian traffic in a street, in the course of solicitation." Again, it is quite likely that minor, unintended obstruction of pedestrian traffic will result if someone is to use a sidewalk to panhandle, and writers of the legislation and the police enforcing it in Vancouver are likely aware of this as are their counterparts in other cities. At the same time, however, to ensure there would be no confusion in its application (if indeed that was ever a real problem), the new Vancouver bylaw includes an exception for charitable solicitations. Obstructive solicitation is a problem of the poor and unemployed, not charity volunteers.

The Vancouver bylaw also broadens the definition of obstruction to include solicitation "from an occupant of a motor vehicle in a manner which obstructs or impedes the convenient passage of any vehicular traffic in a street." The aim here is to prohibit squeegeeing entirely, since anyone stepping into traffic to clean windshields is likely to be deemed to be impeding traffic. The new bylaw is obviously not the same as the original and is perhaps less preferable in the eyes of police and lawmakers. Still it effectively criminalizes the act of begging. The broad definitions make it difficult for the visibly poor and unemployed to pass unnoticed on the street or escape unwelcome attention from police.

By Any Laws Necessary

Panhandling bylaws are not the only instruments used to target the able-bodied unemployed and beggars. Proponents of the crackdown on begging and loitering have also availed themselves of already existing laws. In Vancouver, for example, the Motor Vehicle Act (MVA) has been used to police squeegeers. It was not originally intended for this purpose since it was enacted years before people began squeegeeing. However, section 182 prohibits walking on a street when a sidewalk is available. Such a clause has provided police with an effective complement to the Obstructive Solicitation bylaw, suggesting the importance of stopping begging, especially squeegeeing (Cst. Wooldridge, 2004). Police appear willing to employ whatever laws they can — even laws that are not related to or intended for squeegeeing or panhandling — to achieve their goal. This effectively shows how laws become subordinate to the higher aim of maintaining public order.

In Toronto, where panhandling and squeegeeing by the late 1990s had, in the eyes of politicians, police and media, become an epidemic plaguing the city, no panhandling bylaw has actually been adopted. Proponents of more coercive strategies towards begging and squeegeeing were concerned about legislation strong enough for their liking facing a constitutional challenge, like the initial bylaws in Winnipeg and Vancouver did. They happily conceded this legislative effort to a provincial government that was more than willing to bring in tough legislation that would provide a uniform approach to the problem across the province. But this did not stop the Toronto police, like their counterparts in Vancouver, from using other laws, municipal and provincial, towards the same end before the SSA came into effect. By the summer of 1998, Toronto police were engaged in a systematic campaign to drive young panhandlers, squeegeers and the visibly poor from public spaces (Esmonde, 1999: 128). A similar pattern emerged in all the police divisions, suggesting "a deliberate and planned strategy." As Esmonde explains, police handed out tickets:

> for such diverse things as "soliciting business on a road," "impeding traffic," "blocking a sidewalk," "urinating in public," "jaywalking," and "operating a bicycle without a bell." One squeegeer was charged with littering for leaving his squeegee on the ground while taking a break. (1999: 130)

In his affidavit submitted for a constitutional challenge to the SSA, squeegeer Kolin Davidson provided a similar account of the use of various bylaw offences to target the poor in Toronto. He also listed these intimidation tactics: burning a squat built by poor youth to the ground, confiscating blankets and backpacks, and illegally detaining people to take photos of youth (Davidson, 2000, par. 10, 11, 19). The nature of these charges suggests that they often had little do with any particular actions of beggars. Instead, the police adopted whatever tactics were necessary to remove squeegeers and beggars from the streets. The police had intensified the campaign by mid-summer. The aim, Esmonde argues, seems to have been not only to make it difficult to solicit, but also to intimidate the visibly poor, making it clear to them that they would be targeted regardless of what they were doing in public areas. For instance, police began charging poor people who were sleeping or gathering in parks with "trespassing," a provincial offence that can entail jail time. Police also judiciously used a "dwell-in-park-without-a-permit" prohibition, which appears in the section of the city's municipal code pertaining to the use of public parks. In some cases, police would sit in their cruisers on a street corner, waiting for squeegeers to arrive. As soon as a squeegeer turned up, they would confiscate the individual's materials. Esmonde also notes that, according to squeegeers themselves, the Cherry Beach Specials were also increasing at this time (Esmonde, 1999: 131–33).

The adoption of new bylaws relating to various forms of solicitation and loitering, together with the use of already existing bylaws and provincial laws, represent the renewal of the vagrancy offence in Canada — in spirit if not in letter. We should also recall that this development has been taking place in the context of the overall increase in zero-tolerance philosophies of policing. Public-order offences such as begging or being visibly poor and hanging out in public spaces became a top priority in the fight against "crime." An explicit status offence relating to begging or being unemployed may be less acceptable today from a legal standpoint than it was in the nineteenth and earlier part of the twentieth centuries. The first constitutional challenge to the SSA, based on similar arguments raised against the original Winnipeg bylaw, was itself unsuccessful, however. But the questionable legal legitimacy of a vagrancy status offence has not stopped the use of bylaws and certain provincial laws — often supported in many cases by aggressive public-order policing campaigns — from making it very difficult to be able-bodied and beg or, in some situations, even appear in public spaces. The bylaws are certainly not as far-reaching as the old vagrancy statute, nor do they carry the clout of criminal law as it once did. And some lawmakers and police might desire even stronger legislation that unambiguously criminalizes begging by the able-bodied and unemployed in public to stamp out the problem once and for all. But the recent bylaws and enforcement practices are important nonetheless and clearly go some way to reviving vagrancy law in Canada. Thus they are bound up with the neoliberal project of prohibiting behaviour that undermines market relations. Their purpose is to undermine alternative ways of earning money. A vagrant is a vagrant no matter what century we're looking at.

The Renewal of Vagrancy Laws and Sex-Trade Workers
Sex-trade workers have also been affected by the renewal of vagrancy-type laws and policing. As we saw earlier, the historical targeting of prostitution by police, especially under the vagrancy law, continued until the 1970s. Women's sexuality, as expressed in prostitution, has been viewed by the state, moral reformers and police as a threat to a paternalistically constituted public order. Despite the removal of the prostitution-related offences from the vagrancy statute in 1972, sex-trade workers continue to be targeted by federal legislation. Since the mid-1980s the soliciting law has been most often used. They have not had the benefit of any reprieve from the watchful eye and coercive arm of the state.

But the increasing concern with public order of the neoliberal era likely means an increased emphasis on the policing of sex-trade workers, giving the return of vagrancy law a gendered character. In Toronto, for instance, just as police have applied existing bylaws, as well as the SSA, to remove beggars from city streets, they have also used existing bylaws and intimidation tactics to target sex-trade workers (Committee to Stop Targeted Policing, 2000: 8). The desire to remove them from the streets becomes quite explicit when they are identified as an important threat to public order under the popular zero-tolerance philosophy of policing. Deeply embedded in the contemporary perception of public order, then, is the long-standing fear of prostitution and women's sexuality in general. The focus on sex-trade workers suggests that the state and police are still concerned with controlling the sexual behaviour of some women, particularly the poor.

The Safe Streets Act

The Ontario Safe Streets Act (SSA) is the clearest example yet of the return of vagrancy-type legislation in Canada, and for this reason is worth focusing on specifically. It includes many of the most coercive features found in the different municipal bylaws and much harsher punishment for transgressors. At the same time, a number of things converged quite publicly around its adoption, which suggest it needs to be understood as part of the same state project of which the old vagrancy law was a part. Surrounding the SSA's adoption were very sharp cuts to public services in Ontario, which complemented the steady increase of badly paid and insecure flexible work; an increase in poverty, particularly among youth; and a growing fear, sometimes bordering on hysteria, at the increase in crime (vaguely defined and unsubstantiated). This hysteria was linked to the "dangerous" poor, a perception of the poor as a social and physical pollutant. At the centre of this convergence was a group of mostly able-bodied youth — squeegeers: they were primarily young people who were washing car windshields for money, seemingly avoiding work and seeking an alternative to the market for income. The SSA is about criminalizing behaviour that does not correspond to the demands of market discipline, as opposed to targeting criminals who are running rampant on city streets harming the public, as proponents might suggest. While limited evidence has been provided to suggest this hysterical reaction over the "dangerous" squeegeers is justified, the targeting of the young poor in general, and squeegeers in particular, under the SSA does clearly express the way certain forms of public disorder are viewed by the state and reformers as criminal. There is little real physical danger to the public represented by unemployed youth such as squeegeers; but being young and without work — and seeking to survive in this way — has long been perceived as a threat to capitalist order. It is here where the link to criminality lies, just as it did with vagrancy law.

The adoption of the SSA in 2000 followed the dramatic course of restructuring pursued by the Tories since their election in 1995. The political and economic restructuring of the period, as discussed in the previous chapter, led to a general decline in living standards and to a rise in poverty. The economic restructuring, expressed in the generalization of flexible labour, was reinforced by sharp cutbacks to social-assistance programs. Welfare, for example, was cut by 22 percent overnight. Eligibility was likewise moved out of the reach of most working people. The growth in poverty was experienced by all ages, but increased noticeably among youth. Young people have been hit particularly hard: they are overrepresented in the worst-paying and most insecure jobs.[4] The real wage levels for people under twenty-five have nose-dived. Tory changes to welfare were also aimed at making it nearly impossible for youth to get benefits. It is in this context that a section of the hardest-hit youth turned to squeegeeing, begging or even sleeping in parks in order to survive. Their presence on streets and in parks then became more noticeable (Esmonde, 1999). In some cases, these youth openly expressed their desire to avoid dead-end work and identified squeegeeing or begging as a means to that end.[5]

The Safe Streets Act and Poor Youth Gone Wild

This is the situation in which the SSA came into being in Ontario. In Toronto, however, a very vocal group of city councillors were wary of a successful constitutional challenge to bylaws like those mounted in Winnipeg and Vancouver. They wanted even stronger laws with harsher penalties to ensure that the public in general, and the squeegers and panhandlers in particular, knew without a shadow of a doubt that they were serious about forcefully imposing order on the streets. They lobbied the provincial government to enact such legislation. The push for a bylaw to solve the problem turned instead into a push for provincial legislation. At the same time, the ideological defence of more coercive measures grew more intense.

The Harris government was only too happy to oblige. The Tory government (and its predecessor the Rae government), after all, had adopted a restructuring agenda for a purpose. It certainly would not brook such open contempt, especially from the ranks of the poor. Indeed, as calls for more coercive legislation grew louder from politicians, police and media, same groups made a concerted effort to portray squeegers as criminals. The outcry reached a fevered pitch, surpassing earlier campaigns leading to the adoption of the municipal bylaws. The sense conveyed by get-tough-on-crime advocates is that only the criminally inclined would choose soliciting over a legitimate job. Such people would stoop to anything to avoid the responsibility of work. It was thus necessary to respond strongly to such lawlessness and blatant disregard for public order. Once the squeegers and loiterers are pegged as quasi-criminals in the public mind, it was only a short step to the kind of hysteria underlying discussions leading up to the SSA's implementation — of portraying squeegers as completely violent, out of control and unscrupulous. Indeed, it reached such a point by the summer of 1998 that the onus was clearly on the squeegers and young unemployed to prove — to an increasingly incredulous audience among politicians, police and the media — that they were not a violent criminal element.

During this period, the provincial government established the Ontario Crime Control Commission. Headed by three Tory MPPs with an unrivalled fixation on law and order, they traveled the province to study crime and develop policy responses for the government. After touring a few different cities in the province — but spending much of their time in Toronto — they issued their "Report on Youth Crime," which was a thinly veiled effort to increase the ideological assault on young squeegeers and beggars.

> Crime represents a serious threat to society. In Ontario, much of that crime is committed by young people. The Government of Ontario is committed to dealing aggressively with youth crime and the serious social and economic consequences.[6]

Statistics backing up such claims are not prominent in the report, nor is the exact nature of the "social and economic consequences."

Indeed, the Commission attacked Statistics Canada for suggesting that crime rates had gone down. According to the three MPPs, a walk in downtown Toronto would suggest the opposite to any right-minded observer. But their understanding of crime, and youth crime in particular, became clear when they argued:

> *Disorder needs to be dealt with.* There is important new evidence that social disorder such as aggressive panhandling, street solicitation, and graffiti, cause fear and are precursors to crime and community decay.[7]

The "new evidence," while not provided, is presumably the writings of Wilson and Kelling, who had advanced the theory of broken windows. The point of the Crime Control Commission is clear: crime, in the form of public disorder, is on the rise; the main culprits are young people who beg and solicit; and aggressive measures must be taken to halt it.

The criminal association attributed to squeegeers and poor youth spread beyond the Crime Control Commission, however much the latter helped the government provide a sharp focus on the issue. In fact, the Commission's observations in some instances appear restrained when compared to those of others. Jim Brown, the chair of the Commission, did his best to independently whip up a frenzy about squeegeers whenever the opportunity presented itself. In his article in the weekly *Our Toronto*, Brown declared, in response to critics:

> Mayor Mel's war on squeegees is a war on bad behaviour. Squeegeers, he argues, "break whatever laws they want to.... The root causes of their condition is a lack of respect for others, a lack of respect

for any rule and a general overwhelming selfishness that they can do what they want with what we all pay for and share.... If we continue to let anti-social or bad behaviour persist it will grow. (Brown, 1998: 1–2)

This sentiment was shared by other Conservative members of the provincial government. In the parliamentary debate on the SSA, for example, one MPP argued:

These people target the most defenseless members of our community: the elderly, mothers with young children, as well as others. They will attempt to intimidate them into giving them money. This is an issue of public safety, not of homelessness... these are not homeless, these are thugs who want money that they have not earned and that they do not deserve. (Mazilli, MPP, Hansard, l. 1600)

Gerry Martinuk, MPP for Cambridge, even invoked Sir Robert Peel, the British Home Secretary who reorganized the police force into peelers and bobbies in the nineteenth century. Sir Robert Peel, Martinuk commented:

spoke about his fear of crime and disorder, not just crime as we know it but also disorder on the streets. Graffiti, public displays of drunkenness, squeegee persons, aggressive panhandling: These are all signs of disorder on our streets that lead to fear and to lack of co-operation with the police, and are not to be tolerated in a democratic society. (Martinuk, MPP, Hansard, l. 1950)

Clearly, Martinuk was very much inspired by the broken-window theory.

Examples of this conflation of begging and crime, or disorder and violence, litter the parliamentary debates on the SSA. The *Toronto Sun*, meanwhile, an ardent supporter of stricter law-and-order policing, referred to squeegeers as "herds of locusts who have made it almost impossible for ordinary taxpayers to drive downtown without having their cars descended upon."[8] Any solid evidence was seldom advanced to prove the threat squeegeers represented to public safety. Indeed, in some of their diatribes against squeegeeing, commentators unwittingly betrayed their presumption. During the parliamentary debate, for example, Tory MPP Gary Stewart recounted walking down a main street in Toronto, where he had the misfortune of coming across "a fairly aggressive solicitor soliciting me and sitting on the sidewalk" (Stewart, MPP, Hansard, l. 1600). Stewart went on to comment on a Help Wanted sign that he saw above the solicitor's head, without any awareness of how contradictory his remarks had been. How threatening could a seated person be?

Likewise, in an opinion piece in the *Toronto Star* in the summer of 1998, political commentator Michael Taube admitted to never having been attacked. He nevertheless felt "very uncomfortable while driving in certain areas of Toronto, a city once known as being fairly safe. And that's enough for me to state that the squeegee kids should be taken off the streets." Squeegeers, he adds for good measure, "are vagrants, plain and simple" (1998: A21).

Underpinning the squeegeer-and-poor-youth-as-dangerous-criminals rhetoric is the fear that they are a moral or physical pollutant of the urban environment. In the second chapter we discussed the historical identification of the poor and colonized with the physical and moral contamination of the social order. This was centred on the fear, on the part of the authorities, that the indigent's or colonized's wariness of wage work and criminality would spread to others among the labouring class. The authorities also feared that their habits expressed a lack of sanitation and a disregard for personal hygiene and licentiousness. These could all lead to the spread of vice and disease among the rest of the population. The attack on the perceived lack of sanitation by reformers, public health officials and police was part of the project of constituting a healthy and disciplined supply of wage labour for capital, and of distancing the affluent from the "body-peoples."

Similar sentiments are found in the critique of squeegeers, often connected to the concerns about their criminal behaviour. Advocates of the SSA focused on the supposedly squalid living conditions of squeegeers and poor unemployed youth as one strategy to justify harsher policing measures. At the height of the controversy, during the summer of 1998, the *Toronto Star* reported that Toronto's mayor, Mel Lastman, had accused many squeegeers of intimidating the public and defouling parks with human waste (DeMara, 1998: B3). The same newspaper article quoted Jim Brown, the chair of the Crime Control Commission, who focused on the supposed lack of hygiene: "Their lifestyle does not include the discipline of cleaning up after themselves," he said. "The syringes, decayed food, used condoms, defecation and garbage is left wherever they ply their trade." So dangerous are they, according to Brown, "City maintenance men have to wear bio-medical hazardous suits to clean up after the squeegee people" (Brown, MPP, 1998: 1). Complaints by police and politicians about squeegeers' lack of sanitation are common throughout the debates on the SSA, although the evidence here, too, is anecdotal at best. But the frenzy whipped up by such comments was real, as the unhygienic "lifestyle" of these youth became bound up with violent proclivities as part of a general lack of respect for public safety and order.

Criminalizing the Vagrant Through the Safe Streets Act

Despite the fears about criminality expressed above, the aim of the SSA is fairly clear. The Tories, of course, sought to use any fear whipped up to gain political support, and the implementation of the SSA was a part of their re-election platform in 1999. There was also a small constituency of small business owners claiming that squeegeers and other poor were bad for business. But when we look closely at the Act, and put it in its proper context as we have done above, its goal cannot be reduced to political opportunism, however opportunistic Tory politicians might have been, or to retailing interests. The SSA, like the panhandling bylaws, is clearly part of the broader state project of re-imposing market relations on working people. It criminalizes behaviour that enables people to find income independent of the market. Indeed, it has the character of a criminal law status offence. It expresses, on the one hand, the desire of the state to eradicate alternatives to wage work, and, on the other, the historically rooted identification of unemployment and living outside market relations with criminality and the undermining of public order.

The Act begins with a very broad definition of "solicit." Soliciting is not only performed by oral communication or signs, but as with Vancouver's bylaw, also by "a gesture or other means" (Safe Streets Act, s. 1). In a legal study of the Act, Esmonde argues, "The legislative definition of 'soliciting' is so broad as to include any conduct that communicates need" (Esmonde, 2002b: 70–71). Like Vancouver's bylaw, this broad definition leaves open the possibility that the visibly poor could be targeted simply for their presence on a street; they would have to prove they are not in public for the purposes of soliciting.

Section 2 of the Act, where it defines and prohibits "aggressive" solicitation, is equally broad in scope. Aggressive soliciting, according to the Act, "means a manner that is likely to cause a reasonable person to be concerned for his or her safety or security" (s. 2 (1)). Once again we have the important question: who is "reasonable"? Is reasonable defining someone who is sitting down as aggressive, or is it admitting that you have never been threatened by a squeegeer but nevertheless just do not feel safe around them? "Reasonable" is a highly relative term whose meaning can shift to suit the purposes of those employing it.

Subsection 2(3) gives possible examples of aggressive solicitation, though it states that these examples do not limit its meaning:

1. Threatening the person solicited with physical harm, by word, gesture or other means, during the solicitation or after the person solicited responds or fails to respond to the solicitation.
2. Obstructing the path of the person solicited during the solicitation or after the person solicited responds or fails to respond to the solicitation.
3. Using abusive language during the solicitation or after the person solicited responds or fails to respond to the solicitation.
4. Proceeding behind, alongside or ahead of the person solicited during the solicitation or after the person solicited responds or fails to respond to the solicitation.

5. Soliciting while intoxicated by alcohol or drugs.
6. Continuing to solicit a person in a persistent manner after the person has responded negatively to the solicitation.

These examples are sufficiently vague to give police broad discretionary authority. Consider subsection 2(3)(1), for instance, which includes threats by "gesture or other means," when we have already seen how innocuous behaviour is nevertheless deemed threatening. Further, Esmonde points out with respect to subsection 2(3)(2):

> Because homeless people must carry their belongings with them wherever they go, it would be difficult to avoid violating the Safe Streets Act even soliciting in the most polite and respectful manner — the belongings are likely to constitute an obstruction. (2002b: 71)

Also, subsection 2(3)(4), like some of the bylaws we have seen, prohibits walking while soliciting, suggesting that it is done with the intent of threatening or harming someone. This puts visibly poor people in jeopardy of being targeted simply for being on a street.

Subsection 3(2) covers the solicitation of a "captive audience." It prohibits soliciting from persons using, waiting to use or leaving an ATM; using or waiting to use a pay phone; waiting at a public transit stop; entering or exiting a vehicle; or in a "stopped, standing or parked vehicle." Like bylaws with similar prohibitions, this subsection assumes that poor people are more likely to engage in criminal behaviour than others. It thus bans them from spaces where they can potentially solicit more effectively, since people likely have change available in these areas.

It also bans the squeegeer outright, by prohibiting soliciting from cars. This subsection can be interpreted broadly by police, as suggested by an official communication from Constable Horton, an Ottawa police officer. According to the officer, the "captive audience" provision:

> May very well restrict panhandling significantly in the downtown core. Arguably, panhandling on the sidewalk adjacent to parking meters would mean that every person entering their car to leave or exiting their car as they take over the parking spot would have been unlawfully solicited. We have been interpreting this section liberally and applying it in just that fashion. (Horton, 2000)

Constable Horton raises further questions about the possibility of interpreting this subsection of the Act broadly so as to target as many people as possible. He notes that "the presence of persons being solicited" would normally be required for the "completion of the offence." He continues:

> We have noticed that a number of persons (the majority of whom, it seems, are women or seniors), who appear to be intent on using that bus stop or ATM, will instead walk away and use another bus stop or ATM rather than have to face or deal with the panhandler at the original location. What has happened in these cases is that the mere presence of the "solicitor" is enough to drive persons away from that location and, thus, they are not really "waiting" at the bus stop and may not meet the technical definition of the offense. The intent of the Legislation, we believe, was to ensure that people feel safe and comfortable standing at any bus stop or ATM or any other of the proscribed locations. If someone is being driven away from a location because of the presence of the panhandler, then the intention of the law is not being met.

The officer suggests the "intent" and "spirit" of the Act is to target this broadly, including targeting the "mere presence of the solicitor." Whether someone has avoided a bus stop or ATM because a poor person is present is at the discretion of police, who in this case are willing to fulfill the spirit of the Act.

The perception of squeegeers and poor youth as social and physical pollutants is also incorporated in section 4 of the Act, which prohibits the disposal of condoms, hypodermic needles and syringes, and broken glass in "an outdoor public place." "An outdoor public place," however, is not limited to streets, but also includes a swimming pool, beach, conservation area, park and playground, and school grounds (s. 4 (2) (a) and (b)). Playing on the fear of the poor individual's lack of regard for sanitation or the health of others, this section of the Act does not even pretend to being about the safety of streets. It targets public spaces broadly and thus puts poor people, who may be living or congregating in such places, under a more comprehensive police microscope.

Emerging out of a vitriolic and concerted campaign identifying squee-geers and poor unemployed youth as criminally inclined and threats to public safety (Esmonde, 1999: 123 ff.), the law incorporates some of the most far-reaching and coercive aspects of different municipal bylaws relating to panhandling and the poor. Moreover, if the official comments of the Ottawa police officer quoted above offer any indication of the police approach to the Act, it is that they may be willing to interpret it as loosely as possible to give themselves as much sweeping power as they can. At the same time, because it is provincial legislation, it creates the possibility for a systematic and uniform response that municipal bylaws obviously cannot.

The repercussions for violating the SSA are also much greater than they are for the bylaws. The SSA, as provincial law, allows for the imprisonment of violators, sending a very clear signal to poor and unemployed youth. A second conviction under sections 2 or 3 of the Act can land a person in jail for six months. In Toronto, at least, multiple convictions for individuals are not uncommon (Leitold, 2004). People have spent time in jail after being charged under the SSA (Davidson, 2000). Remarkably, section 6 allows police officers to arrest suspects without a warrant to establish a person's identity if they reasonably believed the person violated the Act. This is a rather heavy-handed measure for an Act aimed at regulating the streets.

Parliamentary debate on the SSA also suggests the Act is very much about targeting the unemployed poor as a form of social disorder. Proponents invoked the broken-windows theory during debate. Little distinction was made between supposedly aggressive begging and begging or squeegeeing in general as the problem.

Of interest to our analysis here is the exception made for charities in the debates, although this does not exist in the legislation itself. When challenged by some critics of the Act that it would prohibit soliciting for charitable donations, proponents responded with a mixture of resentment that someone could consider such a possibility and assurances that it would not happen. Facing such criticism in question period, Premier Mike Harris retorted:

> What I read into this question is a disgraceful lack of confidence in the police to use common sense in understanding the difference between aggressive panhandling, that which is interfering and causing safety concerns, and the case you raised (Harris, MPP, 1999, l. 1400).

For good measure, Attorney-General Jim Flaherty wrote to the Windsor Goodfellows, a charitable organization that publicly raised concerns about the Act, to assure them they could continue to solicit on streets:

> The Act is not aimed at solicitation that is courteous and takes place in a safe manner and setting. I am confident that charities will be able to continue their commendable work in accordance with the current provisions of the Safe Streets Act. (Flaherty, MPP, 2000)

It is merely "common sense," then, that the Act is not aimed at charities, even if the definition of aggressive could easily include some of their actions. Aggression, however broadly defined in the Act, or non-courteous solicitation, is clearly the mark of other kinds of solicitors, namely the squeegeers and visibly poor. The issue thus does not appear to be strictly that of soliciting, but who is soliciting. The able-bodied unemployed youth is not a legitimate solicitor, while people representing charities are acceptable.

This gives the Act the character of a status offence. Esmonde and Schneiderman, who have written legal criticisms of the Act, both share this perspective, suggesting that while the Act is provincial, and nominally about safe streets, it is clearly an invocation of criminal law power, which is federal and not provincial in jurisdiction. Schneiderman argues that the Act "has more to do with regulating behaviour found to be offensive by some ... than the regulation of streets and sidewalks" (2002: 85). Similarly, Esmonde points out that the government could claim the Act is about road safety, which is within provincial jurisdiction, but the Act does little to address such issues. "By prohibiting squeegers from engaging in income-generating activities in public space, the Safe Streets Act has much in common with vagrancy laws of the past" (2002b: 78). The heavy penalties proscribed in an Act supposedly about regulating the use of streets also add to its criminal law character.

Invoking a status offence similar to the old vagrancy statute, the SSA has been an effective weapon in the hands of police. While exact numbers of charges laid under the Act are difficult to come by, as police departments do not keep such records, evidence suggests the Act has been fairly successful. Soliciting still occurs, but the number of able-bodied youth found begging in urban centres has noticeably declined. Squeegers have almost disappeared. Even on a casual stroll through Toronto parks on a warm summer's day, one cannot help but notice the absence of the unemployed poor and of poor youth in particular, who only a few years ago were commonly found hanging out or sleeping in them. The same is true of Ottawa. According to Constable Horton of the Ottawa Police Service, "Prior to any consistent or regular enforcement, a person walking the length of Elgin Street may have been solicited 12-15 times over the course of their 15-minute walk" (Horton, 2000).

In Toronto, the Ontario Coalition Against Poverty (OCAP) has been collecting tickets issued by police to beggars and poor youth since the summer of 1998. Since the passage of the SSA in 2000, the coalition has found that the majority of the tickets police give are under the SSA. They estimate that they have collected approximately 1500 tickets over the five-and-a-half years between the summer of 1998 and early 2004, which works out to approximately 1200 or so under the SSA (Leitold, 2004). This number is only a conservative indication of the use of the Act, since not everyone who receives a ticket will take it to OCAP. The aggressive use of the Act by police and the rather harsh penalties contained in it have sent an unequivocal message to the able-bodied and unemployed poor.

The SSA has been effective enough to draw the attention of some police services and politicians outside Ontario who are looking for even stronger legislation than that found in bylaws. In Calgary, for example, the panhandling bylaw does not target squeegeeing directly, and the city council feels the penalties are not harsh enough to deter all beggars. They are considering asking the Alberta government to enact legislation modeled on the SSA (Walton, 2003: A10).

The Vancouver Police Department, meanwhile, has conducted an internal study of the SSA, which expresses a view favourable to the adoption of similar legislation in British Columbia:

> A new piece of legislation modeled after the Ontario Safe Streets Act would give police more ability to effectively deal with the squeegee people, panhandlers and other nuisance individuals who continue to disrupt the lives of citizens. (Vancouver Police Department, 2003: 3)

While the existing Vancouver bylaw dealing with panhandling is broad, Vancouver police nevertheless note a number of reasons why the Ontario legislation may be more useful. It would provide police across British Columbia with the framework for a more consistent response to begging and "nuisance individuals," and thus send a clear message to these individuals about what to expect wherever they go in the province. It would provide, in the form of a single piece of legislation, a less cumbersome way of addressing these issues of public order and, importantly, would give the police the ability to incarcerate law-breakers. While the current use of bylaws offers "no long-term resolution to the issue," the SSA, they maintain, appears to be much more effective in this regard. The police are not alone in their interest in Ontario's SSA, however, as it now looks at though the British Columbia government will pass its own SSA legislation modeled directly on the Ontario law.

Imposing the Work Ethic

In illuminating the role of the SSA, it is important to note the way that the issue of work prevails in the discussion surrounding its adoption. Work is often identified, on the one hand, as a key ingredient lacking in the lives of beggars and loiterers, contributing to their criminal character, and, on the other, as a healthy alternative to their current behaviour that will provide a legitimate income and lessons in responsibility and self-discipline. This perception of work in relation to the SSA, of course, echoes the historical identification of work with one's moral character, as we saw in the second chapter. Thus, just as the old vagrancy statute was so expressly aimed at forcing the able-bodied poor, who might have different aspirations, into wage work, so too clearly is the SSA.

The typical sentiment of proponents of the SSA was expressed by former Toronto Mayor Mel Lastman, who after complaining about squeegeers "defouling parks," asked angrily: "Is it bad to earn a living? What's happening? These people don't want to work" (quoted by DeMara, 1998: B3). In parliamentary debates, proponents of the Act kept coming back to the lack of work ethic found among squeegeers and other unemployed youth. Gary Stewart, who was quoted earlier, remarked with frustration about passing the "aggressive solicitor… sitting on the sidewalk" and added this comment:

About two feet from the top of his head, on the inside of the window, was a Help Wanted sign. I wanted to go back, and take a picture of that. Here was a person who found it much easier to be part of the underground economy, not to go to work. (Stewart, MPP, 1999: 1. 1600)

Another Tory MPP focused his intervention in the debate on the contrast between squeegeers and the members of his riding, who "are very hardworking; they're honest; they have a great work ethic" (Wettlaufer, MPP, 1999: 1. 1620). MPP Garfield Dunlop suggested that "Perhaps some of our panhandling people could get employment at a car wash and use it as a stepping stone to a better job with self-esteem and with dignity." He added another common thread to the discussion: "Since 1995, our government has been putting in place the right economic conditions to create more jobs for Ontarians" (Dunlop, MPP, 1999: 1. 1930).

These attitudes betray the historic link between unemployment and crime, and between public-order policing and the constitution of wage labourers, since nominally the SSA is supposed to be about safe streets, and not whether or not someone is working. Yet the issue of work was very prevalent in the discussions surrounding the Act and often came up in the same context in which the criminality of squeegeers and other poor unemployed was discussed. This suggests that proponents viewed the absence of work among these youth as a serious problem and clearly saw the SSA as one way of forcing them to work. The work ethic is a crucial concern of proponents of today's vagrancy laws. The only legitimate income in the eyes of these proponents is earned through the sweat of one's brow — produced of course through market relations.

The connection between the SSA and the desire to impose wage work on able-bodied and unemployed youth is explicitly stated in the City of Toronto's Diversion Program. It was established in 1999 to train squeegeers to become reliable wage earners. The Diversion Program was advanced as complementary to the SSA. The program, costing approximately three-quarters of a million dollars, was supported by most members of the city council, including the NDP-affiliated councillors. The city dressed it up as charitable: it provided the poor youth with an opportunity to find "honest" work. Implicit in this idea is that wage work is the only legitimate way to earn an income. Moreover, the central goal of the training was not to provide them with the kind of hard skills necessary to ensure they would find secure work, but to teach them the discipline and responsibility required to find and keep whatever work is out there. This is similar to most employment-training people receive through the Employment Insurance Program or in public schools (Sears, 2003). According to Geraldine Babcock, coordinator of the program,

The object is to create someone with transferable skills. This in-

cludes life skills, and self-discipline and getting to work on time...
they need to understand that they are selling their labour for a
wage, that the employer has certain needs that need to be met....
We are talking about young people without any work skills. They
are taking part in the program to learn how to work, to understand
the expectations of work. They need to be motivated.[9]

Hundreds of youth have participated in the program. According to progress
reports, only a very small proportion could reasonably be considered to
have steady work with good wages or be on the path to finding it (City of
Toronto, 2001). They lack the hard skills that can land them such work and
they no longer have the option of finding an alternative source of income.
Beyond the training to be a good disciplined worker and accept what the
market has to offer, the Diversion Program does not offer much. The end
result is not very promising for most participants: at the end of the day
whatever employment they are likely to find will be poorly paid, unsteady
and unrewarding. Furthermore, it is useful to recall that many squeegeers
expressly chose squeegeeing over a paid job, and in some instances were
able to eke out a living comparable to minimum wage work but without
many of the rigid structures that come with it. The SSA, together with the
Diversion Program, makes this impossible, forcing them into a situation
where the only option for survival may be to find whatever kind of paid
employment they can.

Conclusion

While no vagrancy statute has been put back into the Criminal Code, the
municipal bylaws discussed in this chapter and Ontario's Safe Streets Act
represent a considerable step in the direction of vagrancy law. In this respect
they represent one important form that law-and-ordering policing is taking.
These laws and the police practices accompanying them are clearly designed
to target beggars and carry with them, in some instances, the potential to
make it difficult for the visibly poor, especially youth, to simply be in, or
gather in, public spaces.

As we have seen, the bylaws and the SSA draw on the historical identification of the able-bodied unemployed as criminal and aim to force the wage
relation on indigents. This is especially clear in the case of the SSA, given
the focus on the supposedly missing work ethic of beggars and squeegeers
found in the comments of the Act's proponents and in the City of Toronto's
Diversion Program, whose coordinator bluntly stated the program's goal
of teaching the kind of responsibility and discipline necessary to sell one's
labour for a wage. But it is also clear insofar as the prohibitions found in the
bylaws and the SSA in their own ways make it extremely difficult to obtain
subsistence outside of a wage. Even when begging is not banned outright,
it is usually narrowly circumscribed. Monetary social relations, as a result,

are driven deeper into people's social lives, making it harder and more dangerous to live outside the market, which of course was the explicit aim of vagrancy legislation. With this the state has taken important strides in its effort to reconstitute the working class in Canada into a cheaper and more flexible labour force.

Notes

1. On the targeting of racialized immigrants via vagrancy law, see also Brannigan and Lin (1998) and Mosher (1996).
2. Faraday (1991). See also Canada (1970) or, for a history of prostitution laws during Canada's first forty years, McLaren (1986).
3. See Schafer (1998: 3–4); Schneiderman (2002); and Esmonde (1999).
4. On the impact of labour market restructuring in terms of the decline in wage levels and growth of non-standard labour through the 1990s, see Burke and Shields (2000). The Centre for Policy Alternatives, Centre for Social Justice and National Council on Welfare also publish reports on incomes and the growth of inequality in Canada. Much of their data is taken from Statistics Canada <www.statscan.ca>, the government's arms-length official statistical body.
5. See O'Grady, Bright and Cohen (1998). See also Moloney and Infantry (1998: A3).
6. Ontario's Crime Control Commission (1998: 5).
7. Ontario's Crime Control Commission (1998: 6). Emphasis in original.
8. Quoted in O'Grady and Bright (2002: 23).
9. Quoted in Esmonde (1999: 140).

5. Criminalization, Race and Neoliberal Order: Policing Immigrant Communities

Throughout this book we have looked at the relation between the constitution of wage labourers in capitalist society and the criminalization of large numbers of this class. This process of criminalization is especially virulent with respect to immigrants. For this reason it is important to focus on the policing of immigrant communities in order to better understand state power and the criminalization of working people as it relates to the demands of the capitalist market under neoliberalism.

Aggressive, racist policing of immigrants in Canada is not new, of course. It has a history as old as the country itself. It must therefore be understood not as a mere corollary to state power but rather as an integral part. State power in Canada materialized through racist social relations. Not surprisingly, then, we find these same dynamics at the heart of the neoliberal order. The state power mobilized today to recompose the working class into a cheaper and more flexible form, like its mobilization in earlier periods of Canadian history, is not race-neutral. Furthermore, it is also very much framed by the gendered nature of capitalist restructuring and the impact this has on Canada's immigration policy.

This chapter will explore the different strategies by which the state polices immigrants in Canada today, mobilizing its resources to turn them into an extremely vulnerable, cheap and exploitable class of workers whose labour is increasingly pivotal to the success of Canadian capitalism. The policing analyzed in this chapter should be viewed, on the one hand, within the context of neoliberal restructuring and the role of police in fashioning a new political and economic order, as detailed in previous chapters. On the other hand, it should be viewed as a process that takes on a dynamic unique to the experiences of its targets. Immigrants (and people of colour more generally, though in the eyes of the state and police there is often little distinction here — a point we will return to below) not only attract a great deal more attention from police and state authorities than do other Canadians, but the attention they do receive, bound up with their historical relationship to the Canadian state, is influenced today by the "exigencies" of the post 9-11 period. The attention is also in important ways specific to them as immigrants.

The task of analyzing all the different ways in which the state polices immigrants deserves an entire book to itself. This chapter will try to underline a few of the more salient features. The chapter will begin first by situating immigration generally within the changing needs of the Canadian labour market. It will then look at the way in which immigration has been conflated with criminality in political discourse and the public imagination, and how this strategy is used by the state and others to justify the harsh conditions imposed on immigrants in Canada and to increase their social and economic vulnerability. We will then examine the "war on drugs." This is a central component of the state's pursuit of bourgeois order in immigrant communities. The chapter will conclude with a brief look at the increasing use of incarceration against immigrants — another means of reinforcing their vulnerability and the state's nearly unencumbered authority over them.

Globalization and Migration

Migration is not unique to the period of globalization and neoliberal restructuring. "Throughout the history of capitalism," Nigel Harris (1980: 38) notes, "workers have moved in search of work, or been driven to work, in areas other than those where they were raised." The largest and fastest-growing capitalist economies, particularly those of Western Europe and North America, have relied on immigration to fuel their economic expansion. For a country like Canada, that immigration has stemmed partly from Britain, as part of the project of building the white Anglo-Saxon nation. However, British immigration could not keep pace with the labour needs created by the industrial expansion in the late nineteenth century. Canada began drawing heavily from labour pools in so-called lesser-developed countries.

One could trace the historical and geographical dynamics of uneven global capitalist accumulation through patterns of transnational migration. People from poorer regions of the globe have historically crossed international borders in search of work and a better standard of living. The situation in Canada is no different. In the late nineteenth and early twentieth centuries, Canada drew part of its labour supply from China and Eastern Europe. In the early postwar period, following the economic destruction of sections of Eastern and Southern European industry and the heavy human displacement caused by the war, Canada attracted thousands from these regions. Today, Canada draws immigrant workers from such places as the Caribbean, the Philippines and once again Eastern Europe and China. This historical process amounts to what Harris (1980: 39) describes as "a continual redistribution of a margin of each national labour force in response to changes in the geography of capital accumulation."

The demand for immigrant labour in advanced capitalist countries like

Canada is driven by a few key factors. One crucial factor has been the declining growth rate of the native labour pool. The slowdown has been caused by "a decrease in the number of hours worked per week; an increase in holidays per year; an increase in the number of years of full time education... [and] early retirement" (Harris, 1980: 44). Many of these factors emerged in the postwar period, and despite pressure from the state and employers to change the pattern, still exert influence on the Canadian labour market.

The declining birth rate has also had an important influence on the demand for migrant labour. Pension plans for the elderly, widely available and affordable contraception, and laws banning the use of child labour have contributed to a significant decline in the birth rates of Europe and North America in the past fifty years. Current birth rates are not high enough to provide enough new workers to sustain economic expansion — and governments are fully aware of this fact (McNally, 2002: 137–38).

The annual *Report of the Demographic Situation in Canada*, for instance, has repeatedly noted the country's steadily declining birth rate (compounded by the ageing of the population), and the role increased immigration will have to play in response to this problem.

> With each year that passes, the growth of the Canadian population depends a little more on the contribution of migration, and this trend is likely to continue in the coming decades. (Ministry of Industry, 2003: 1)

Another factor driving Canada's need for immigrant labour is the historical increases in the average levels of labour productivity. To sustain these increases, increases in the cost of reproducing the labour force must follow a similar pattern, even though certain industries will remain below the average in productivity levels. The average cost of reproducing the labour force is shaped by the levels of health and education needed to maintain or increase average levels of productivity. The more educated and healthy the labour force, the more productive it is. But because productivity levels vary from industry to industry, the state has helped through its funding of education and social programs, maintaining the average level for the reproduction of labour power necessary for the growth of the economy. The consequence is that wages and working conditions in those sectors whose level of productivity is lower than the national average tend to be worse than what native-born workers might be inclined to accept. Typically these sectors are labour-intensive rather than capital-intensive.

Of course, the state and employers have sought to drive down wages and working conditions across sectors, or dramatically reduce the expectations of native-born workers, as we saw in the third chapter. The pressure to do so is not the same across different sectors, however. There is less pressure in capital-intensive industries, such as the auto industry, and greater pressure in labour-intensive industries, like garment manufacturing or services. In the former industries, technologies and machinery eat up a much greater proportion of costs borne by employers than in the latter. The profits, in other words, are less wage-sensitive. Thus their profit rates can be more readily improved by introducing advanced technologies (increasing, as Marxists would say, the value composition of capital). Capital-intensive industries also tend to have bigger workplaces with a larger number of workers under a given roof, spaces that have been historically more conducive to unionization. For these reasons, capital-intensive industries today tend to have higher wages and better working conditions better than the national average. Conversely, wages and working conditions for labour-intensive sectors typically remain well below that average.

None of this should suggest, however, that more labour-intensive industries, such as large parts of the service sector, are forever doomed to be highly exploitative. What is being described here is a pattern to better show the current parameters within which certain industries operate. This pattern, even in lower-productivity sectors, is not immune to the collective struggles of workers for better working conditions. Throughout the twentieth century, some industries like mining, which used to rely on cheap immigrant labour from non-British source countries, have seen wages increase above the national average as a result of hard-fought struggles and the steady adoption of new, more sophisticated technologies.

In any case, employers tend to have difficulty in filling the worst kinds of jobs with native-born workers. Typically, these jobs are found in the more labour-intensive areas — the service sectors and seasonal work such as agriculture. Most native-born workers gravitate to sectors where wages and working conditions are better and more stable. And while a concerted effort has been made, with some success, by the state and employers to reduce the expectations of native-born workers stuck at the bottom end of the labour market and to force them into the more poorly paying jobs with the worst working conditions, they also tend to rely heavily on immigrant workers here.

Historically, immigrants, especially those racialized as non-white, have helped to fill the worst jobs Canada has to offer. They have faced racist persecution. When unemployed, they have struggled hard to support themselves either because they cannot access government benefits, don't have familial or friendship networks to fall back on, or lack possessions that can be sold or pawned. For these reasons they have been very susceptible to highly exploitative work conditions, typically "reproduced at costs below the average" in a destination country like Canada. The above factors in fact explain the "extreme mismatch" between the education levels of immigrants and the work they actually perform (Harris, 1980: 46-7). Nevertheless, the historical role of immigrants in the Canadian labour market continues to this day. Given the country's steadily declining birth rate, it is as important as ever.

Equally important for our consideration, however, are the reasons people would travel great distances, often risking their lives in the process and leaving family members and loved ones behind, to work in extremely exploitative working conditions (relative at least to other work available) in places like Canada. Mainstream economists call these reasons the push factors. The picture painted by mainstream economists is often a sanguine one, presented via the cold calculus of an abstracted model of supply and demand: the Global North has a need for skilled labour; the Global South has the supply because it is unable to provide enough work for its skilled workers. What we never see is the real impact upon human beings of global capitalist restructuring, or the role countries like Canada play in driving people to migrate in search of work in the Global North in the first place.

Migration must be understood historically as a product of unequal relations — imperialist relations — between countries of the Global North and those of the Global South. It is not by accident that large pools of migrant workers are drawn from the Philippines or Caribbean nations, for example. These countries have witnessed a long history of colonial subjugation at the hands of the West. This continues today in the form of International Monetary Fund (IMF) structural adjustment policies supported by Canada. Structural adjustments, using debt-relief as the wedge, force the targeted nation to cut back on much-needed food subsidies; open the domestic market to more competitive capital from the Global North; and privatize public services, driving millions into unemployment and greater poverty. The destructiveness of these programs is compounded by the extensive use of protectionist tariffs and agricultural subsidies by Canada, the U.S. and the European Union. Such tactics, on the one hand, make it extremely difficult for agricultural producers of the Global South to access lucrative markets of the North. On the other, they allow agricultural producers of the North to undercut producers of the South by flooding the world market with their produce and thus driving down prices. Since governments in poorer countries can't subsidize their agricultural producers to the same extent as those in richer countries, the former cannot survive the price depression (McNally, 2002: 135–36).

It is in this context that emigration becomes a strategy for economic survival: people leave their native country, often destined for the Global North, in search of an income that can help support family back home. Indeed, David McNally (2002: 136) has shown the concrete link between the destruction of specific agricultural industries in Third World nations as a result of protectionist measures used in the North, and the rise in emigration levels from those very same countries. As structural adjustment policies, protectionist measures and subsidies by advanced capitalist countries take their toll on countries of the South, literally hundreds of millions of people are left unemployed and displaced.

One major consequence of the crisis of displacement is the exponential increase in levels of cross-border movements of people. In the year 2000, over 150 million people were engaged in international migration. This is a doubling of the figures from the mid-1980s and this number is expected to double again by the end of this decade. To put this into perspective, about 1.5 billion people have crossed nationalized borders over the last decade alone. In absolute numbers ... this rate of migration is more than that which occurred in the nineteenth and early twentieth centuries: the great "age of mass migration." (Sharma, 2003: 56)

The dynamics of global capitalism, facilitated by the active intervention of states in advanced capitalist countries, are creating an extremely racialized and gendered international division of labour, integrating increasing numbers of Global South labourers into the economies of the North as a growing army of desperate and cheap workers. The result has led to the creation of an extremely racialized and gendered international division of labour. An increasing number of workers from the Global South have been integrated into the economy of the Global North.

The More Vulnerable the Better:
Canada's Immigration Strategy

Canada's immigration strategy exploits global imperialist conditions — conditions for which it is partly responsible. Canada does not welcome immigrants with open arms. Rather, it sets conditions whereby increasing numbers of migrants, forced from their home countries in search of economic survival for themselves and their families, join the ranks of vulnerable and cheap labour, helping to drive the Canadian economy from the bottom end of the labour market. Key immigration policies in the state's constitution of migrant labour in this manner have been well analyzed by commentators elsewhere. We will cover the basic themes only briefly here in order to get a sense of the broad strategic continuum on which the policing and criminalization of immigrants operates.

It is worth noting the economic status of immigrants in Canada. Their income in Canada is considerably lower than that earned by the rest of the population; in fact it has declined significantly over the past few decades. This is particularly the case for immigrants from "non-traditional source regions" — for immigrants of colour from outside of Britain and Southern Europe. They now comprise the majority of newcomers to Canada. The steady decline in income has occurred even though recent immigrants have more education than they had in the past. Their educational background is higher than that of the Canadian average (Palameta, 2004, Keung, 2004a). Statistics Canada notes these trends:

- immigrants arriving between 1986 and 1990 earned on average 18 percent less than Canadians;
- immigrants arriving after 1990 earned on average 36 percent less.

The increase in this income differential between immigrants and non-immigrants has occurred over the last few decades as increasing numbers of immigrants are likely to be of colour. This trend also helps to explain the significant income discrepancy between racialized and non-racialized Canadians in general: by 1995, 80 percent of the former group were immigrants (Galabuzi, 2001: 63–64). The troubling economic experience of immigrants, despite their education, can be explained by the systematic racist policy of the Canadian state.

The Points System and Beyond

In the 1960s, Canada dropped its official whites-only immigration policy in favour of a new, purportedly race-neutral points system. Canada had been taking small steps in this direction since the 1950s, when it began admitting large numbers of immigrants from Central and Southern Europe, people whom it was reluctant to accept previously and whom it had considered a non-white threat to the Anglo-Saxon character of the nation. This change in immigration policy in the 1950s was not an anti-racist-inspired act, however, but was a response to the rapid postwar economic boom. As immigration from Britain dried up, employers actively lobbied the federal government to loosen its eligibility restrictions to let in people from Europe's displaced person's camps (Troper, 2003: 29 ff.).[1] These new immigrants joined the ranks of a rapidly growing working class and played a vital role in the economic boom.

With the adoption of the points system, following increased challenges to overtly racist immigration policy from civil rights activists and the postwar decline in influence of the eugenics movement, formal reference to a prospective applicant's race was abandoned. Entry was to be decided by points accumulated for such things as job skills, educational background and the ability to communicate in the two official languages. But race, as many observers have pointed out, was never far from the surface. Developed by subsequent governments, the points system has made it extremely difficult for immigrants from Third World countries to enter Canada as permanent residents with full status and the opportunity to become legal citizens. Language requirements impact the ability of many individuals to gain permanent status and become citizens, while certain jobs that the government requires migrant labour to perform, such as domestic work, have been purposely accorded very low points in terms of occupational skill and experience. Sedef Arat-Koç argues:

> One of the factors working against domestic workers in immigration

policy had to do with racist concerns about Caribbean immigration. Archival research on internal memos in the Ministry of Immigration and Citizenship reveals that throughout the 1960s... there was a great deal of ambiguity and anxiety about immigrants from the Caribbean. (1999b: 217)

Before the 1960s Britain was one of the main sources of domestic workers. There was no citizenship restriction placed on them. The restriction only occurred after as the source of British domestics dried up. Part of the fear of immigration officials in the 1960s was that Caribbean domestics would sponsor family members to come with them, expressing once again the historical tension in Canada between the need for immigrant labour and the desire to maintain the country's Anglo-Saxon character (Arat-Koç, 1999b: 215–18).

This also highlights the very gendered character of the points system, which intersects sharply with its racist premises. Officials feared that the licentiousness and fecundity of racialized Caribbean domestics would also upset the nation's delicate racial balance if their status and ability to sponsor others was not narrowly restricted. About the only way most female immigrants from the Third World can actually enter Canada is by applying to programs such as the one established for domestic workers. The points system is also a significant barrier to female applicants, because the system does not award points for many of their skills. The points system emphasizes workplace skills acquired by holding paid jobs as opposed to childcare or other skills that go unpaid. The remaining option is to be sponsored by a male breadwinner in the family, which reinforces a woman's dependency.

The points system, however, also makes it hard for Third World men to enter as permanent residents and thus be able to sponsor their wives or daughters. Moreover, government policy over the last decade has changed the criteria enabling permanent residents to sponsor family members, an issue we will come back to in the next section (Thobani, 2001: 62). One of the few real options for Third World women is therefore a program like the one created for domestic workers, which reproduces a sharply gendered division of labour and restricts women's rights on racist and sexist grounds.

But even when immigrants do manage to "pass" the points system, they face significant hurdles, which increase their vulnerability. Starting in the early 1990s, both the federal and provincial governments have cut back on services, like ESL classes, settlement support and other programs to help newcomers establish themselves. The period has also seen funding cuts to welfare and employment insurance. At the same time, the federal government requires sponsors to sign documents guaranteeing financial support for the sponsored person. The sponsor is also liable to hefty fines if the sponsored person applies for welfare or unemployment benefits (Thobani, 2001: 62; Basok, 1996: 145). These measures are designed to pressure permanent residents to find work regardless of its quality or take on a second job, and may explain why even immigrants with permanent residency status also end up at the bottom end of the labour market.

The Citizenship Wedge: Fabricating a Non-status Working Class
What should be clear from the discussion above is that the legal status associated with full citizenship — or its denial — is a central tool in the state's arsenal to create a cheap and flexible working class today. As international migration from the Global South to the Global North increases by historic proportions, the Canadian government, like the U.S. government and the European Union, has adopted increasingly restrictive measures against immigrants. The goal is not to shut the doors to the Third World immigrants; the goal is to increase their vulnerability when they do arrive. This is accomplished by making it harder and harder for immigrants to enter Canada legally or to attain full citizenship. Over the last three decades, the Canadian state has been directing its immigration policy towards favouring temporary and non-status labour.

> In 1973, 57% of all people classified as workers destined to enter the Canadian workforce came with permanent resident status. By 1993, of the total number of workers admitted to Canada... only 30% received this status while 70% came in as migrant workers on temporary employment authorizations. (Sharma, 2001: 5)

These numbers do not include those who are here illegally, or without status (an issue discussed below).

The denial of citizenship to growing numbers of immigrants is made possible by historically derived and racially inspired notions of who is a "real" Canadian and who is not. The definitions of "citizen" and "Canadian" emerged out of colonialist and white supremacist relations, which we discussed in some detail in the second chapter. In the past the state has used denial of citizenship to lower the status of much-needed non-British immigrant labour, such as with Chinese workers in the late-nineteenth and early-twentieth centuries. By the late 1980s, 70 percent of the total number of immigrants came from Africa, Asia, the Caribbean and South America. By this time, too, the government had made the denial of citizenship rights a common policy (Arat-Koç, 1999b: 209).

The reality of this strategy undermines the ideal notions of citizenship in liberal democracies and its progressive evolution, as found in the writings of people like T.H. Marshall.[2] The category of citizenship has always developed simultaneously with that of non-citizenship. The conceptual and material significance of one relies on the existence of the other, and are both shaped by social relations of class, race and gender. According to Stasiulis and Bakan:

> The maintenance of the ideal type of liberal citizenship relies upon the creation of its opposite, the derogatory ideal of the dangerous, criminal and economically burdensome non-citizen. (1997: 118)

Not until the twentieth century were working class women and Aboriginals allowed to vote, which is considered a pillar of citizenship rights, and only through struggle was that right won. The same struggle took place for social rights like welfare or health care (which, as we saw earlier, are now under threat). Today migrant workers represent a forceful example of the non-citizen Other, betraying the deep-seated racist and colonial nature of white-settler Canada. The government has been able to systematically deny them the full rights of citizenship, which "ensures their vulnerability in all aspects of life in Canada" (Baines and Sharma, 2002: 76).

Migrant workers who are unable to become permanent residents enter Canada through the Non-immigrant Employment Authorization Program (NIEAP). The NIEAP was established in the early 1970s. By the early 2000s over four million temporary work authorizations had been issued under the program by the Canadian government (Baines and Sharma, 2002: 76). The program establishes very strict conditions over the terms of employment: it constitutes migrant workers as an extremely vulnerable and cheap labour force highly suitable to the demands of neoliberalism. Persons entering the country under this program must "work at a specific job for a specific period of time for a specific employer."[3] Temporary migrant workers:

- cannot change their jobs without the written permission of an immigration officer, and face deportation if they do so;
- can renew their work visa if their employer agrees, but their status will always be temporary, as they can't apply to be permanent residents;
- are not entitled to social services like health care, welfare, Employment Insurance or workplace safety insurance, even though they pay taxes and make EI contributions.

Predictably, migrant workers end up in the lowest-paying occupations with some of the worst working conditions, where they are not even covered by the minimum wage and other labour standards, and where it is either illegal or extremely difficult to unionize. The Live-in Caregiver Program for domestic workers is a good example. To fill the demand for domestic workers, the government has turned to women from the Caribbean and, increasingly, women from the Philippines. In addition to the conditions imposed on them through NIEAP, the women also have to live with their employers. These conditions create a toxic mix for domestic workers.

> According to a survey answered by approximately 600 foreign domestic workers in Toronto in 1990, very long working hours with no proper compensation, lack of privacy, poor quality room and

board, restrictions placed on social and sexual life by employers, and vulnerability to sexual abuse were among typical conditions for many domestic workers on temporary status.[4]

Seasonal agricultural work is also another occupation heavily reliant on temporary migrant workers. It has been receiving media coverage in recent years due to workers' efforts to win the right to unionize. Like domestic workers, agricultural workers are extremely vulnerable to abuse at the workplace. The conditions range from low wages to unpaid overtime, from the inhalation of pesticides to physical abuse from managers.[5]

Illegal Labour

Illegal immigrant workers are another important source of cheap labour. It is difficult to determine the precise numbers of such labourers, given the understandable concerns they might have about disclosing their status to government officials; as a result there is a dearth of research and statistics on their plight. However, it should not come as a surprise to find that illegal labour, common in the U.S. and European Union, may be on the rise in Canada since immigration laws have become increasingly restrictive (McNally, 2002: 132–34, 138).

An immigration and refugee lawyer interviewed for this chapter suggests that there are a few key ways illegal workers enter a country like Canada, which unlike the United States does not have a border contiguous to a major source country for such labour. Perhaps the most common way has to do with expired visas. There is no systematic way in which the government ensures students, workers or visitors leave after their visas expire.[6] This provides an opening for those who wish to remain in Canada. Instead of leaving after the visa expires, immigrants stay; because they are now here illegally, they cannot legally find work. It has been estimated that of 800,000 individuals given visas in 2002, at least 8 percent stayed past their legal limit (Jiminez, 2003). Failed refugee claimants are also another source of illegal labour.

Despite international obligations regarding the treatment of people looking for sanctuary from political, religious, racial or gendered persecution, Canada has made it very difficult for refugees to enter the country legally. Immigration officials require claimants to provide identification documents. Typically, however, it is common for refugees to not have proper identification because they need to hide their identity from the government they are fleeing or because such documents are not available. (In the case of Somalia, there is effectively no central government.) At the same time, immigration officials often downplay the dangers of certain regions. Female refugee applicants were deported to Taliban-ruled Afghanistan in the 1990s, for example. The government no longer hears second claims if the first were unsuccessful on the grounds that it is reducing the number of people who abuse the system. The original claim may have been unfairly denied or the conditions in the applicant's country may have worsened in the interim.

Many failed claimants choose to stay in Canada illegally rather than face deportation to a country in which their personal safety or that of their family members is at serious risk. Some prospective immigrants claim refugee status to get into the country and go underground to avoid deportation. According to the immigration and refugee lawyer interviewed for this chapter, some claims — though certainly not all — are false, especially claims from countries like Mexico or Pakistan, where human rights abuses are not as widespread as they are in other countries, like Sri Lanka or Somalia. To be clear, most refugee claimants, many of whom are denied legal entry to Canada, are in fact fleeing persecution. Because the country's immigration system is so structurally biased against Third World persons, however, many claimants will pursue whatever options they can to enter, despite the kind of life in Canada these options mean, in order to eke out a decent and socially just existence for themselves and their family. It has been estimated that at least 36,000 applicants whose claims failed have not been deported (Jiminez, 2003).

Governments officially condemn illegal migrants rather than their employers. However, the persistent use of illegal labour and some industries' dependence on it suggest the opposite: governments tacitly approve of the practice. Illegal workers can be found in the ranks of domestic workers, according to Stasiulis and Bakan (1995: 321), among Caribbean workers who, after beginning to organize against working conditions in the 1980s, began to be replaced by Filippina domestics in the temporary-worker program. Illegal workers are also typically hired in garment sweatshops, in restaurants and hotels, and on construction sites. According to Ontario's Construction Secretariat, for example, some 76,000 illegal workers worked in the building trades in 2001 — approximately one-quarter of the industry (Jiminez, 2003). Clearly the construction industry would collapse without the availability of these workers.

That officials in the construction industry publicly acknowledge their reliance on illegal labour reveals the state's "see-no-evil, hear-no-evil" attitude. According to Jiminez, the police know where workers get picked up for the day's work. The state's tacit approval of illegal labour, in fact, is not out of step with its effort to restructure the working class in a manner suitable for neoliberalism. Illegal workers are even more vulnerable than temporary workers. Conditions for the latter are exploitative, but for the former they are even more so. There are absolutely no regulations of employer practices, especially if the entire workplace is "under the table." Illegal workers are in no position to complain to any authority for fear of being denounced, and thus face arrest, detention and deportation. An illegal immigrant can actually apply to the Ministry of Immigration and Citizenship for a work permit, and may even be granted one. The Ministry, however, may well issue an arrest warrant for that same person, upon learning of their status (or lack thereof). On the one hand, the Ministry offers the nominal hope of status;

on the other, it effectively discourages such individuals from applying for a work permit, thereby condemning them to miserable wages and working conditions. In the construction industry, for instance, undocumented workers may earn less than half the wages of other workers (Jimenez, 2003). This situation likely also puts downward pressure on the bargaining position of legal workers, something looked on favourably by employers.

Migrant workers, then, are central to the success of neoliberal economic order in Canada. Thousands of native-born workers have experienced a significant shift for the worse in their own work experience over the last twenty years. Immigrant workers, however, are far more likely to face the worst wages, hours of work, benefits, workplace conditions and legal rights. It is important to stress here that their predicament is far from a natural process of "the market" or its "invisible hand." They have the skills and education to meet the demand. It is not a matter of Third World labour being particularly unskilled or uneducated, as we have seen, or not being in demand. The state is actively *producing* a subclass of cheap Third World migrant labour for use on the bottommost rungs of the Canadian labour market. The production of this subclass of workers is reinforced, as we will see, through the law-and-order agenda.

The Immigrant as Criminal

In the eyes of the state, police and media there is a very fine line between being an immigrant and being a criminal. Often these two categories are conflated with each other: being an immigrant is sometimes tantamount to being a criminal, or at the very least potentially criminal, and thus worthy of suspicion and special attention from authorities. This attitude has defined the dominant attitude towards non-British immigrants throughout Canada's history. Underpinning this perspective is a toxic mix of a fear of, and anger and resentment towards, the immigrant Other. In the Canadian imagination the non-British immigrant has often been seen as a licentious, morally bereft repository of repressed white Anglo-Saxon desires writ large, but also as unhealthy: both a moral and physical pollutant potentially contaminating Canada's social environment. Thus while these immigrants were necessary for the development of industrial capitalism in Canada, they were met with outright hostility, on the one hand, and close observation by state agencies, on the other. As Yeager (2002: 179) observes: .

> One of the hallmarks of Canadian immigration policy has been the periodic outcries over the settlement of foreigners, who were often characterized in the press and Parliament as "riff raff," "refuse" and "physical and moral degenerates." (2002: 179)

Sears (1990) meanwhile locates the growth of the concern with hygiene and disease, and the initiation of systematic public-health inspections in working-class communities in the early twentieth century, with increasing levels of non-British immigrants. This fear was exacerbated by immigrants' living conditions. It was common for police, politicians and moral reformers to fret about immigrant ghettos and enclaves where dangerous habits — of both a moral and physical kind — flourish in defiance of Canadian "civilization." These fears and resentment underlying the traditional hostility to immigrants are not just a strategy of the ruling class. They are part of a deeply embedded racist world view shaping the attitudes of many Canadians across all classes. This was expressed, for example, in the exclusionary practices of some trade unions in the early twentieth century, or the generalized public hostility towards Chinese migrants who arrived by boat on the shores of British Columbia in 1999 looking for refuge. Many Canadians saw them simply as queue jumpers who would drain our social services rather than as refugees fleeing dictatorship or poverty in China.

Immigration and Crime: The Contemporary "Epidemic"
The conflation of immigration and crime in the Canadian imagination gained particular resonance in the 1990s (Razack, 1999). This social dynamic has a special significance for illegal immigrants. Their situation is worth noting not simply because they have been a target of public venom for supposedly queue-jumping or cheating the system, which indeed they have. It is also that they are here — illegally. Their very existence in Canada without status, in other words, makes them illegal. They transgressed Canadian law, not to mention arbitrarily imposed Canadian standards of forthrightness and honesty, to even stay here in the first place. Restrictive immigration policies and the need for cheap labour have produced a subclass of workers who are, by definition, criminal. They are scorned on the one hand but desired for their labour power — a seemingly contradictory situation that leaves them extremely vulnerable. Any step out of line — say, challenging their status or complaining of an employer's unfair treatment — and they risk being jailed or deported. The heavy but predictable presence of police in their communities reminds them of the danger.

But the link between immigration and crime extends beyond illegal immigrants. The very category of immigrant, like that of unemployed, represents a threat to public order embodied in the potential criminality of a racialized Other. This stereotype, while never entirely absent from the Canadian political and social landscape, gained renewed vigour with the fall of the postwar order and the rise of neoliberalism in the 1980s, as the need for labour-market restructuring intensified and immigration from the Third World increased. As early as the 1970s, the Trudeau government began linking immigration with issues of crime, security and political stability (Sharma, 2001: 8). By the late 1980s this linkage had become a much more salient feature of public discourse. It was reinforced by the public paranoia engendered by the federal Conservative government and media regarding the interdiction of boatloads of Tamils and Sikhs who landed on the east coast; the deep recession of the early 1990s; and the increasing representation of Global South countries such as Somalia, Afghanistan, Sri Lanka and the Philippines in Canadian immigration patterns (Basok, 1996: 149).

Bound up with these things is the phenomenon of globalization. Although its effects on nation states and local communities may be overstated in public discourse, the fears mobilized in response to it are quite real. At the heart of these fears is the perceived "dangers" of increased transnational migration accompanying globalization. This is seen by many politicians, academics and reporters as contributing to the weakening of state sovereignty and security in all senses of the word: political, cultural, ecological and personal. Global South immigrants are sometimes portrayed as the modern barbarians at the gate of Canadian civilization, ready to tear apart our social fabric and overwhelm our ecology (see, for example, Abell, 1996). But the danger of transnational migration has also been given more concrete portrayal for some in the shootings that occurred in a Just Desserts restaurant in downtown Toronto and the murder of the police officer Todd Bayliss. Both incidents involved young black males (some of them illegal immigrants) and white victims — in the first case, a young woman, and in the other, a young police officer. At the same time, after they began organizing in the 1980s, Caribbean domestics quickly earned a reputation as "aggressive" and "cunningly criminal," further contributing to racist stereotypes of Caribbean migrants (Stasiulis and Bakan, 1995: 320).

Among those keen to exploit this historical context and promote fears of "dangerous" immigrants are the media and racist, opportunistic politicians. As sociologist Sherene Razack (1999: 160) finds, "the criminal attempting to cross our borders" was a central theme in discussions on immigration policy in the 1990s. The "bad immigrant" versus the "good immigrant," she argues, served to reconfirm "the national character of white goodness and civility" while portraying the Global South migrant as threatening. The media were quick to use isolated incidents of violent crime, like those mentioned above, to portray the increase of Caribbean immigrants as tantamount to a social crisis undermining community safety.

> In these narratives, the line between immigrant and Canadian-born citizens is sharply drawn and clear distinctions are made between foreign-born villains and Canadian-born victims. (Wortley and Kellough, 1998)

The Reform Party, who made the "dangers" of immigration a central plank in their platform in the early 1990s, was perhaps the most overtly racist of the major political parties. Its members though were far from the only ones conducting themselves in such a manner. The federal Conservative government under Mulroney reacted strongly to the Tamils and Sikhs who landed in the Maritimes in the late 1980s. The next government under the

Liberals also drew on the theme of the "dangerous" immigrant. Commenting on proposed changes to immigration legislation in 1997, then Immigration Minister Eleanor Caplan asserted the following:

> Our number-one priority is stopping people from coming to Canada who are bad people, who don't have proper documentation, and those who might pose any kind of risk to Canada. (quoted in Waller, 2002: 13)

The cynicism of such a statement cannot go without comment. After all, as Caplan would surely know, many individuals seeking refuge arrive without proper documentation either because they are unable to obtain it for fear of getting killed or because they are fleeing a cruel war and there is effectively no central government to provide it. Such phrases as "bad people" who pose "any kind of risk" are vague and help to promote stereotypes. Even the Ontario provincial Conservatives under Premier Eves hopped on the bandwagon in the fall election of 2003, despite the fact that immigration law falls under federal, not provincial jurisdiction. Tellingly, the Conservatives placed their discussion of immigration issues in the crime section of their campaign literature. It was entitled, "Safe Communities in a Secure Ontario." They talked of "bringing good people into Ontario while keeping bad people out," and criticized the federal Liberals under Chrétien for failing to keep "criminal elements and potential terrorists out of our country" (quoted in Walkom, 2003: A1).

Of course, little in the way of hard evidence is ever presented to support the link between immigrants and criminality. Such evidence does not exist. According to Yeager (2002), even those immigrants who have criminal records before coming to Canada are far more likely to be convicted of public-order charges and/or shoplifting or petty theft than violent crime. For the majority of individuals this was their only offence. "This is not the kind of imagery," Yeager remarks, "complained of by the tabloids or critics in the body politic" (2002: 183–84).

Connected to the "dangerous" immigrant theme is the assertion that they are an excessive burden on our (that is, white Canadians') social services, draining the system of precious resources. An immigration policy review leading up to the introduction of the new Immigration and Refugee Protection Act asks these questions to participants:

> Should newcomers receive materials explaining the rights and responsibilities of consuming public services? How far are Canadians prepared to go to ensure their generosity and openness are not abused? (quoted in Thobani, 2001: 52)

Implicit in these questions is the assumption that immigrants are less deserving of social services, and more likely to take advantage of them regardless of whether they have been paying taxes. As Basok has noted, refugees and family-class migrants are especially portrayed as threats to social services (1996: 145). Refugees, she argues, no longer serve the ideological needs of a country defending "freedom" against the communist "threat" during the Cold War. They are far less warmly received and more quickly deemed a burden if they try to access public services. Family-class immigrants and their sponsors would constitute a far less vulnerable class of immigrants if they were allowed unrestricted access to public services.

The threadbare nature of the argument that immigrants overburden the country's public services is displayed in a recent government study reported in the media. An article in the *Toronto Star* (Keung, 2004b: A14), entitled, "Immigrants put strain on city services," dutifully reported that increases in immigration would increase the stress on education, housing and transit services. Immigrants, it maintained, are more likely to upgrade their education, have housing troubles and use public transit. Even if this portrait is factually accurate, it does not mention what percentage of new immigrants use these services compared to other Canadians. Nor does it suggest why upgrading education, in an era when upgrading and re-skilling are supposed to be pivotal to the "knowledge" economy (leaving aside for the moment the usefulness of that description of the economy), should be seen as a strain on the health of the economy and thus public services rather than a boon. It also fails to mention that large numbers of immigrants have above-average levels of education, though Canadian employers often do not recognize the degrees because foreign standards are supposedly not good enough.

The article does not say why any of these problems are immigration problems rather than problems caused by poorly funded public services — or racist policies keeping immigrants in low-paying jobs so they are forced to use public transit instead of cars (which may in fact be good for the environment — but "immigrants improve environment" is not likely to appear as a newspaper headline anytime soon) or access public housing. The racist discrimination facing immigrants and people of colour in the housing market has been documented, but is nowhere mentioned in this *Toronto Star* report.

The portrayal of immigrants as criminals or burdens on social services speaks, on the one hand, to a real racist fear of the non-white Other, rooted in European and Canadian colonialist history. On the other hand, it facilitates more restrictive and punitive laws towards immigrants. How else, could what Sharma (2003: 57) rightly refers to as a system of global apartheid be justified? Global South migrants in North America or the European Union have few if any rights and are relegated by state law to the most exploitative forms of wage labour. Who but the criminally inclined immigrant, who has no respect for or understanding of the Canadian way of life and will, if given an inch, abuse our generosity, deserves to work without possibility of union rights or a minimum wage, or to have to pay taxes but be denied access to services paid for by those same taxes? Since the 1970s the ongoing criminalization of Third World migrants in the public imagination has allowed governments to maintain the extremely punitive temporary-worker program; it has also allowed the government to intensify restrictions on all classes of immigrants.

A previous section looked at how the points system has made it difficult for most would-be immigrants to enter as permanent residents. The state has also made it harder for family members of permanent residents to enter the country. It now requires sponsors of family-class residents to sign a document ensuring financial support for their relatives for ten years. If they fail to do this, they can be prosecuted and fined if their relative seeks social assistance. In addition, federal immigration-department and provincial social-service agencies have been working more closely with one another since the 1990s to increase surveillance of sponsored immigrants who seek social assistance (Basok, 1996: 145; Thobani, 2001: 62).

Potentially assisting in the surveillance of immigrants are proposals for a new permanent resident card, which, Sharma notes, will allow "the government to more closely monitor, track and ultimately deport permanent residents" (2000: 8). Citizenship and Immigration Canada's most recent proposal is for a single card that is embedded with the holder's biometric data (Bronskill, 2004: A1, A12). Such a card is intended for immigrants *with* permanent status, namely people who have entered through the legitimate governmental channels. With respect to deportations, the government reserves the right to deport not only immigrants who have overstayed a visa or whose refugee claim has been denied, but also those who have been granted full citizenship if they are found guilty of a criminal offence. In other words, the government reserves the right to deport certain citizens who are most likely racially stigmatized. This is an extremely heavy-handed power that speaks to the view of immigrants in Canada, including those who become citizens, as second-class.

Policing the Immigrant Other
The criminalization of immigrants also helps us to further understand the observation we made in the first chapter about the heavy street policing faced by immigrants and communities of colour. Study after study has found that racially stigmatized individuals — particularly members from the Black community — are far more likely to be stopped by police while walking or driving or hanging out in public places than are whites, regardless of any evidence that they have committed an offence. Even though this practice is seldom discussed in the same context as other methods used by the state to target immigrants, its analytical separation is really an artificial one. Racist street policing is part of the same agenda; it is facilitated, like other punitive measures towards immigrants, by the far-reaching criminalization of them, while at the same time reinforcing that criminalization.[7] It serves as another

important tactic in keeping them vulnerable and susceptible to the worst forms of wage labour. Intense policing of immigrant communities — in the form of the stop-and-chats, arbitrarily pulling over drivers, or aggressively removing individuals from public spaces — is another reminder that they are viewed as a threat to order by their very existence. Order, in this case, means accepting the conditions of flexible wage work, not being a burden on public services, relinquishing any hope of rights accorded to non-immigrant Canadians — in general, quietly enduring the racist and exploitative conditions of their existence in the country. Policing is central to the state's efforts to produce these extreme relations of dominance and subservience, especially when immigrants are not so willing to docilely play along.

It is important to point out here that while not all persons of colour in Canada are immigrants, in the eyes of the criminal justice system "immigrant" and "person of colour" are often the same thing. According to census data, many persons of colour are indeed immigrants (four of five income earners of colour). Police and judges, however, commonly assume persons of colour are immigrants and are quick to question them about their status (Ontario, 1995: 225). It is not uncommon for police to simply stop a person of colour to question them about their status (Anonymous, 2004). This reality suggests that problems of immigration are seen by state authorities as a problem of race. In the minds of police, the targeting of people of colour on the streets and in public spaces is the targeting of immigrants.

The questioning of persons of colour about their status raises another point worth considering briefly. It highlights the selective nature of the policing of immigrants. In the previous section we noted that police deliberately refrain from targeting illegal immigrants who are waiting to be picked up for a day's work. But the officers go out of their way to harass individuals about their status when they are traveling or hanging out in public spaces. Waiting to go to work is permissible, but being in public space for other reasons necessitates intervention. Waiting for work, they show respect for order; in public spaces they represent disorder.

As a further expression of the state's preoccupation with immigration and public order, immigrants are also policed by special immigration "enforcement" officers. These officers are charged with enforcing the Immigration and Refugee Protection Act and have the power to arrest for immigration violations and deportations. They are now a part of the Canada Border Services Agency (CBSA), established in December 2003 to more efficiently coordinate the policing of migrants. Interestingly, The CBSA does not operate under the authority of the Immigration Ministry, but rather under the new Department of Public Safety and Emergency Preparedness, clearly suggesting that migration represents a threat to Canada. The stated responsibility of the officers, furthermore, is "to ensure the twin goals of economic security and public safety," expressing here the intimate connection for the state between economic and public order (Citizenship and

Immigration Canada, 2004a: 1). A threat to economic security is thus perceived as a threat to public order.

Immigration officers are charged with working at Canada's borders to watch for people who are attempting to enter the country fraudulently or whom they deem to be a risk to public safety. The policing of borders, according to Sherene Razack, increased substantially through the 1990s (1999). At the same time, immigration officers have also stepped up their enforcement activities of immigrants inside the country. In addition to targeting individuals deemed threats to public security, they can also arrest and detain persons whose identity they suspect, or whom they believe will not appear at future immigration proceedings (these proceedings may decide on a person's right to stay in the country or determine their status or identity). Immigration officers work closely with the RCMP, Canadian Security Intelligence Service (CSIS) and municipal police forces. In fact, much of the work they do is based on information received from local police, who in their routine stopping of people of colour on the street or in public spaces often check up on their immigration status. Local police may choose to detain a person whose status is in question, or simply pass the information on to immigration officers who will then make the arrest.[8]

The attacks on the World Trade Centre on September 11, 2001, encouraged the government to strengthen the link between immigration and security, thus facilitating the adoption of increasingly tough legislation.[9] However, 9-11 does not represent a watershed in policy implementation. More accurately, it expedited processes that were already underway. While Canada set up the new Department of Public Safety and Emergency Preparedness after 9-11, immigration officers are not new. The change is perhaps best seen as a rationalization of enforcement functions, collapsing customs and other tasks under the new CBSA. The Orwellian-named Immigration and Refugee Protection Act, and the government discussions leading up to its introduction — criticized by some immigrant advocates for exploiting the identification of immigrants with criminality and making it harder for Global South migrants to enter under the points system — was already designed and under discussion when 9-11 occured. The state has enacted specific legislation dealing with terrorism and threats to national security, called the Anti-Terrorism Act, which was discussed in the first chapter. But law regarding terrorism — and a vaguely defined terrorism — had been in place before 9-11 in the Immigration Act (Macklin, 2001). The standard of proof under immigration law to determine whether someone is a threat is "very low." It is simply the "reasonable grounds to believe" on the part of the immigration Minister. The law allows for the "automatic, indefinite, warrantless, preventative detention of a non-citizen" if the Minister and Solicitor General sign a security certificate. Macklin also suggests that the definition of terrorism and the broad investigative powers under the new Act will eventually be incorporated into immigration legislation. But the post-9-11 developments must be seen as part of a long development of tougher legislation and publicly promoted racist sensibilities.

The Endless War at Home: Pursuing the "War on Drugs"

It has been argued throughout this book that, as an expression of contested social relations, policing typically intensifies towards individuals who do not readily except the unjust, alienating or racist conditions of their existence. Policing, it has been stressed, is an administrative feature of state power historically developed in response to class struggles at the heart of capitalist social relations. This, as we have seen, takes on a particular dynamic relating to people of colour and immigrants.

While the individual immigrants the police meet on the street may represent a threat to order to them, this is amplified when it is seen to be embodied not by an individual but by a community of people. A certain urgency occurs in policing when, in the eyes of the state, the collective behaviour of immigrant communities runs counter to the morals or norms thought to represent proper "Canadian" order. There is a long history of concern on the part of police and moral reformers about specifically immigrant communities. Often overcrowded enclaves, they have typically been viewed as cesspools oozing with vice, crime and disease which may infect the broader Canadian population in both the moral and physical sense.[10] Because of these enclaves, "the social distance and related distrust were increased."[11] That the creation of immigrant neighbourhoods is a response by immigrants to discrimination in the housing market and is a way of coping with a strenuous life as a non-Anglo Saxon in Canada is not the concern of state officials and police. It is the roles these communities come to play for their members that is the real issue, woven together as they are with their bonds of kinship, common understandings of the hostile life its members face, and sometimes relations of solidarity. Integration into the "Canadian" way of life on the state's terms can never be achieved on this basis. Thus the state's promotion of racist attitudes and exclusionary policies towards immigrants leads to the very kinds of community developments that worry them greatly. These neighbourhoods, and the state's response to them, express the contradictory nature of the state's strategy towards immigrants.

If immigrants were to remain effectively invisible to the state and police, in the sense of meekly accepting their conditions of life here in Canada while providing a source of cheap labour, then the anxiety would not be so great. But the development of immigrant neighbourhoods in Canada has represented a certain collective visibility and with it an independence — or perhaps non-conformity — which the state and its police see as a potential undermining of public order. Through their communities, immigrants find ways of enduring in Canada. What can develop out of this context are often subtle, though sometimes not, or unconscious, but other times quite conscious, ways of responding to the harsh reality of life facing them here.

That these patterns of behaviour are a response to their conditions suggests that for the state immigrants exist outside of or opposed to the "Canadian" social fabric. And so these patterns of behaviour — which may range from simple cultural practices brought by immigrants to Canada to forms of play and pleasure (which may also have been brought from "outside," and so are doubly dangerous as such) or to community organizing — become primary targets in the policing of public order.

While many concrete examples of this policing dynamic could be given, we are going to highlight the so-called "war on drugs." Historically, the war on drugs has dominated police efforts to produce bourgeois public order in Canada. It has focused largely, though not exclusively, on immigrant communities. While the war on drugs and policing-of-immigrant-communities nexus have been empirically well documented by commentators on Canadian drug policies, explanations for its historical development and persistence up to the present remain limited. The way in which the war on drugs has facilitated the production of a class of wage labourers also needs greater attention.

The war on drugs is as much about drugs as, say, the Safe Streets Act is about safe streets. The sale of contraband substances provides a financial alternative to market relations; their consumption, a source of "play" or pleasure. Both fly in the face of bourgeois expectations of working-class discipline and responsibility. This is doubly the case when the immigrant Other is involved.

A Short History of the Drug War

The history of Canada's war on drugs does not consist of the prohibition of narcotics because they have been deemed physically or mentally harmful (nicotine, we should remember, is perfectly legal), or because they are associated with a widespread pandemic of abuse. Instead, the state has selectively prohibited drugs and police enforced that prohibition — with an unparalleled degree of power and authority — precisely because the narcotics in question have been associated with immigrant communities. Drug prohibition as it emerged in the early twentieth century reflected a fear of the impact the communities and their narcotics might have on white Canadians and their moral order. Drug prohibition was an attempt to control immigrant communities and draw them into the bourgeois order on the state's terms.

At the time of their criminalization, narcotics such as opium, cocaine and cannabis were used largely by specific immigrant communities and not Canadians of British descent, and so represented to the authorities an assertion (consciously or not) of non-conformity or independence from the broader "Canadian" moral order. This is the real reason for the prohibition. It is clear from the discussions surrounding their criminalization that scientific proof of the harmful effects of the different drugs was not central to support the passage of legislation. Nor could it have been. Despite their continued criminalization, many researchers have shown that the dangers of these drugs — addictive qualities, effects on motor skills and short-term memory, or their propensity to a have a long-term impact on our physical health — have been greatly overstated, to say the least (Erickson, 1998a: 266). Drugs found to be much more physically harmful and addictive, such as nicotine and alcohol, are still legally available.

The criminalization of opium (first in 1908) was a direct response to Chinese immigration. As we saw in the second chapter, Chinese immigrants were pivotal to the growth of industrial capitalism in Canada in the late nineteenth and early twentieth centuries, but they were far from warmly welcomed. The growth of Chinese immigration in Canada, particularly in British Columbia, was accompanied by the growth of anti-Chinese senti- ment and eventually tougher immigration measures directed towards them. Chinese migrants were perceived as morally inferior and a threat "to the survival of the white British ethnic domination" of Canada (Giffen, Endicott and Lambert, 1991: 53). Bound up with this view was the role Chinese workers performed as a source of cheap labour, drawing the wrath of large segments of the trade-union movement, especially the craft unions. Morally threatening and seen as economically undermining the conditions of the white working class, Chinese immigrants were barred from most unions (the One Big Union was a notable exception). They were likewise the subject of deportation campaigns. The attack turned violent in the infamous 1907 riot in Vancouver: an anti-Chinese rally involving union members marched into Chinese neighbourhoods where they smashed shops and homes and physically assaulted people (Comack, 1991: 79).

For many white Canadians, particularly state officials, police and moral reformers, the use and sale of opium symbolized the Chinese "problem":

> In the popular ideology, opium smoking tended to be one among several items exemplifying the alien, inferior and inassimilable nature of the Chinese.... [It was not regarded as] a habit harmful in itself.[12]

It was feared the practice would spread like a disease — and with it perhaps aspects of Chinese culture — to the white population.

The testimony of a police officer given to an 1885 government com- mission on Chinese immigration typifies the attitude of many officials and reformers towards the immigrants' use of opium:

> Opium is the Chinese evil... used in every house without exception. This evil is growing with the whites... principally working men... and white women prostitutes.... I have seen white women smoking in the Chinese dens myself.[13]

Note that there is no mention of any dangerous physical side effects here. The concern is with a habit expressive of Chinese immigrant culture, one which may be taken up by working-class whites. The potential interaction between white and Chinese workers likely also concerned authorities. As Elizabeth Comack (1991) has argued, the state actively promoted anti-Chinese racism to divide and weaken the working-class movement. The prohibition of opium was clearly one means pursued by then-cabinet minister Mackenzie King to accomplish that goal by fostering white fears of Chinese immigrants.

But we should be careful not to place too much stress on the divide-and-conquer strategy as a reason for the criminalization of opium. No doubt it played a role. The fact that a fear of the Chinese community in general, and opium in particular, contaminating the white Canadian social fabric was there to be exploited by King in the first place, however, suggests the reasons are a little more complex. The state and moral reformers, as suggested above, were clearly concerned about opium as a dangerous expression of an immigrant culture that showed signs of non-conformity with "Canadian" order, and that this vice of bodily pleasure might infiltrate the ranks of the white working class. Further, the comments of the police officer above and of other moral reformers betray the historical fear of the over-sexualized racialized Other, ready to prey on and contaminate the purity of white women and, by extension, the white race. Emily Murphy was Canada's first female judge and one of the country's most strident moral reformers obsessed with drug prohibition. In her book *Black Candle* she suggested that from the use of opium:

> The seduction of the women addicts becomes easy.... Under the influence of the drug, the woman loses control of herself; her moral senses are blunted, and she becomes a "victim" in more senses than one.[14]

For Emily Murphy opium use was "an attempt to injure the bright browed races of the world" (quoted in Boyd, 1991: 10).

Both cocaine and cannabis were banned in 1911 and 1923 respectively because they were identified with Black immigrants. Cannabis was also identified with Mexican immigrants. Marijuana, according to police, was used by Black jazz musicians, who in their eyes were hardly examples of moral fortitude and who displayed a desire for pleasure that did not strictly conform to bourgeois expectations for them in Canada. These drugs were "elevated to the status of a social problem" (Boyd, 1991: 10). The drugs also threatened to contaminate white Canada: once again a main point of entry, moral reformers feared, was women preyed upon by immigrants. In *Marihuana: A New Menace*, Murphy's follow-up to *The Black Candle*, the stereotype of the "dangerous" promiscuous immigrant looms once again.

> The ultimate degradation that could befall any woman as a result of narcotic drug use was sexual contact with a member of the Black or yellow races.[15]

Not only does marijuana alleviate the user of moral responsibility, she adds for good measure, it also drives the user "completely insane" (quoted in Boyd, 1991: 10). Neither insanity nor moral laxity could be allowed to threaten public order.

In the early part of the twentieth century there were movements banning tobacco and alcohol as well. Alcohol was seen as a potentially dangerous vice for the working masses. It was potentially disruptive of public order itself and was prohibited for a brief period in the 1930s. But because these drugs were used much more broadly, and thus not identified with simply a non-British immigrant community, the movements against tobacco and alcohol never had the same resonance as the ones against opium, cannabis and cocaine, where the threat of contamination by racialized immigrants and the compromising of the innocent white women could be mobilized to great effect. Eventually tobacco and alcohol were defined as permissible recreational drugs, though alcohol use would be regulated under provincial laws with respect to the licensing of bars and setting the legal age for drinking. Workers who were visibly drunk in public would also be policed heavily (Giffen, Endicott and Lambert, 1991: 49; Boyd, 1991: 10).

With the persistence of virulent propaganda against opiates, cocaine and cannabis, attitudes towards users hardened, and the "social distance" between users and sellers and other citizens widened. This facilitated the adoption of very tough drug laws and rather sweeping police powers accompanying them. This in turn led to a further hardening of attitudes towards the drugs and their users, as particular communities came under intense police scrutiny. Indeed, the criminalization of opium, for instance, which is associated with a specific immigrant community, but not other drugs that are associated with whites, was tantamount to criminalizing the immigrant community. The very use of the drug comes to represent criminality.

This dynamic is also suggested by the selectivity with which police enforced drug laws. Mosher and Hagan's (1994: 635) research on the enforcement of drug laws in the early part of the twentieth century indicates that more than two-thirds of those arrested were "of visible minority background." Giffen, Endicott and Lambert (1991) found that in British Columbia, where most convictions under the various opium laws were made, Chinese offenders constituted 82 percent of convictions. These numbers do not account for police interventions on the pretence of drug law violations that do not actually lead to arrest, which in communities of colour can be a common occurrence.

The link between narcotics and their users may help to explain the harsh character of the different drug laws, as well as the extensive powers given to police under them. Some of the severest penalties on the law books since opium was first prohibited in 1908 are for possession or trafficking of banned narcotics. They have only been surpassed by offences such as assault or murder. As early as 1921, amendments to the drug law at the time, the Opium and Drug Act, contained a reverse-onus provision, formally superseding in law the much-heralded liberal right of being innocent until proven guilty.

It was likewise an offence to be in a building in which there were narcotics, "unless the accused could prove 'the drugs were there without his [sic] authority, knowledge or consent'" (quoted in Alexander, 1990: 31). This amounts to guilt by association. In the 1950s, police were also given the authority to charge someone with trafficking if that person possessed small amounts of an illegal drug. The penalty for trafficking was far more severe than that for possession. Again, it was up to the accused to prove they were not in possession for the intent to sell. The rule of law, as we have noted throughout the book, does not stand in the way of the police's effort to produce order. They use the law as a means in this effort.

In terms of police powers, however, this is the tip of the iceberg. Throughout the twentieth century, following the introduction of the Opium Act in 1908, police powers to wage their war on drugs have steadily increased through legislative dictates and court rulings. Writing in reference to the Narcotics Control Act, the predecessor to the current Controlled Drugs and Substances Act, Solomon (1988: 263) argues that the "police have far broader enforcement powers in even a minor drug case than they have in a murder, arson, rape or other serious criminal investigation." He notes, for instance, that Canadian courts have ruled that, in effect, police who enforce drug laws should not be expected to follow the rules typically expected of officers during an arrest — including identifying themselves, making a formal arrest, citing reasons for the arrest and, in some cases, permitting the accused to submit peacefully. "In their attempt to facilitate drug enforcement," he writes (1988: 269), "our courts have suspended several fundamental safeguards of citizens' rights and freedoms." Legal technicalities framing a police officer's responsibilities around arrest procedures, in other words, should not encumber the enforcement of drug laws. In fact, while The Charter of Rights and Freedoms states in section 24(2) that evidence found during an illegal arrest should be excluded if it were to bring the administration of justice into disrepute, courts consistently admit evidence that the police have obtained illegally.

On top of this, the police have special powers granted under drug laws for search and seizure. According to Solomon (1988: 274), drug laws "authorize police to search without a warrant, day or night, any place other than a dwelling-house in which they reasonably believe an illicit drug is present.... The basis of the officers' beliefs are not subject to judicial scrutiny, either before or after the search is made." Moreover, police can search any person in the premises they enter in the course of drug enforcement, whether or not they have evidence that person has broken the drug law. These rules accord police a degree of discretion and power unmatched in the Criminal Code, allowing them to "legally break into homes at night, without warnings, warrants, or explanations, to smash the furnishings, to manhandle and beat the occupants and to punch and choke people who are suspected of trying to swallow drugs" (Alexander, 1990: 36). In this respect, the "war" of the war on drugs really is much more than metaphor expressing the seriousness and commitment of the state in its drug policy. It is a reality for many of the targets, and as with any war, the prospect for human rights violations or collateral damage looms large.

The war on drugs was stepped up a notch in the 1980s under the leadership of Prime Minister Brian Mulroney. In 1986 Mulroney declared that "drug abuse has become an epidemic that undermines our economic as well as our social fabric" (quoted in Erickson, 1998b: 218). Under the guise of a national strategy aimed at harm reduction, the Conservative government increased funding for law enforcement. Mulroney's Conservatives then introduced a new drug bill involving stronger punitive measures for offenders. While the bill died on the order paper when the election was called in 1993, it was picked up in essentially the same form and eventually passed by the Liberal government in 1997 as the Controlled Drugs and Substances Act.

> [T]he new drug law ensconced the severe maximum penalties and extensive police powers found in the previous Narcotic Control Act, and added resources to aid even more efficient arrest and prosecution of illicit drug users and sellers. (Erickson 1999: 275)

> Police also got some new powers to aid them in their fight for order, including the ability to sell drugs in reverse sting operations and the expansion of seizure provisions. (Erickson, 1998a: 271)

The War Without End: Reflections on the Persistence of Prohibition

So the drug war continues apace, despite the social cost in terms of erosion of civil liberties and violence towards the accused, and despite the fact that it has demonstrably failed to stop the use of prohibited drugs like cannabis, cocaine and opiates. Indeed, in the case of cannabis, since the 1960s more and more people report having used it at least once, and growing numbers support changing the laws. Some members of Parliament and the Senate have discussed decriminalization; a bill to this effect was introduced in 2004, but died with Parliament's dissolution in the fall of that year. At this point, it is very unlikely that such legislation will be introduced by the new Conservative government. Prime Minister Harper has discussed introducing minimum sentences for the possession and sale of cannabis. But the decriminalization of the possession (and note, not the sale) of cannabis would by no means signal the end of the drug war, including on cannabis itself, as will be suggested by the argument below.

Two reasons are typically exposed to explain why the war on drugs continues. First, the different actors involved profit directly from it. In one version of this argument, police, bureaucrats and crown prosecutors have a vested interest in maintaining the anti-drug campaign because it directs a lot of public funds their way.[16] Another version blames it on political opportunism. Jensen and Gerber (1993), for instance, suggest Mulroney declared a new drug epidemic in an effort to boost flagging popularity. A more philosophical argument, on the other hand, cites the long-standing (perhaps innate?) human need to assign blame for all the troubles or misfortunes of the world. In this scenario, the "drug warriors" (police and government officials) can blame drug users and sellers as responsible for many of our societal ills because of their blatant disregard for public morals and safety. Drug users and sellers decry the authoritarian impulses to infringe on individual liberty, which are always lurking beneath society's surface (Alexander, 1990).

There may be some truth to these arguments, particularly as they relate to the motivations of self-interested players in the criminal justice system or of Mulroney's attempt to opportunistically play off of an emotionally charged issue. Nevertheless they are rather functionalist arguments, the form of which we critiqued in the second chapter. It is of only very limited use for us to reduce the drug war to the interests of particular social groups. Although they may benefit from funds garnered in the name of the war on drugs, police budgets do not stand or fall on drug enforcement. Moreover, the targeting of drug users or sellers is not always executed as drug enforcement per se, with officers organized and funded specifically for that task. Instead it is performed as part of the broader project of producing public order on the streets. Furthermore, while Mulroney may have been optimistic, the Chrétien government implemented the Controlled Drugs and Substances Act in 1997 despite a public outcry, especially relating to cannabis laws, and passed it into law after largely avoiding meaningful debate. Contrary to these views, the war on drugs cannot properly be understood without considering the efforts of the state to administer the working class, especially immigrants, by producing public order. Drug enforcement is one important means to that end.

The other common argument for the drug war's persistence is linked to an argument used to explain the policing of the poor on the streets. This is a version of the fear-of-the-Other syndrome (Oscapella, 1998; Erickson, 1998a: 271). Insofar as drug prohibition is rooted in racist attitudes towards particular immigrant communities, this argument makes some sense. But it needs to be developed further. What underlies this fear? Is it inevitable, a feature of modernist rationalizing logic, as a postmodernist might argue, or is it rooted in a certain historical dynamic relating to the social construction of whiteness and bourgeois order? If the latter, it is not inevitable, but the product of a complex historical process by which the non-British working class came to symbolize criminality as a non-conformist threat to bourgeois order. In this respect, it is an expression of the social relations of struggle, with the war on drugs being one feature of this dynamic. Relating the drug war to the contradictory character of capitalist accumulation fills the argument out more, while refusing, by emphasizing the processes of struggle, the fatalism implicit in many of the fear-of-the-Other arguments.

Taking a closer look at some of the dynamics of the war on drugs will help to better illuminate its goals and the consequences for those targeted, and thus better explain why the state and police continue to pursue it with vigour despite its failure to eradicate illegal drug use. The war on drugs is about much more than eradicating the use of prohibited narcotics, and unless we understand that, we will never really make sense of its persistence. It developed historically, as we have seen, out of racist social relations underlying the state's efforts to administer immigrant communities that were perceived as signs of disorder. While not the only expression of that disorder, narcotics associated with specific communities became a focus of concern for reasons we have discussed. Negative attitudes among state officials and some of the public today towards drugs like cocaine, opiates and, to a much lesser degree, cannabis are a product of this historical process, however conscious or not people may be of this. Racism, we have noted throughout this book, is deeply woven into the social fabric of Canadian society, and while taking different, and often less explicit, forms, it is as prevalent today as it was a hundred years ago.

As part of this process, drug enforcement became an excellent excuse for police, in their pursuit of the production of bourgeois order, to intervene in and assert their control in communities, on streets and in public spaces — regardless of whether those being targeted are actually violating drug laws. This is a pattern that continues to this day, influenced no doubt by the extensive arrest, search and seizure privileges granted to them for drug enforcement. Moreover, that narcotics are seen as undermining the sobriety and discipline expected of wage workers, and as expressive of a desire to escape its drudgery, are also no doubt motivations for the state and police to continue the drug war.

The loss of productivity as a result of drug use is monitored closely in Canada. Annual productivity losses due to substance abuse are estimated to be $11.8 billion for all drugs, with $823.1 million of that for illegal drugs. Absenteeism and loss in productivity are most often witnessed in young workers:

> Lower-status workers, young persons and males are most likely to experience a workplace problem due to their use of alcohol or other drugs. (Canadian Centre on Substance Abuse, 1999)

At the same time, the selling of drugs is a potential means to avoid wage work. Many individuals sell drugs because the hours are more flexible; they do not have a boss standing over them eight or more hours a day; and the remuneration is likely better than that received for wage work at the bottom end of the labour market (see, for instance, Bourgois' (1995) insightful study of drug dealers in Harlem). The war on drugs, then, is an ongoing fight against perceived moral laxity and the threat of its spread. It cuts out an important avenue to avoid working represented by the use and sale of narcotics.

It is notable that since Mulroney's declaration of a new drug epidemic, and especially since the early 1990s, there has been a considerable increase in charges under Canada's drug acts. The majority of the changes relate to cannabis:

- According to government data, the police-recorded drug-crime rate has increased by approximately 42 percent since the early 1990s.
- In 2003 the rate reached a twenty-year high.
- Increases in charges for cannabis possession account for this increase.
- Offences relating to cannabis climbed 80 percent from 1992 to 2002.
- In 2002 three out of four cannabis charges were for possession.
- The charges were the highest for those between eighteen and twenty-four, followed by teenagers between twelve and seventeen (Statistics Canada, 2004).

Although Canadians' attitudes towards cannabis have softened, there has been an increase in policing.

The statistics also suggest that drug enforcement is largely directed towards working-class individuals and youth. Because of its availability, price and reputation as a less dangerous drug, cannabis is one of the most accessible illegal narcotics available to the poor, working-class individuals or young persons. This policing dynamic is also suggested by studies that have found that drug enforcement is disproportionately directed towards persons of colour. In 2002 the *Toronto Star*'s exposé of racial profiling by the Toronto police found, that although Blacks make up only 8 percent of the city's population, they account for nearly 25 percent of those charged for simple drug possession. It is worth recalling here that 75 percent of all income earners belonging to visible minorities are immigrants, according to census data. The *Toronto Star*'s study, as well as that of Ontario's Commission on Systemic Racism in the Criminal Justice System, highlighted these interesting findings:

- Blacks reported that the police often stopped them on the assumption they had illegal drugs.
- Blacks are three times more likely than whites with a similar criminal

record to be refused bail and ordered detained before trial (Ontario, 1995: 124 ff.).

• Blacks detained for drug possession are far more likely not to be released by police than whites.

Charges for minor possession and pretrial detention, moreover, are extremely police-sensitive. Drug crimes, especially for minor possession, are seldom reported to the police. Thus arrest patterns are the result of a conscious policy (Tremblay, 1999: 1; Wortley, undated: 23). Police strategy, in other words, is a significant factor determining the increase in charges for simple possession and for these charges to be disproportionately skewed towards persons of colour and immigrants.

In his field research with police, Richard Ericson (1982: 82–83) made similar findings. He also found that police often stop individuals, who have done nothing identifiably illegal, on the pretence that they may be carrying prohibited substances (see also Wortley, undated: 24). Of course, if a certain segment of the population is disproportionately scrutinized for something like illegal drug possession, then they are more likely to be found with a prohibited substance and to make up relatively more of the number charged than are groups that receive far less police attention. But the point here for police is perhaps not whether the targeted individual actually has drugs, but that the enforcement of drug laws, with the wide discretion granted by the law and the courts, provides a very good excuse for intervening on the streets and in public spaces. No doubt the police are aware that not every person they stop on the pretence of violating drug laws will actually be found to be doing so, as experience certainly proves. Drugs are a specific threat to order that must be targeted by police, while drug enforcement is a useful excuse for the ongoing general production of "order" in communities through assertion of police power.

Patterns relating to the policing of drug trafficking are also worthy of note here. Police are far more prone to target small-time street sellers than they are major actors in the drug trade (Erickson, 1998a: 219). Charges for cannabis trafficking are highest among those aged eighteen to twenty-four, followed by those aged twelve to seventeen (Statistics Canada, 2004). Individuals in these younger age cohorts are more likely to be selling small amounts on the street than to be major players in the drug trade, who have established networks, as well as the resources and ability to move large quantities of illegal narcotics. Ontario's research (1995: 156) also suggests that the majority of trafficking charges are for "minor actors in the drug trade," while Blacks are disproportionately charged with trafficking offences, as is the case with possession. But not only are small-time dealers and Blacks more likely to be targeted: "such people are easily replaced by those who control drug supplies, imprisonment of minor dealers and couriers has a negligible impact on the availability of illegal drugs to users" (Ontario,

1995: 156) The report also notes that this fact is not lost on either police or courts. Thus police consciously target minor dealers in a strategy they and the criminal justice system know is ineffective in stopping the drug trade.

The Auditor General of Canada in 2001, Sheila Fraser, in fact lambasted the government for what she described as an enormous waste of money and a drug-enforcement policy that was unaccountable, which no one involved could rightfully say was succeeding. While her findings are telling, her assessment misses the point. What we are seeing here is more than just an irrational waste of money by self-serving bureaucrats. Clearly, if police and other actors in the criminal justice system realize that their tactic of targeting small-time dealers has a negligible impact on the drug trade yet continue to do so, then their first aim must not really be to stop the drug trade per se. Rather, it must be to stop small-time dealers, who represent disorder. As with squeegeeing or panhandling, a central objective is to impose market relations on individuals who can get a better income selling drugs than they can selling their labour power — and without the more structured hours and bosses that come with a job. At the same time, however, the questions raised about the moral character of the person choosing to absent himself from market relations to sell drugs are no doubt also framed by the very racialized history of drug prohibition and enforcement.

The policing dynamic of drugs discussed here helps explain why the war on drugs continues, despite its failure to stop drug sale or use. To properly comprehend the importance of this war, we need to understand both its historical origins and the patterns by which it is pursued today. Even if marijuana were to become decriminalized so that the possession of small amounts would entail fines rather than charges, there is no reason to assume the drug war would stop. Many drugs would still be illegal, while decriminalization would not make it legal to possess cannabis and certainly not to sell it. Indeed, one of the arguments often advanced for decriminalization is that the prohibition of cannabis unfairly gives otherwise law-abiding citizens a record (or potentially so). This argument has gained currency as more groups of people — namely, white, upper-middle-class adults — have become cannabis users. With decriminalization, they would be less likely to be targeted than immigrants, persons of colour and/or the poor. The latter could still be fined, or given a reverse-onus charge such as trafficking. And if these groups of people are already disproportionately targeted under the excuse of a drug offence, it is not unreasonable to expect that the police will continue to stop them under other pretexts. They can still use cannabis as an excuse or make reference to other illegal drugs. The key issue here is the pursuit of bourgeois order. If we understand this, we can also understand that the law is a tool used flexibly by police rather than a barrier to their operation.

Khat: A Particularly Somalian Danger

But these particular policing patterns give us only part of the contemporary picture. A look at the criminalization of khat provides us with further insight into the persistence of prohibition and its continued usefulness for the police pursuit of order in specific communities, and brings us full circle in our discussion of the drug war. Khat is a plant indigenous to East Africa and parts of the Middle East and is used by some members of the Somalian community in Toronto. Khat offers a contemporary example of the dynamic we discussed earlier in this section: a drug associated with a relatively new immigrant community in Toronto that has been criminalized, although medical evidence on its reputed danger is weak. This criminalization has been used, furthermore, as an excuse by police for greater and, according to some Somalians, more violent intervention into their community.

Somalian migration (primarily as refugees) to Canada increased in the late 1980s and early 1990s as a result of a civil war and the collapse of the central government. Like many immigrants before them, Somalians in Toronto clustered in particular neighbourhoods (or "ethnic enclaves") as a response to discrimination in the housing market (an experience not unique to Somalians [see Galabuzi, 2001: 124–26]) and as a way of coping with life as new immigrants of colour in Canada. The growth of the Somalian community in Toronto occurred during a time of recession and an increasing racist backlash towards new immigrants, intensified by a couple of high-profile incidents mentioned earlier in the chapter involving members of the city's Black community. Statistics taken from the Canadian census report of 1996 show that the Somalian community, nearly half of which is under the age of twenty-four, faces some of the worst employment prospects and highest rates of poverty in Toronto. Almost one-quarter of Somalians in Toronto are unemployed. Those with work are most likely to be represented in the lowest-paying and least skilled jobs the city has to offer. The median income of Somalian women is $15,000, while for men it is only marginally better, at $17,000. Not surprisingly, Somalians face a very high incidence of poverty, with 63 percent of their families living below the official poverty line (Ornstein, 2000).

The response of police to the Somalian community is not atypical of the way in which it has historically reacted to the development of non-white immigrant neighbourhoods. The Somalian community is very poor, with a high rate of young members facing hostility, bleak job prospects and poverty. This experience has no doubt helped to shape the development of Somalian neighbourhoods and shared sentiments about Canada. At the same time, a large number of Somalians have not been in Canada very long: half arrived in 1986 or after. They have brought with them a language and customs alien to most Canadians. Moreover, Somalians are identified in the public consciousness with Islam. All these factors suggest why Somalians are seen as non-conformists and thus a danger to Canadian order.

It is here that khat becomes a problem in the eyes of the state and police. Somalians describe it as a very mild narcotic, the buzz from which is not unlike a strong caffeine rush. It is commonly used in social situations (not unlike alcohol for many Canadians). Users typically chew on its shoots for its intoxicating effects. Khat was legal in Canada until 1997 when it was included in the drug schedule of the Controlled Drugs and Substances Act.

It is crucial to recognize that the state did not criminalize khat based on medical evidence of its harmful effects on users. One official from Health Canada has defended its prohibition, saying that it "creates a sense of euphoria in the user; it elevates the mood and sometimes causes hallucination" (Jones, 2001: F5). The exact danger of euphoria is unclear, while hallucination is not the property of criminalized drugs alone. This description of khat's effects is also contradicted by members of the Somalian community, as we have seen. It is clear, furthermore, that Health Canada did not do serious research into khat's effects before the drug was banned. In the agency's publication *Straight Facts Sheet About Drugs and Drug Abuse*, the section on long-term effects states "insufficient research" for khat. It does note elsewhere in the sheet, however, that "prolonged use can result in withdrawal symptoms such as lethargy, depression, nightmares and tremors," which are symptoms common to withdrawal from legal drugs like nicotine or alcohol (Health Canada, 2000). A spokesperson for the Canadian Centre on Substance Abuse has offered this assessment: "on a scale of addictive substances in this country, khat's impact doesn't even make a bleep on the radar screen" (Jones, 2001: F5).

With no meaningful evidence of its physical dangers, why did it get banned in 1997? The reason becomes clear if we situate khat's criminalization within the long historical context of the war on drugs in Canada. The problem for the state and police is less the drug in itself than what it represents. Khat is a visible symbol of a community that in many ways is foreign to them. Indeed, as the Toronto-based Somali writer, Ali Sharrif, noted in a news article on the banning of khat, "it has a strong cultural connection in the Somali community" (Sharrif, 1996: 3).

A foreign substance used by an immigrant community for festive pursuits, it is one sign of that community's willingness to try to carve out a space for itself and its own traditions and practices from Africa here in Canada. It is an expression, in other words, of the Somalian community's non-conformity, and to the state and police, producers of our public order, that cannot be tolerated. Not used by white Canadians, but only poor Somalians? Khat must be dangerous. This danger grows, furthermore, when we consider that like other drugs, this new drug is used by a specific immigrant community for festive pursuits. The fear of cultural independence strongly intersects again with concerns that it will undermine immigrants' discipline and responsibility, increasing the threat to Canada's bourgeois order. As one officer assigned to patrol the Somalian community said:

> If people get involved in this type of thing [khat], we are going to end up with a lot more people on welfare. They are going to become no good to go to work. (quoted in Sharrif, 1996: 2)

Thus police have been empowered to stamp out its use and sale. According to Sharrif, half of Somalis use it, making it a common substance. But banning the drug has the effect of potentially criminalizing a big section of the community. Thus, at the same time, the police have seized the banning as an excuse to intervene in the Somalian community. Looking for khat has become a convenient pretext for stopping people and removing them from public spaces, and for entering Somalian homes, restaurants and coffee shops. Khat's role as a pretext for broader intervention is suggested by the fact that, as one community worker has noted, the police presence seems to be well out of line for the number of individuals actually using the drug. This is not lost on other community members as well, who suggest the police are using it as an excuse to harass them (Jones, 2001: F15).

Whether they are using khat or not, as Somalian immigrants they are potential criminals, targets of the police's efforts to impose order on them. Police authority over the Somalian community, though, is asserted with not only a broad scope but an aggressive intent as well. It is like a chain reaction: as the putative danger of khat has escalated for police, the stakes for stamping it out have gotten higher and the subsequent reports of brutality have increased. It's been reported that:

- Police have burst into homes without search warrants, assaulted the occupants, and left without laying charges.
- Individuals have been assaulted on the street and in plazas for not immediately displaying the requisite subservience demanded by police.[17]

In one incident, a man reported (with corroboration from eyewitnesses) that police had smashed his door down, threw him on the ground, kicked him in the head, knocked him unconscious, broke his elbow and hog-tied him with telephone cord. An officer then said, "Fucking Somalians, why don't you do something with your lives?" (Rankin, 2000: B1). No khat was found but he was charged with assaulting the police. The crown attorney subsequently withdrew the charge without explanation. The victim made an official complaint with the Toronto Police Services, the avenue of recourse since the Ontario Conservatives eliminated the independent complaints system. It was rejected by the investigator due to insufficient evidence (apparently Somalian eyewitnesses do not count as sufficient). The situation has deteriorated so far that in some instances police harassment has led to violent responses in which police are surrounded and challenged by angry Somalians who are unable to endure aggressive assertions of control over them (Yelaja, 2001: B4).

Somalians in Toronto are a current example of the police's history of dedicated targeting of specific immigrant communities. Their experience goes some way to help explain the continuation of the war on drugs. Together with the policing patterns discussed above, it suggests the key to understanding the drug war is to grasp the racialized campaign for the production of order at the heart of white settler bourgeois society. As long as this production of order is a central feature of state power, the likelihood of the drug war continuing in some form is fairly good.

A Note on the Use of Detention

Detention is the term the government uses for incarcerating or jailing immigrants. It is a tactic being employed more widely as immigration policy and is thus worth considering briefly here. This important feature of the control of immigrants should be situated within the broader context of imprisonment and its relation to law-and-order policies. As the law-and-order agenda picks up steam, we see incarceration being employed more readily against those who defy the state's imposition of public order. It may not be the first choice the state makes; police resort to issuing tickets and fines or physical threats to produce order. Such practices are cheaper and less time-consuming than drawing further on legal resources to put someone in jail. But jail remains an option. We saw, for instance, that people have reportedly faced jail time for repeated violations of the Safe Streets Act. The majority of those charged with minor drug possession pay hefty fines rather than ending up in jail. Some of those convicted, particularly if they are Black, however, do still sometimes end up behind bars. The Ontario Tories, while in power, made prisons an important part of their law-and-order agenda. In 1997 they opened a new "boot camp" for young offenders in Medonte Township. They also oversaw the building of a private jail for adult offenders, which opened in 2001 in Penetanguishene. In Manitoba, all incarcerated youth are subjected to boot-camp-style conditions. The use of incarceration in Canada is not on a scale with its use in the United States, where private prisons are a rapidly growing industry and the incarceration rate is the highest in the world, but it is still of relevance for Canada.[18]

This is especially the case for immigrants, and so is deserving of attention here. Immigrants are increasingly facing incarceration simply for being immigrants. Unfortunately there is currently not a lot on this issue in the academic literature in Canada, so what follows is only a rough outline of the phenomenon. It is in fact a trend developing in many advanced capitalist countries, which are in need of greater numbers of immigrants. They are also stepping up the rhetoric about the dangers of immigrants and employing increasingly coercive measures against them. The U.S. and Australia have gained a reputation for their widespread use of detention against immigrants from Global South countries (see, for example, Motta, 2002; Simon, 1998; and Welch, 1996).

But the pattern is occurring in Canada as well, if at a slower pace. Up-to-date statistics on the jailing of immigrants are not readily available. According to the Canadian Council of Refugees, which tries to track incarceration rates, detention has steadily increased through the 1990s into the early part of the present decade. Gauvereau and Williams (2002: 68) report, in what may be a conservative estimate using data a few years old provided by Citizenship and Immigration Canada, that there is an average of 455 persons detained under the immigration law at any one time. Immigrants are held in either of three jails in Toronto and Vancouver used specifically for them, or in regular jails.

The three main reasons given for incarcerating immigrants under the Immigration and Refugee Protection Act are as follows: they represent a threat to public safety; authorities have concerns about their identity; or they might flee the country. According to the immigration and refugee lawyer interviewed for this chapter, these three provisions are used quite broadly. In this lawyer's experience, the threat-to-public-safety provision is used most often for permanent residents accused of minor crimes, such as drug possession or theft. Despite their permanent-residence status, they are commonly placed in immigration jails and face the threat of deportation. In this respect they are not only persons accused of a crime, but are immigrants accused of a crime.

The rules about identity documents, meanwhile, effectively condemn many refugee claimants to jail time. People fleeing a country may have forged documents or none at all because they face persecution or there is no central government from which to obtain them, as in the case of Somalia. Despite this reality, refugees may remain in prison for many months waiting for immigration officials to verify their identity.

With respect to the third reason for detention, the lawyer interviewed suggests that the simple act of making a refugee claim makes one a flight risk (that is, unlikely to show up for interviews or deportation if released) and thus a candidate for detention. The formal determination of a flight risk, however, is more specific: the person has "no fixed address," or their "removal is imminent" (Citizenship and Immigration Canada, 2004b). Some persons might make refugee claims as a way of entering the country and staying here illegally. If officials suspect this is the case, they are likely to detain them as a flight risk. Persons caught overstaying their visa likewise will be detained as a flight risk. However, persons detained as a flight risk can be released if they can get a family member or close friend to post a bond for them, an important point we will return to in a moment.

The increasing use of imprisonment is part of a context in which the state has been pursuing coercive measures against certain groups of immigrants more generally and, with the media's assistance, promoting the image of these groups as dangerous to Canada. While this propaganda facilitates the use of imprisonment in the first place, the increasing recourse to imprisonment itself reinforces the very view of immigrants as criminal. It further isolates them as the dangerous and unrespectable working-class. This isolation, while political or social, on the one hand, is also increasingly material, as real buildings surrounded by barbed wire literally contain the threat and potential social contamination posed by the Third World Other.

Detention also serves as a very stark reminder to immigrants of the power of the Canadian state and the lengths to which it is willing go to punish what it sees as disorder. And, indeed, it takes its toll. According to the immigration and refugee lawyer we interviewed, incarceration can be absolutely devastating for people, leading to feelings of desperation and hopelessness. For many refugees and their families, including sometimes young children, who have traveled across continents to flee persecution, their first experience in Canada is jail. This not a warm welcome, but rather an early warning of how the state views them.

But it can be equally devastating for those who are imprisoned for overstaying their visa, many of whom have spent years in Canada building a life and raising a family. Some are shocked that the government would jail them, separating them from their families and Canadian-born children (who can be turned over to Children's Aid) and/or threatening to deport them. The devastation is compounded by the conditions they face in jail. The immigration detention centres in Toronto, for example, were originally built as hotels. They have no facilities for young children or for outdoor exercise. Alternatively, some, such as those whose visa has expired and have a criminal record, will be sent to a regular jail. In Toronto, many immigrants are put in the Don Jail. Built in the nineteenth century, it now holds four persons in cells meant to hold one and has even been described by one judge as medieval.

Eventually, most people are released, but under strict conditions. Often they have to report to an immigration enforcement officer on a weekly basis and to keep the officer informed of their whereabouts. Given their experience in jail and the emotional cost involved, challenging the conditions or refusing to abide by them are not real options. These individuals thus end up, in effect, monitoring themselves for the state. The lesson here, both for those who have spent time in detention and those who have thus far been lucky enough to avoid it, is to accept their conditions of existence in Canada, keep quiet and stay out of trouble. The consequence of failing to do so is obviously great. There are plenty of police officers patrolling their communities to see to that.

Conclusion

In the end, there is little respite for immigrants in Canada from the watchful eyes and coercive hands of the state. From their entry at the border to their communities and the harsh reality of prisons, immigrants face unparalleled scrutiny from authorities. This treatment, it must be noted, is premised in part on an increased hostility from the white Canadian public, derived from deeply embedded colonialist assumptions about the Global South Other and years of racist propaganda and fear mongering directed towards them, especially, as we have seen, since the emergence of neoliberalism.

The rise of neoliberalism brought with it the pressing need for cheap and flexible labour, which in turn is a fillip to Global South immigration, drawn from a large pool of easily exploitable workers created by the ravages of globalization. This dynamic brings the contradictions of white settler Canada's approach to immigration into sharp relief, as the country needs Global South labour but fears and despises it. A body-peoples expected to engage in both the least desirable wage work (and perhaps seen as undermining the wages and working conditions of native workers) and customs alien to white Canadians, Global South migrants are an ever-present threat of non-conformity to the historical project of the white Anglo-Saxon bourgeois order as well as the contemporary project of neoliberalism and its demands for a subservient and disciplined labour force. Understood in this light, the special focus on immigrants, bound up with the contemporary law-and-order regime, is no mere corollary of state activity but a pivotal moment in the exercise of its power.

Notes

1. Displaced person camps were refugee camps for persons displaced by the Second World War.
2. Stasiulis and Bakan (1997: 115).
3. Quoted in Baines and Sharma (2002: 87).
4. Arat-Koç (1999b: 218). See also Stasiulis and Bakan (1995). Several Caribbean-born writers have documented in literature the unique experiences of domestics. Novelist Austin Clark, for example, has documented their plight in his short-story collection *When He Was Young and Free and Used to Wear Silks* (1971).
5. Min-Sook Lee's *El Contrato* (2003), a documentary film released by the National Film Board (NFB) on workers in the tomato growing industry in Leamington, Ontario, exposes the harsh conditions facing migrant farm workers. See also Ferguson's (2004) report on migrant farm workers.
6. On September 9, 2004, an interview for this chapter was conducted with an Toronto immigration and refugee lawyer who requested anonymity. See also Jiminez's (2003) interesting report on illegal labour.
7. By maintaining such a heavy presence in the targeted communities, public perception of them may be shaped negatively, while racial profiling, as we noted in the first chapter, is a self-fulfilling prophecy: the more police focus on one community over another for illegal activities, the more likely they are to find it in that community as opposed to the other.
8. The police role here has come under some public scrutiny of late, after a few cases in which police gave immigration authorities the names and addresses of women here illegally who reported being victims of domestic abuse. See, for instance, Levy (2004: A2).

9. Some members of the media have worked hard to support this as well. John Ibbitson's (2002: A15) article in the *Globe and Mail*, "Why racial profiling is a good idea," is an excellent example of racial fear mongering passing as serious journalism. Racial profiling is defended as a necessary step against the ubiquitous Arab terrorist. The logic of his argument, not surprisingly, is extremely confounded: old white ladies tend not to be terrorists, so it makes no sense to profile them, but most terrorists are Arabs, therefore we should profile them. "Healthy cultures examine their flaws," he adds, whereas Arab cultures, susceptible to violence and extremism, do not. There is no mention of the impact of Western imperialism on Arab people, or of the historical violence exacted by the West around the world, which might, by the same logic, imply the need to profile white people. Nor is there the acknowledgement of the fact that most Arab people do not engage in "terrorism." Moreover, he refers to the Arab region's cultural rather than racial flaws, yet it is not cultural profiling he is calling for.

10. Troper (2003: 34) provides an interesting look at the way in which this same hostile attitude was directed toward Italian neighbourhoods in Toronto in the 1940s and 1950s, when the communities were still relatively new in Canada, and Italians were not considered white. The new outdoor sidewalk cafes associated with Italians were viewed as a threat to the city's hygiene, while Italians drinking wine in parks (an act not associated with Anglo Saxons) were targeted by police as a representation of disorder.

11. Giffen, Endicott and Lambert (1991: 47).

12. Giffen, Endicott and Lambert (1991: 57).

13. Giffen, Endicott and Lambert (1991: 58).

14. Quoted in Giffen, Endicott and Lambert (1991: 152).

15. Quoted in Giffen, Endicott and Lambert (1991: 154).

16. See Oscapella (1998), for example.

17. See for example, Rankin (2000: B1); Yelaja (2001: B4); Jones (2001: F5).

18. See Parenti's (1999) very insightful discussion of the emergence and rapid growth of the U.S.'s "prison industrial complex" in the 1980s and 1990s. See also his interesting analysis of private prisons, where he effectively challenges the more traditional left arguments that they are driven by large returns to corporate investors or the cheap labour they provide via inmates. Instead, he argues the most salient and enduring reason for the rise of prisons, including the private prison industrial complex, in the last twenty years in the U.S. is terror and punishment as class struggle from above.

Conclusion

Law-and-order policing is at the core of the neoliberal project in Canada today. It is not enough to simply assert its passing relevance, as if it is useful but not necessary to the success of neoliberalism. Instead, it is part of the neoliberal state form, as essential as cuts to welfare or monetarism. To grasp this, it is important to emphasize the state's aggressive pursuit, in Canada and other advanced capitalist countries, of political and economic restructuring over the last couple of decades. This has involved the effort to support the restoration of capitalist profitability following the economic downturn of the 1970s by facilitating the generalization of lean production methods and the restructuring of the working class. People's dependence on market relations, i.e., on money, has been reinforced by the drastic reduction of alternatives to workers. People, in other words, have increasingly few options but to enter the market in order to seek a living. This deepening commodification of social relations has helped to reduce incomes. It has put increased pressure on bargaining positions more generally at the lower end of the labour market, as avenues to avoid the worst forms of wage labour have been systemically closed off. This forceful measure has been pursued by the state in response to people's reluctance to dramatically alter expectations fostered by decades of struggle and steady improvement in living and working conditions. Law-and-order policing is at the heart of this process. It is, as Bonefeld remarks, "the other side of a policy of state austerity" (1993: 158).

Commonly advanced explanations for the rise of law-and-order policing are seriously limited. To suggest that it is merely about gentrification, for instance, or sweeping the castoffs of neoliberal society under the carpet — out of sight and therefore out of mind — is to miss the deeper dynamics at play, including the central constitutive role of state power over capitalist society today. As we have seen, it does not occur only in neighbourhoods at the cutting edge of gentrification. And while being visibly poor and on the street may increase one's likelihood of receiving unwanted police attention, it is certain groups of the visibly poor found in public spaces — namely the able-bodied, young people, as well as immigrants of colour — face by far the greatest scrutiny.

But to draw out some of the key dynamics of law-and-order policing as we have done — its role, as a moment of neoliberal state power, in establishing contemporary bourgeois order by producing a cheap and flexible class of wage labourers — is really, in one important respect, to situate it properly within the broad historical context of the state power and policing that emerged with industrial capitalism. This is worth emphasizing, since there is so much mythology about the supposedly natural occurrence of capitalist social relations as a fulfilment of human development, when they are no more natural than, say, historically specific laws targeting particular social practices deemed disorderly. Forcefully separated from the means of production and subjected to extremely alienating working conditions and the often autocratic authority of employers, the working class has to be created. This task has been a vital feature of state power under capitalism. The police have emerged as the front line in this battle, searching for and destroying whatever incentives people can find — financial, festive or both — to avoid wage labour, and criminalizing a broad range of working class activities in the process. The struggle discussed here is not against violent offenders run amok, but the everyday signs of disorder that may undermine the wage form, which, from the capitalist state's point of view, are much more threatening to bourgeois civilization. Without an orderly and disciplined class of workers ready to enter the market and sell their labour power for a wage, there is no capitalism.

This policing dynamic has been forcefully reasserted over the past twenty-five years in several advanced capitalist countries. It has really picked up momentum in Canada since the 1990s. If the targeting of forms of public disorder such as vagrancy declined in the postwar period in Canada, it has escalated, reaching a near fever pitch, with our entry into the neoliberal era. As the success of Canadian capitalist order became increasingly wedded to the drastic restructuring of the labour market and the assault on working-class expectations, the law-and-order agenda became that much more pressing. Any hint of non-conformity to market relations brings a swift response. Activities that clearly are not dangerous in themselves — squeegeeing, panhandling or hanging out in public spaces, for example — are criminalized and made the subject of vitriolic moralistic rants, lest someone get the idea that it might be acceptable to engage in activities that provide relief from the drudgery of life at the bottom of the new labour market. The resentment towards the young and able-bodied who don't work is profound. It underlies the righteous indignation of the proponents of the Safe Streets Act, and the verbal (and sometimes non-verbal) assaults of police officers directed towards the new vagrants.

As sweeping as the law-and-order agenda has been in some ways, however, it is not gender- or race-blind. Since its emergence modern policing has been extremely gendered and racialized. Poor working-class and colonized women, especially those in the sex trade or those without proper paternal authority, as defined by the new truancy laws — the failure-to-comply offences — discussed in the second chapter, constitute an important policing target today. But the pursuit of public order is perhaps most pronounced in immigrant communities. Increasing numbers of immigrants, we noted, are criminalized simply by virtue of being here because of their status (or, more precisely, their lack of status). There has been a trend since the 1970s towards the criminalization of all Global South immigrants, who comprise the majority of migrants to Canada today. While their cheap labour is desperately needed, the immigrant Other is typically viewed as a danger to the safety, social services and ecology of Canada. Their customs and languages are unfamiliar to many Canadians of British and French descent; they don't fit in and thus pose a menace. They are seen as "body-peoples" — the repositories of physical desires repressed by whites in order to achieve respectability within bourgeois civilization, and so they are a threat to Canada's order. From their entry at the border, to their communities and to the jails in which increasing numbers of them end up simply for being immigrants, they are under constant and extensive physical surveillance, reminded daily via the harsh assertion of state power of their place in Canada.

The fact of the violent production of order in immigrant communities is also a sharp rebuke to the panoptic theories so trendy in the academic literature today. Policing is no more done at a distance than it is done simply to facilitate gentrification. The former assertion, however, is much more dangerous, and any responsible study of the law-and-order agenda, or of power in the neoliberal era, has to acknowledge that it is a very material, directly physical process pursued by the state. Order is not the result of a metaphysical power emanating from multiple sites and weaving its way through self-reproducing docile bodies. It is the result of an aggressive state policy imposed on real human beings who sometimes aspire for alternatives to, or distractions from, the alienating and exploitative experience of dead-end jobs. Zero-tolerance policing and the enforcement of the Safe Streets Act and immigration policy are direct, harsh and sometimes quite violent exercises of power. The fact that the panopticon theory completely misses these dynamics of contemporary policing is not surprising, given its roots in a theoretical framework that eschews class and state analysis that it deems passé. But the critique of this literature provided in the first chapter demonstrates its gaping holes, reminding us that a class-struggle-oriented Marxist theory of state power, which pays attention to social relations of racism and sexism, is as relevant today as it has ever been. Indeed, it has enabled us to illuminate the law-and-order agenda from a different angle and thus to provide insights that are simply not possible with panoptic theory.

This Marxist angle also forces us to consider the likely persistence of public-order policing. Although it certainly has ebbs and flows in terms of how extensively or pressingly it is pursued, our location of policing within the very form of the capitalist state as an expression of the contradictory relationship of labour in-and-against capital suggests it will continue to be a forceful presence in poor people's and immigrants' lives. As the political mode of existence of those contradictory relations, there is a demand on the state to administer labour and ensure it is decomposed into an available and orderly class of wage workers. The current importance assigned to law-and-order policing, moreover, is unlikely to abate any time soon. It is doubtful that the development of something comparable to the postwar period and the kind of labour relations regime that emerged within it will occur any time in the near future. Like other advanced capitalist countries, Canada will likely become more dependant on cheap Global South immigrant labour to help fuel its economy.

None of this is to suggest that criticism of policing is irrelevant. Consider the work of community activists who have persistently demanded greater civilian oversight of police or the campaign of the victims of aggressive law-and-order policing to hold police accountable for their actions. Their work has been invaluable in shedding light on the harsh reality of policing and reminding the state that its practices cannot be pursued unchecked or unchallenged. Even limiting the room within which the police operate by only a small amount is a positive step forward in this respect.

But the analysis offered in this book should challenge us to dig a little deeper when considering what is at stake. While greater civilian oversight of police or checks on police power are certainly welcome, the issues involved here go to the core of capitalist social relations. Modest reform of policing practices or of police administration are one place to start. It is necessary, however, to consider more seriously the social organization of the society in which we live, which relies on the aggressive use of power to impose its unequal, exploitative and indeed racist and sexist form of order on people. Only by considering the implication of policing in the production of capitalist social relations and focusing our critical attention on those social relations themselves can we really begin to develop a meaningful challenge to it that extends beyond necessary but insufficient reforms.

This is neither an easy nor a short-term task. But for those who are seriously concerned about the power of the state and its increasingly aggressive penetration by means of the police into their communities, it is one that cannot be ignored. Indeed, any form of social organization that necessitates such measures to be sustained is clearly sick. As with any illness, it is not the symptoms alone that must be targeted. And to the extent the analysis presented here forces us to consider the persistence of public-order policing, it also hints at alternative possibilities. As we have argued throughout this book, policing is an expression of contradictory social relations that lead people to struggle for better conditions in their workplaces and communities. So the other side of its persistence as a moment of the capitalist state form is the aspirations of poor and immigrant men and women for a life without subjection to the alienating and oppressive relations that shape their daily experiences. These aspirations for a better and more socially just world are a basis upon which the struggle against policing, or indeed the system driving it, will rest. With them lies the possibility — distant, perhaps, but a possibility nonetheless — of a world where social relations are not shaped by a violent state power with a pathological drive to produce its notion of order. This, in other words, is a world based on relations of social justice, equality and dignity, and thus one in which law-and-order policing has no part.

Bibliography

Abell, Neil. 1996. "The Impact of International Migration on Security and Stability." *Canadian Foreign Policy* 4, 1.

Adams, Howard. 1989. *Prison of Grass: Canada From a Native Point of View.* Saskatoon: Fifth House.

Adler, James. 1989. "A Historical Analysis of the Law of Vagrancy." *Criminology* 27.

Alberta. 1991. *Justice On Trial: Report of the Task Force on the Criminal Justice System and Its Impact on the Indian and Metis People of Alberta*, vol. 1. Edmonton: The Task Force.

Albo, Greg. 1994. "'Competitive Austerity' and the Impasse of Capitalist Employment Policy." In R. Miliband and L. Panitch (eds.), *Between Globalism and Nationalism: Socialist Register.* London: Merlin Press.

Alexander, B. 1990. *Peaceful Measures: Canada's Way Out of the 'War on Drugs.'* Toronto: University of Toronto.

Anonymous. 2004. Interview conducted by author, September 9.

Arat-Koç, Sedef. 1999a. "'Good Enough to Work but Not Good Enough to Stay': Foreign Domestic Workers and the Law." In E. Comack (ed.), *Locating Law: Race/Class/Gender Connections.* Halifax: Fernwood.

_____. 1999b. "Gender and Race in 'Non-discriminatory' Immigration Policies in Canada: 1960s to the Present." In E. Dua and A. Robertson (eds.), *Scratching the Surface: Canadian Anti-racist and Feminist Thought.* Toronto: Women's Press.

Auditor General of Canada. 2001. "Illicit Drugs — The Federal Government's Role." Press Release. Ottawa: Office of the Auditor General of Canada.

Baines, D., and N. Sharma. 2002. "Migrant Workers as Non-Citizens: The Case of Citizenship as a Social Policy Concept." *Studies in Political Economy* 69.

Bakker, Isa. 1996. "The Gendered Foundations of Restructuring in Canada." In I. Bakker (ed.), *Rethinking Restructuring: Gender and Change in Canada.* Toronto: University of Toronto Press.

Bannerji, Himani. 2000. *The Dark Side of the Nation: Essays on Multiculturalism, Nationalism and Gender.* Toronto: Canadian Scholars' Press.

Bannister, J., N.R. Fyfe and A. Kearns. 1998. "Closed circuit television and the city." In Clive Norris, Jade Moran and Gary Armstrong (eds.), *Surveillance, Closed Circuit Television and Social Control.* Aldershot: Ashgate.

Basok, Tanya. 1996. "Refugee Policy: Globalization, Radical Challenge, or State Control?" *Studies in Political Economy* 50.

Bonefeld, Werner. 1993 *The Recomposition of the British State During the 1980s.* Aldershot: Dartmouth.

Bonefeld, W., R. Gunn and K. Psychopedis (eds.). 1992. *Open Marxism, Volume 1: Dialectics and History*, London: Pluto Press.

_____. *Open Marxism, Volume 2: Theory and Practice*. London: Pluto Press.
Bonefeld, W., R. Gunn, J. Holloway and K. Psychopedis (eds.). 1995. *Open Marxism, Volume 3: Emancipating Marx*. London: Pluto Press.
Bonefeld, W., and J. Holloway. 1995. "Introduction: The Politics of Money." In W. Bonefeld and J. Holloway (eds.), *Global Capital, National State and the Politics of Money*. New York: St. Martin's Press.
Boritch, H., and J. Hagan. 1987. "Crime and Changing Forms of Class Control: Public Order Policing in 'Toronto the Good', 1859–1955." *Social Forces* 66, 2.
Bourgeault, Ron. 1988. "Race and Class Under Mercantilism: Indigenous People in Nineteenth Century Canada." In B. Bolaria and P. Li (eds), *Racial Oppression in Canada*. Toronto: Garamond.
Bourgois, Phillippe. 1995. *In Search of Respect: Selling Crack in El Barrio*. Cambridge: Cambridge University Press.
Boyd, Neil. 1991. *High Society: Legal and Illegal Drugs in Canada*. Toronto: Key Porter Books.
Boyle, T. 1995. "Deaths raise doubts on pepper spray." *Toronto Star*, October 17, A19.
Bradford, Neil. 2000. "The Policy Influence of Economic Ideas: Interests, Institutions and Innovation in Canada." In M. Burke, C. Mooers and J. Shields (eds.), *Restructuring and Resistance: Canadian Public Policy in an Age of Global Capitalism*. Halifax: Fernwood.
Brannigan, A., and Z. Lin. 1998. "'Where East meets West': Police, immigration and public order crime in the settlement of Canada from 1896 to 1940." *Canadian Journal of Sociology* 24 (December–February).
Bratton, W.J. 1998. "Crime is Down in New York City: Blame the Police." In N. Dennis (ed.), *Zero Tolerance: Policing a Free Society*. London: IEA Health and Welfare.
Bright, D. 1995. "Loafers are not going to subsist upon public credulence: Vagrancy and the law in Calgary, 1900–1914." *Labour/Le Travail* 36 (Fall).
Bronskill, J. 2004. "I.D. proposals spark concern." *Toronto Star*, September 6, A1 and A12.
Brown, J. 1998. "Squeegee People: Urban Guerillas." *Our Toronto Free Press*, August, 1–2.
Burke, M., and J. Shields. 2000. "Tracking Inequality in the New Canadian Labour Market." In M. Burke, C. Moores and J. Shields (eds.), *Restructuring and Resistance: Canadian Public Policy in an Age of Global Capitalism*. Halifax: Fernwood.
Burke, R. 1998a. "A Contextualisation of Zero Tolerance Strategies." In R. Burke (ed.), *Zero Tolerance Policing*. Leceister: Perpetuity Press.
_____. 1998b. "Begging, Vagrancy and Disorder." In R. Burke (ed.), *Zero Tolerance Policing*. Leceister: Perpetuity Press.
Calgary Herald. 2000. "Native complaints of harassment pour in." *Calgary Herald*, February 24, B10.
Canada. 1970. *Report of the Royal Commission on the Status of Women in Canada*. Ottawa: Information Canada.
Canada. 2-3 Elizabeth/1954. Parliament. House of Commons. 22nd Parliament, 1st Session Official Report, vol. 3. Ottawa: Queen's Printer.
Canada. 55 Vict./1892. Vagrancy. *Criminal Code*. C. 29. S. 207 and 208.
Canadian Centre for Justice Statistics. 1997. *Private Security and Public Policing in Canada*. Ottawa: Statistics Canada.

_____. 1998. *Police Personnel and Expenditures in Canada, 1996–97.* Ottawa: Statistics Canada.

_____. 2001. *Crime Stats in Canada, 2000.* Ottawa: Statistics Canada.

_____. 2002. *Police Resources in Canada, 2001.* Ottawa: Statistics Canada.

Canadian Centre on Substance Abuse. 1999. "Canada Profile." Ottawa: Canadian Centre on Substance Abuse, 1–4. Available at <www.ccsa.ca/index>.

Chambliss, William. 1964. "A Sociological Analysis of the Law of Vagrancy." *Social Problems* 12 (Summer).

Citizenship and Immigration Canada. 2004a. "Creation of the Canada Border Services Agency." Ottawa: Citizenship and Immigration Canada. Available at <www. cic.gc.ca/english/department/notice-cbsa.html> (accessed May 2004).

_____. 2004b. "Admissibility Hearings and Detention Review Proceedings." Ottawa: Citizenship and Immigration Canada. Available at <www.cic.gc.ca/manuals-guides/english/enf/> (accessed May 2004).

City of Calgary. 1990. By-law to Regulate Panhandling. No. 3M99.

City of Hamilton. 1997. Panhandling By-law. No. 97-162.

City of Oshawa. 1994. Public Nuisance By-law. No. 72-94.

City of Toronto. 2001. *Squeegee Youth Work Mobilization Program. Summary Results.* Toronto: City of Toronto.

City of Vancouver. 1998a. *Report of the Urban Safety Commission.* February 24. Vancouver: Urban Safety Commission. Available at <www.city.vancouver. bc.ca/ctyclerk/cclerk/980305/PE4.HTM> (accessed October 2003).

_____. 1998b. *Report on Panhandling.* April 21. Vancouver: City Manager. Available at <www.city.vancouver.bc.ca/ctyclerk/cclerk/980430/pe4.htm> (accessed October 2003).

_____. 1998c. Panhandling By-law. No. 7885.

_____. 2000. Obstructive Solicitation By-law. No. 8309.

City of Winnipeg. 1995. A By-law of the City of Winnipeg to regulate and control panhandling. No. 6555/95.

_____. 1998. "Stronger Police Presence and New Programs Will Make Downtown Safer." News Release. February 23. Winnipeg: City of Winnipeg. Available at <www.winnipeg.ca/cao/media/news/nr1998/nr_19980223.stm> (accessed October 2003).

_____. 2000. The Obstructive Solicitation By-law. No. 7700.

Clairmont, D. 1991. "Community-Based Policing: Implementation and Impact." *Canadian Journal of Criminology* 33.

Clarke, John. 1991. *New Times and Old Enemies: Essays on Cultural Studies in America.* New York: Harper Collins.

Clarke, Simon. 1983. "State, Class Struggle and the Reproduction of Capital." *Kapitalistate* 10, 11.

_____. 1988. *Keynesianism, Monetarism and the Crisis of the State.* Aldershot: Edward Elgar.

Coleman, R., and J. Sim. 2000. "'You'll never walk alone': CCTV surveillance, order and neoliberal rule in Liverpool city centre." *British Journal of Sociology* 51, 4.

Collins, D., and N. Blomley. 2001. "Private Needs and Public Space: Politics, Poverty and Anti-Panhandling By-laws in Canadian Cities." *Legal Dimensions* (May). Ottawa: Law Commission of Canada.

Comack, Elizabeth. 1991. "'We will get some good out of this riot yet': The Canadian State, Drug Legislation and Class Conflict." In S. Brickey and E. Comack (eds.), *The Social Basis of Law: Critical Readings in the Sociology of Law*. Toronto: Garamond.

Committee To Stop Targeted Policing. 2000. *Who's The Target?* Toronto: Committee to Stop Targeted Policing.

Crowther, C. 1998. "Policing the Excluded Society." In R. Burke (ed.), *Zero Tolerance Policing*. Leceister: Perpetuity Press.

Davidson, Kolin. 2000. Defendant's Book of Affidavits. R. v. David Banks et al.

Davis, Mike. 1992. *City of Quartz: Excavating the Future of Los Angeles*. New York: Vintage.

De Lint, W. 1999. "A Post-modern Turn in Policing: Policing as Pastiche?" *International Journal of the Sociology of Law* 27.

DeMara, B. 1998. "Squeegee plan put off until October." *Toronto Star*, July 30, B3.

Dougherty, J. 2000. "Pepper-spray study set up: But public-security minister won't issue moratorium on its use by cops." *Montreal Gazette*, July 27, A5.

Drainville, André. 1995. "Monetarism in Canada and the World Economy." *Studies in Poltical Economy* 46.

Dunlop, G., MPP. 1999. Hansard. 1st Session, 37th Parliament, November 15, Toronto: Queen's Printer for Ontario.

Eck, J.E., and D.P. Rosenbaum. 1994. "The New Police Order: Effectiveness, Equity, and Efficiency in Community Policing." In D.P. Rosenbaum (ed.), *The Challenge of Community Policing*. Thousand Oaks: Sage

Elias, P. 1988. *The Dakota of the Canadian Northwest: Lessons in Survival*. Winnipeg: University of Manitoba Press.

Erickson, P. 1998a. "Neglected and Rejected: A Case Study of the Impact of Social Research on Canadian Drug Policy." *Canadian Journal of Sociology* 23, 2/3.

_____. 1998b. "Recent Trends in Canadian Drug Policy: The Decline and Resurgence of Prohibitionism." In T. Hartnagel (ed.), *Canadian Crime Control Policy*. Toronto: Harcourt and Brace.

_____. 1999. "A Persistent Paradox: Drug Law and Policy in Canada." *Canadian Journal of Criminology* 41, 2.

Ericson, Richard V. 1982. *Reproducing Order: A Study of Police Patrol Work*. Toronto: University of Toronto.

Ericson, Richard V., and K.D. Haggerty. 1997. *Policing the Risk Society*. Oxford: Clarendon Press.

_____. 1999. "The Militarization of Policing in the Information Age." *Journal of Political and Military Sociology* 27 (Winter).

Esmonde, Jackie. 1999. "Neoliberalism, Youth Poverty and Washing Windshields: An Ethnographic Study of Squeegeeing in Toronto," MA thesis, York University: Toronto.

_____. 2002a. "The Policing of Dissent: The Use of Breach of Peace Arrests at Political Demonstrations." *Journal of Law and Equality* 3, 2.

_____. 2002b. "Criminalizing Poverty: The Criminal Law Power and the *Safe Street Act*." *Journal of Law and Social Policy* 17.

Esping-Anderson, G. 1990. *The Three Worlds of Welfare Capitalism*. Princeton: Princeton University Press.

Faraday, C. 1991. "The Debate About Prostitution: A History of the Formation and Failure of Canadian Laws Against the Sex Trade," PhD thesis, University of Toronto: Toronto.

Ferguson, Sue. 2004. "Hard Time in Canadian Fields." *Maclean's*, October 11.

Available at http://205.150.121.181/xta-asp/storyview.asp?viewtype=brows e&tp1=browse_frame&vpath=/2004/10/11/canada/90409.sthml> (accessed December 2004).

Fischer, B. 2000. "'Community Policing': A Study of Local Policing, Order and Control," Ph.D. thesis, University of Toronto: Toronto.

Flaherty, J.M., MPP. 2000. "Letter to City of Windsor Mayor Michael D. Hunt Re. Safe Streets Act." March 24. Toronto: Attorney General's Office.

Foucault, Michel. 1977. *Discipline and Punish*. New York: Vintage.

Gabriel, Christine. 2001. "Restructuring at the Margins: Women of Colour and the Changing Economy." In E. Dua and A. Robertson (eds.), *Scratching the Surface: Canadian Anti-Racist Feminist Thought*. Toronto: Women's Press.

Galabuzi, Grace-Edward. 2001. *Canada's Creeping Economic Apartheid: The Economic Segregation and Social Marginalisation of Racialised Groups*. Toronto: Centre for Social Justice.

Galati, Rocco. 2002. "Canada's globalization, militarization and police state agenda." *Briarpatch* 31, 1.

Gavereau, C., and G. Williams. 2002. "Detention in Canada: Are We on the Slippery Slope?" *Refuge* 20, 3.

Giffen, P. J., S. Endicott and S. Lambert. 1991. *Panic and Indifference: The Politics of Canada's Drug Laws*. Ottawa: Canadian Centre on Substance Abuse.

Gill, P. 1998. "Making Sense of Police Intelligence? The Use of A Cybernetic Model in Analysing Information and Power in Police Intelligence Processes." *Policing and Society* 8 (April).

Glyn, A., A. Hughes, A. Lipietz and A. Singh. 1990. "The Rise and Fall of the Golden Age." In S. Marglin and J. Schor (eds.), *The Golden Age of Capitalism: Reinterpreting the Postwar Experience*. Oxford: Clarendon.

Gordon, Diane. 1987. "The Electronic Panopticon: A Case Study of the Development of the National Criminal Records System." *Politics and Society* 15, 4.

Gordon, P. 1987. "Community Policing: Towards the Local Police State?" In P. Scraton (ed.), *Law, Order and the Authoritarian State*. Philadelphia: Open University Press.

Greaves, G. 1986. "The Police and Their Public." In J. Benyon and C. Bourn (eds.), *The Police: Powers, Procedures and Proprieties*. Oxford: Pergamon Press.

Greene, J.A. 1999. "Zero Tolerance: A Case Study of Police Policies and Practices in New York City." *Crime and Delinquency* 45, 2.

Gregoire, L. 2001. "Excessive police force? Lawyers want answers in deaths of 2 men." *Edmonton Journal*, May 23, A1.

Hall, S., C. Critcher, T. Jefferson, J. Clarke and B. Roberts. 1978. *Policing the Crisis: Mugging, the State, and Law and Order*. London: MacMillan.

Harring, S. 1993. "Policing a Class Society: The Expansion of the Urban Police in the Late Nineteenth and Early Twentieth Centuries." In D. Greenberg (ed.), *Crime and Capitalism: Readings in Marxist Criminology*. Philadelphia: Temple University Press.

Harris, M., MPP. 1999. Hansard. 1st Session, 37th Parliament, November 2. Toronto: Queen's Printer for Ontario.

Harris, Nigel. 1980. "The new untouchables: the international migration of labour." *International Socialism Journal* 2, 8.

Harvey, David. 1990. *The Condition of Postmodernity*. Oxford: Blackwell.

_____. 1999. *The Limits to Capital*. London: Verso.

Haythorne, G.V. 1973. "Prices and Income Policy: The Canadian Experience, 1969–1972." *International Labour Review* 108.

Health Canada. 2001. "Straight Fact Sheet about Drug Abuse." Available at <http://www.hc-sc.gc.ca/ahc-asc/pubs/drugs-drogues/straight_facts-faits_mefaits/tables-tableaux_e.html> (accessed May 2004).

Hermer, Joe. 1997. "Keeping Oshawa Beautiful: Policing the Loiterer in Public Nuisance By-law 72094." *Canadian Journal of Law and Society* 12.

High, S. 1996. "Native Wage Labour and Independent Commodity Production During the 'Era of Irrelevance.'" *Labour/Le Travail* 37.

Horton, Cst. M. 2000. Memo Written By Constable Horton, Ottawa-Carleton Regional Police Service, On the *Safe Streets Act*, November 10. Vancouver: Office of the Information and Privacy Commissioner, Vancouver Police Department. Information and Privacy reference: 04-0455A.

Ibbitson, J. 2002. "Why racial profiling is a good idea." *Globe and Mail*, June 3, A15.

Jakubowski, L.M. 1999. "'Managing' Canadian Immigration: Racism, Ethnic Selectivity, and the Law." In E. Comack (ed.), *Locating Law: Race/Class/Gender Connections*. Halifax: Fernwood.

Jeffs, A. 1996. "Pepper spray had no impact." *Calgary Herald*, June 18, B3.

Jensen, E., and J. Gerber. 1993. "State Efforts to Construct a Social Problem: The 1986 War on Drugs in Canada." *Canadian Journal of Sociology* 18, 4.

Jimenez, M. 2003. "200,000 illegal immigrants toiling in Canada's underground economy." *Globe and Mail*, November 15, A1 and A9.

Jones, V. 2001. "Cultures clash on streets over Canada's ban on khat." *Toronto Star*, July 25, F5.

Kelley, Robin D.G. 1994. *Race Rebels: Culture, Politics, and the Black Working Class*. New York: The Free Press.

_____. 1997. *Yo' mama's disfunktional! fighting the culture wars in urban america*. Boston: Beacon.

Keung, N. 2004a. "Newcomers' wages in decline: Study." *Toronto Star*, May 18, A10.

_____. 2004b. "Immigrants put strain on city services." *Toronto Star*, August 19, A14.

Knight, R. 1996. *Indians at Work: An Informal History of Native Labour in British Columbia 1858–1930*. Vancouver: New Star Books.

Kossick, D. 2000. "Death by cold: Institutionalized violence in Saskatoon." *Canadian Dimension* 34, 4.

Laliberte, R., and V. Satzewich. 1999. "Native migrant labour in the southern Alberta sugar-beet industry: Coercion and paternalism in the recruitment of labour." *Canadian Review of Sociology and Anthropology* 36, 1.

Landau, T. 1996. "When Police Investigate Police: A View From Complainants." *Canadian Journal of Criminology* 38, 3.

Leighton, B.N. 1991. "Visions of Community Policing": Rhetoric and Reality in Canada." *Canadian Journal of Criminology* 33, 3/4.

Leitold, Matt. 2004. Personal Communication to author. April 1.

Levy, H. 2004. "Teen in rape case spared deportation." *Toronto Star*, July 28, A2.

Lipietz, Alain. 1987. *Mirages and Miracles: The Crisis in Global Fordism*. London: Verso.

Macklin, Audrey. 2001. "Borderline Security." In R. Daniels, P. Macklem and K.

Roach (eds.), *The Security of Freedom: Essays on Canada's Anti-Terrorism Bill.* Toronto: University of Toronto.

Manitoba. 1991. *Report of the Aboriginal Justice Inquiry*, vol. 1. Winnipeg: Queen's Printer.

Marquis, G. 1994. "Power From the Street: The Canadian Municipal Police." In R. Macleod and D. Schneiderman (eds.), *Police Powers in Canada: The Evolution and Practice of Authority.* Toronto: University of Toronto.

Martinuk, G., MPP. 1999. Hansard. 1st Session, 37th Parliament, November 15. Toronto: Queen's Printer for Ontario.

Marx, Karl. 1977. *Capital*, vol. 1. New York: Vintage.

Mazilli, F., MPP. 1999. Hansard. 1st Session, 37th Parliament, November 15. Toronto: Queen's Printer for Ontario.

McCahill, M. 1998. "Beyond Foucault: Towards a contemporary theory of surveillance." In C. Norris, J. Moran and G. Armstrong (eds.), *Surveillance, Closed Circuit Television and Social Control.* Aldershot: Ashgate.

McLaren, J. 1986. "Chasing the Social Evil: Moral Fervour and the Evolution of Canada's Prostitution Laws, 1867–1917." *Canadian Journal of Law and Society* 1.

McMullan, John. 1998. "The Arresting Eye: Discourse, Surveillance and Disciplinary Administration in Early English Police Thinking." *Social and Legal Studies* 7, 1: 97–128.

McNally, David. 2002. *Another World is Possible: Globalization and anti-capitalism.* Winnipeg: Arbeiter Ring.

Ministry of Industry. 2003. *Report on the Demographic Stituation in Canada, 2002.* Ottawa: Ministry of Industry and Statistics Canada.

Moloney, P., and A. Infantry. 1998. "Mayor says squeegee plan a waste." *Toronto Star*, November 28, A3.

Moon, Richard. 2002. "Keeping the Streets Safe From Free Expression." In J. Hermer and J. Mosher (eds.), *Disorderly People: Law and the Politics of Exclusion in Ontario.* Halifax: Fernwood.

Mosher, C. 1996. "Minorities and Misdemeanours: The treatment of Black public order offenders in Ontario's criminal justice system, 1892–1930." *Canadian Journal of Criminology* 38, 4.

Mosher, C., and J. Hagan. 1994. "Constituting Class and Crime in Upper Canada: The Sentencing of Narcotics Offenders, circa 1908–1953." *Social Forces* 72, 3.

Mosher, Janet. 2002. "The Shrinking of the Public and Private Spaces of the Poor." In J. Mosher and J. Hermer (eds.), *Disorderly People: Law and the Politics of Exclusion in Ontario.* Halifax: Fernwood.

Motta, F. 2002. "'Between a Rock and a Hard Place': Australia's Mandatory Detention of Asylum Seekers." *Refuge* 20, 3.

Murphy, C. 1993. "Community Problems, Problem Communities, and Community Policing in Toronto." In J. Chacko and S.E. Nancoo (eds.), *Community Policing in Canada.* Toronto: Canadian Scholars' Press.

National Anti-Poverty Organization. 1999. "Short-Changed on Human Rights: A NAPO Position Paper on Anti-Panhandling By-laws." NAPO: Ottawa.

Neocleous, Mark. 1996. *Administering Civil Society: Towards a Theory of State Power.* New York: St. Martin's.

_____. 2000. *The Fabrication of Social Order: A Critical Theory of Police Power.* London: Pluto Press.

Norris, C., and G. Armstrong. 1998. "Introduction: Power and Vision." In C. Norris, J. Moran and G. Armstrong (eds.), *Surveillance, Closed Circuit Television and Social Control*. Aldershot: Ashgate.

O'Grady, B., and R. Bright. 2002. "Squeezed to the Point of Exclusion: The Case of Toronto Squeegee Cleaners." In J. Mosher and J. Hermer (eds.), *Disorderly People: Law and the Politics of Exclusion in Ontario*. Halifax: Fernwood.

O'Grady, B., R. Bright, and E. Cohen. 1998. "Sub-employment and street youths: An analysis of the impact of squeegee cleaning on homeless youths." *Security Journal* 11.

O'Mally, P., and D. Palmer. 1996. "Post-Keynesian policing." *Economy and Society* 25, 2.

Ontario. 1995. *Report of the Commission on Systemic Racism in the Ontario Criminal Justice System*. Toronto: Queen's Printer.

_____. 1999. *Safe Streets Act*. Available at <www.e-laws.gov.on.ca/DBLaws/statutes/English/99s08_e.htm> (accessed October 2003).

Ontario Crime Control Commission. 1998. *Report on Youth Crime*. Toronto: Queen's Printer for Ontario.

Ornstein, Michael. 2000. *Ethno-Racial Inequality in Toronto: Analysis of the 1996 Census*. Toronto: Institute for Social Research, York University.

Oscapella, Eugene. 1998. "Profiteers and Prohibition." Address to the International Society for the Reform of Criminal Law Conference, August 11. Available at <www.cfdp.ca/barbados98.htm> (accessed May 2004).

Palameta, B. 2004. "Low Income Among Immigrants and Visible Minorities." In *Perspectives on Labour and Income*. Ottawa: Statistics Canada 5, 4.

Palmer, Bryan D. 1992. *Working-Class Experience*. Toronto: McClelland and Stewart.

_____. 2000. *Cultures of Darkness: Night Travels in the History of Transgression*. New York: Monthly Review.

Panitch, L., and D. Swartz. 1988. *The Assault on Trade Union Freedoms*. Toronto: Garamond.

Parenti, Christian. 1999. *Lockdown America: Police and Prisons in the Age of Crisis*. London: Verso.

Peck, James. 2001. *Workfare States*. New York: Guilford.

Pedicelli, G. 1998. *When Police Kill: Police Use of Force in Montreal and Toronto*. Montreal: Vehicule Press.

Phillips, J. 1990. "Poverty, Unemployment, and the Administration of Criminal Law: Vagrancy Laws in Halifax, 1864–1890." In P. Girard and J. Phillips (eds.), *Essays in the History of Canadian Law, vol. 3*. Toronto: University of Toronto Press.

Pitsula, J. 1980. "The Treatment of Tramps in Late Nineteenth-Century Toronto." *Historical Papers*. Ottawa: Canadian Historical Association.

Pollard, C. 1998. "Zero Tolerance: Short Fix, Long Term Liability?" In N. Dennis (ed.), *Zero Tolerance: Policing a Free Society*. London: IEA Health and Welfare Unit.

Pugilese, D. 1998. "SWAT you're dead." *Saturday Night*, 113, 3.

Quinn, J. 2002. "Police balk at surveillance cameras." *Toronto Star*, March 28, B1 and B3.

Rankin, J. 1998. "Police preferred pepper for force." *Toronto Star*, May 20, B5.

_____. 2000. "Raid leaves painful memories." *Toronto Star*, November 27, B1.

Rankin, J., J. Quinn, M. Shephard, S. Simmie and J. Duncanson. 2002. "Singled out." *Toronto Star*, October 19, A1 and A12–14.

Razack, Sherene. 1999. "Making Canada White: Law and the Policing of Bodies of Colour in the 1990s." *Canadian Journal of Law and Society* 14, 1.

Reitsma-Street, Margaret. 2000. "Justice for Canadian Girls: A 1990s Update." In R.M. Mann (ed.), *Juvenile Crime and Delinquency*. Toronto: Canadian Scholars' Press.

Riches, G. 1989. "Welfare Reform and Social Work Practice: Political Objectives and Ethical Dilemmas." In G. Riches and G. Ternowetsky (eds.), *Unemployment and Welfare: Social Policy and the Work of Social Work*. Toronto: Garamond.

Roberts, W., and J. Bullen. 1984. "A Heritage of Hope and Struggle: Workers, Unions, and Politics in Canada 1930–1982." In M.S. Cross and G.S. Kealey (eds.), *Modern Canada, 1930s–1980s*. Toronto: McClelland and Stewart.

Russell, Bob. 2000. "From the Workhouse to Workfare: The Welfare State and Shifting Policy Terrains." In M. Burke, C. Mooers and J. Shields (eds.), *Restructuring and Resistance: Canadian Public Policy in an Age of Global Capitalism*. Halifax: Fernwood.

Sangster, Joan. 1999. "Criminalizing the Colonized: Ontario Native Women Confront the Criminal Justice System, 1920–1960." *Canadian Historical Review* 80, 1.

Satzewich, V., and T. Wotherspoon. 1993. *First Nations: Race, Class and Gender Relations*. Scarborough: Nelson.

Satzewich, V., and L. Zong. 1996. "Social Control and the Historical Construction of 'Race.'" In B. Schissel and L. Mahood (eds.), *Social Control in Canada: Issues in the Social Construction of Deviance*. Toronto: Oxford.

Schafer, R. 1998. *Down and Out in Winnipeg and Toronto: The Ethics of Legislating Against Panhandling*. Toronto: Caledon Institute of Social Policy.

Schneiderman, David. 2002. "The Constitutional Disorder of the Safe Streets Act: A Federalism Analysis." In J. Mosher and J. Hermer (eds.), *Disorderly People: Law and the Politics of Exclusion in Ontario*. Halifax: Fernwood.

Schuster, E. 2001. "Set tasers on 'stun': A new electric weapon may soon supercede the old police billy club." *Report Newsmagazine* 28, 1. Available at <web7.infotrac.galegroup.com> (accessed June 2002).

Sears, Alan. 1990. "Immigration controls as social policy: The case of Canadian medical inspection 1900–20." *Studies in Political Economy* 33.

_____. 1999. "The 'Lean' State and Capitalist Restructuring: Towards a Theoretical Account." *Studies in Political Economy* 59.

_____. 2003. *Retooling the Mind Factory: Education in a Lean State*. Aurora: Garamond Press.

Sharma, Nandita. 2000. "Maintaining the master-servant relationship." *Kinesis* (May) 8.

_____. 2001. "On Being not Canadian: The Social Organization of 'Migrant Workers' in Canada." In *The Canadian Review of Sociology and Anthropology* 38, 4.

_____. 2003. "Travel Agency: A Critique of Anti-Trafficking Campaigns." *Refuge* 21, 3.

Sharrif, Ali. 1996. "Khat on a hot fed list." *Now* 15, 49. Available at <www.nowtoronto.com/issues/15/49/News/feature2.html> (accessed March 2005).

Siemiatycki, M., T. Rees, R. Ng and R. Khan. 2003. "Integrating Community Diversity in Toronto: On Whose Terms?" In P. Anisef and M. Lanphier (eds.), *The World in a City*. Toronto: University of Toronto.

Simmons, Deborah. 1999. "After Chiapas: Aboriginal Land and Resistance in the

New North America." *The Canadian Journal of Native Studies* 19, 1.

Simon, J. 1998. "Refugees in a Carceral Age: The Rebirth of Immigration Prisons in the United States." *Public Culture* 10, 3.

Skolnick, J. 1966. *Justice Without Trial: Law Enforcement in a Democratic Society*. New York: John Wiley and Sons.

Smith, D.J. 1986. "The Framework of Law and Policing Practice." In J. Benyon and C. Bourn (eds.), *The Police: Powers, Procedures and Proprieties*. Oxford: Pergamon Press.

Smith, G. 2003. "Teens see police as threat." *Globe and Mail*, January 16, A21.

Smith, M.E.G., and K.W. Taylor. 1996. "Profitability Crisis and the Erosion of Popular Prosperity: The Canadian Economy, 1947–1991." *Studies in Political Economy* 49.

Solomon, R. 1988. "The Noble Pursuit of Evil: Arrest, Search, and Seizure in Canadian Drug Law." In J. Blackwell and P. Erickson (eds.), *Illicit Drugs in Canada: A Risky Business*. Scarborough: Nelson.

Stasiulis, D., and A. Bakan, 1995. "Making the Match: Domestic Placement Agencies and the Racialization of Women's Household Work." *Signs: Journal of Women in Culture and Society* 20, 2.

_____. 1997. "Negotiating Citizenship: The Case of Foreign Domestic Workers in Canada." *Feminist Review* 57 (Autumn).

Stasiulis, D., and R. Jhappan. 1995. "The Fractious Politics of a Settler Society: Canada." In D. Stasiulis and N. Yuval-Davis (eds.), *Unsettling Settler Societies: Articulations of gender, race, ethnicity and class*. London: Sage.

Statistics Canada. 2004. "Trends in drug offences and the role of alcohol and drugs in crime." *The Daily*, February 23.

Stewart, G., MPP. 1999. Hansard. 1st Session, 37th Parliament, November 15. Toronto: Queen's Printer for Ontario.

Strange, C. 1988. "From Modern Babylon to a City Upon the Hill: The Toronto Social Survey Commission of 1915 and the Search for Sexual Order in the City." In R. Hall, W. Westfall and L. MacDowell (eds.), *Patterns of the Past: Reinterpreting Ontario's History*. Toronto: Dundurn Press.

Stuart, Donald. 2001. "Time to Recodify Criminal Law and Rise Above Law and Order Expediency: Lessons from the Manitoba Warriors Prosecution." *Manitoba Law Journal* 28, 1.

Supreme Court of British Columbia. 2002. *Federated Anti-Poverty Groups of BC, End Legislated Poverty Society and National Anti-Poverty Organization vs. City of Vancouver and The Attorney General of British Columbia*. March 7.

Taube, M. 1998. "Let's get them off the streets." *Toronto Star*, July 31, A21.

Teel, G. 1997. "Beware of high-speed beanbags: Edmonton's latest crime-fighting tool may turn out to be a killer." *Alberta Report* 24, 17 (April 7).

Thobani, Sunera. 2001. "Closing the Nation's Ranks: Racism, Sexism and the Abuse of Power in Canadian Immigration Policy." In S. Boyd, D. Chunn and R. Menzies (eds.), *(Ab)using Power: The Canadian Experience*. Halifax: Fernwood.

Toronto Police Accountability Coalition. 2002. "Submission to the City of Toronto Budget Committee." Toronto: Toronto Police Accountability Coalition, February 18.

Toronto Police Services. 1984. *Annual Statistical Report*. Toronto: Toronto Police Services.

_____. 1986. *Annual Statistical Report*. Toronto: Toronto Police Services.

_____. 1992. *Annual Statistical Report*, Toronto: Toronto Police Services.

_____. 1996. *Statistical Report*, Toronto: Toronto Police Services.

_____. 1998. *Annual Report*. Toronto: Toronto Police Services.

_____. 1999. *Annual Report*, Toronto: Toronto Police Services.

_____. 2001. *Statistical Report*, Toronto: Toronto Police Services.

Toronto Star. 1997. "RCMP wants armoured column of its own." July 10, A12.

Tremblay, S. 1999. "Illicit Drugs and Crime in Canada." *Juristat*. Ottawa: Statistics Canada 19, 1.

Troper, H. 2003. "Becoming an Immigrant City: A History of Immigration into Toronto since the Second World War." In P. Anisef and M. Lanphier (eds.), *The World in a City*. Toronto: University of Toronto.

Trotter, Gary. 2001. "The Anti-Terrorism Bill and Preventative Restraints on Liberty." In R.J. Daniels, P. Macklem and K. Roach (eds.), *The Security of Freedom: Essays on Canada's Anti-Terrorism Bill*. Toronto: University of Toronto Press.

Valverde, Mariana. 1991. *The Age of Light, Soap and Water: Moral Reform in English Canada, 1885–1925*. Toronto: McClelland and Stewart.

Vancouver Police Department. 2003. "Nuisance Behaviour: Time for New Strategies in British Columbia." Vancouver: Office of the Information and Privacy Commissioner, Vancouver Police Department. Information and Privacy reference: 04-0455A.

Vancouver Province. 2000. "Police in Saskatoon face racial firestorm over Aboriginal deaths." February 22, A27.

Waganese, Richard. 1991. "SQ Rambos On." *Windspeaker* 8, 22.

Walkom, T. 2003. "Immigrants rap Tory plan." *Toronto Star*, September 4, A1 and A8.

Waller, H. 2002. "Security vs. Immigration in Canada." *The New Leader* January/February.

Walton, D. 2003. "'Bum heaven' has had enough." *Globe and Mail*, November 13, A10.

Wanagas, D., and J. Warmington. 1998. "Feds enter squeegee war." *Toronto Sun*, July 28.

Welch, M. 1996. "The Immigration Crisis: Detention as an Emerging Mechanism of Social Control." *Social Justice* 23, 3.

Wettlaufer, W., MPP. 1999. Hansard. 1st Session, 37th Parliament, November 15. Toronto: Queen's Printer for Ontario.

Wilson, J.Q., and George Kelling. 1982. "Broken Windows." *Atlantic Monthly* March.

Winnipeg Police Service. 1998. *Annual Report*. Winnipeg: Winnipeg Police Service.

_____. 1999. *Annual Report*. Winnipeg: Winnipeg Police Service.

Wolfe, D. 1984. "The Rise and Demise of the Keynesian Era in Canada: Economic Policy, 1930–1982." In M.S. Cross and G.S. Kealey (eds.), *Modern Canada, 1930–1980s*. Toronto: McClelland and Stewart.

Wooldrige, Cst. M. 2004. Personal Communication to author. March 15.

Wortley, Scot. Undated. "Under Suspicion: Race and Criminal Justice Surveillance in Canada." Unpublished paper.

Wortley, S., and G. Kellough. 1998. "The 'Probable' Offender: Police and Crown Discretion and the Over-Representation of Black People in the Ontario Criminal Justice System." Unpublished paper presented at the International Conference on Criminology and Criminal Justice in the Caribbean, Barbados, October.

Wright, S. 2001. "Killing me softly." *New Scientist* 17 (Issue 2303, August 11).

Yeager, M. 2002. "Rehabilitating the Criminality of Immigrants Under Section 19 of the Canadian Immigration Act." *International Migration Review* 36, 1.

Yelaja, P. 2001. "Somali 'tempers boiling' after police drug bust." *Toronto Star*, July 23, B4.

Young, Jock. 1979. "Left Idealism, Reformism and Beyond: From New Criminology to Marxism." In B. Fine, R. Kinsey, J. Lea, S. Picciotto and J. Young (eds.), *Capitalism and the Rule of Law: From Deviancy Theory to Marxism*. London: Hutchinson and Co.

Index

Acknowledgements

This book, which began as my Ph.D. thesis, would not have been possible without the support of several individuals. In particular, I would like to give special mention to David McNally, supervisor and friend. David's thoughtful suggestions on earlier drafts of chapters, selfless commitment of time, despite his very busy schedule, guiding me through the thesis process more generally, and overall support for my academic endeavours have been invaluable. Rob Albritton and Bob MacDermid, also members of my thesis committee, were also helpful the whole way through. I am indebted to Marlene Queesenberry, who has very kindly and patiently put up with my many administrative questions and confusions.

Many thanks to my editor, Debby Seed, who worked very hard at the difficult task of transforming a thesis into a much more readable book; and to all those at Fernwood who have helped put this book together.

Jackie and Breton deserve a very special mention. Jackie has been an invaluable source of knowledge on policing, the law and many other things, and indeed her reflections have been a significant resource for formulating the ideas presented here. Her unwavering support made an often difficult and emotionally taxing process much more endurable, and our countless hours spent watching Buffy together was the perfect antidote to the stresses of thesis preparation. My morning walks with Breton were a nice and relaxing way to start days with lots of work lying ahead, while his demands for attention throughout the day were always welcome excuses to take breaks from research and writing.

This book was inspired, in part, by my experience as an activist, hearing stories about, and seeing first hand, poor peoples' unwelcome encounters with police. I hope it will make one small contribution to understanding and perhaps challenging the unjust and dangerous phenomenon of law and order.

Parts of this book have been published elsewhere. A version of chapter three appeared in *Studies in Political Economy* 75, pp. 53–78 and as a chapter in D. Crocker's and V.M. Johnson's (eds.) *Poverty, Regulation and Social Exclusion: Readings on the Criminalization of Poverty*, which is forthcoming in the spring, 2006. A version of chapter four appeared in *Canadian Review of Social Policy*, 54, pp. 34–57, while a section of chapter five appears in a forthcoming issue of *Social Justice* in 2006.

About the Author

Todd Gordon is a social justice activist who completed his Ph.D. in political science at York University in Toronto in 2005. His articles have appeared in *Studies in Political Economy, Canadian Review of Social Policy* and *Capital and Class*. He is also an editor of *New Socialist* magazine.

DATE DUE